Explorers of the Mississippi

The Fesler-Lampert *Minnesota Heritage* Book Series

This series is published with the generous assistance of the John K. and Elsie Lampert Fesler Fund and David R. and Elizabeth P. Fesler. Its mission is to republish significant out-of-print books that contribute to our understanding and appreciation of Minnesota and the Upper Midwest.

The series features works by the following authors:

Clifford and Isabel Ahlgren

J. Arnold Bolz

Walter Havighurst

Helen Hoover

Florence Page Jaques

Evan Jones

Meridel Le Sueur

George Byron Merrick

Grace Lee Nute

Sigurd F. Olson

Charles Edward Russell

Calvin Rutstrum

Timothy Severin

Robert Treuer

TIMOTHY SEVERIN

Explorers of the Mississippi

University of Minnesota Press
MINNEAPOLIS · LONDON

Copyright 1967 by Timothy Severin

First published by Alfred A. Knopf, 1967

First University of Minnesota Press edition 2002

Republished by arrangement with the author.

Published by the University of Minnesota Press
111 Third Avenue South, Suite 290
Minneapolis, MN 55401-2520
http://www.upress.umn.edu

A Cataloging-in-Publication record for this book is available from
the Library of Congress.

Printed in the United States of America on acid-free paper

The University of Minnesota is an equal-opportunity
educator and employer.

12 11 10 09 08 07 06 05 04 03 02   10 9 8 7 6 5 4 3 2 1

For Dobby

PUBLISHER'S NOTE

THE FESLER-LAMPERT MINNESOTA HERITAGE BOOK SERIES is designed to renew interest in the state's past by bringing significant literary works to the attention of a new audience. Our knowledge and appreciation of the culture and history of the region have advanced considerably since these books were first published, and the attitudes and opinions expressed in them may strike the contemporary reader as inappropriate. These classics have been reprinted in their original form as contributions to the state's literary heritage.

PREFACE

THE IDEA OF WRITING A BOOK ABOUT THE EXPLORERS OF the Mississippi occurred to me while I was spending twenty-one months in the United States on an International Fellowship from the Commonwealth Fund. The Mississippi had played no part in the original plans for my stay in North America, but as a student of the history of exploration and travel I was surprised to learn that no one had attempted a survey of the exploration of the "Father of Waters" from the point of view of the explorers themselves. There is, of course, a vast amount of literature about the Mississippi but most of it concerns either the Civil War days or the steamboat era. To a great extent the glamour of the paddle-wheels and King Cotton has swamped the story of the pioneers. This, it seemed to me, was a pity; for while such figures as De Soto and La Salle are well known, the exploits of the lesser men—Hennepin, Carver, Beltrami, and others—also deserve mention. In the following pages I have tried to tell their stories, concentrating as much as possible on the personalities themselves.

In an attempt to appreciate some of the geographical conditions which these explorers encountered, I undertook a boat trip during the summer of 1965 from one end of the river to the other. Starting by canoe from the source in northern Minnesota and then continuing by launch downstream from St. Paul, I managed to see the length of the Mississippi. The following winter I returned to Minneapolis, where a wealth of research material was made available to me at the James Ford Bell Collection. There and at Harvard this book was written. It would not have been possible but for the assistance of many people, and my special thanks are due to Jack Parker, Carol Urness, and their staff at the Bell Collection; to the Ryberg family in Minneapolis; to Martha Bray; to the staff of Widener Library, Harvard University; and to a host of helpers ranging from canoe enthusiasts to barge masters along the Mississippi. Above all I should like to thank the staff of the International Fellowship Division, Commonwealth Fund, in New York; their help and the generosity of the Fund made my project a reality.

TIMOTHY SEVERIN

Harvard, June 1966

CONTENTS

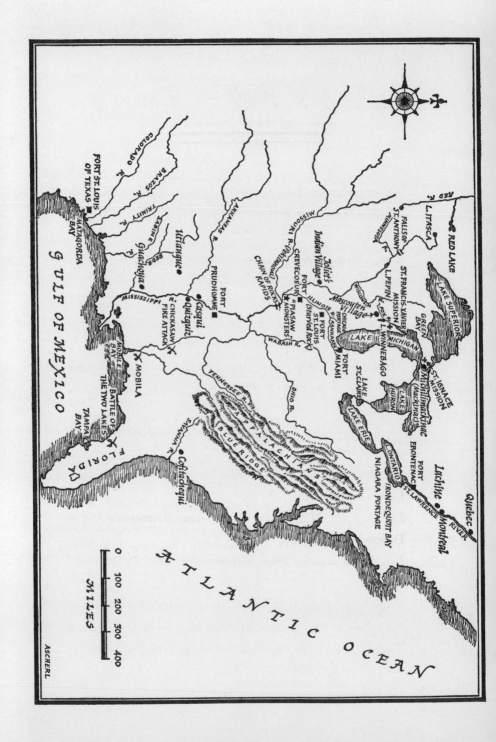

ILLUSTRATIONS

[xi]

Explorers of the
Mississippi

1

Father of Waters

THE ULTIMATE SOURCE OF THE MISSISSIPPI IS A small Y-shaped lake in upper Minnesota about 175 miles from the Canadian border. The lake has a single outlet—a small stream which tumbles from one arm of the Y as a puny riffle swirling between a chain of well-worn boulders. This is a favorite spot for tourists and many of the visitors like to use the boulders at steppingstones so that they can claim to have walked across the mighty Mississippi without getting their feet wet. But few of the tourists are curious enough to trace the stream any farther, for almost immediately it plunges into a maze of willow thickets and is lost from view.

Yet the Mississippi is worth following, even for those first few miles. It must be one of the very few major rivers in the world which develops meander loops within walking distance of its source. Whereas most infant rivers tumble along with great enthusiasm in the early stages, the Mississippi assumes its sedate character at once. Hidden among the pine and birch forests of the north it wriggles like a water snake, throwing its coils in a series of contortions which are miniature copies of its famous downstream oxbows. It is still narrow enough for beavers to build untidy dams of sticks and branches from one bank to the other, but already the Mississippi has settled down to a sober pace, curling interminably through little rocky basins which are cradled between low hills. This is wild country; there are massive fish eagles wheeling in the sky, an occasional moose, clumsy porcupines and white tailed deer, acres of whispering reeds, and the eerie cry of the loon piercing the early morning mist as if some hobgoblin is loose on the river.

It is also Indian country. Dotted along the upper river are tracts of land reserved exclusively for various bands of the Ojibway or Chippewa. They are the last remnants of a tribe which was powerful on the river before the white man. Then, more than three hundred years ago, the Mississippi was an Indian river. Spreading in a vast belt from the Great Lakes to the Gulf of Mexico was a multitude of tribes—Fox, Potawatomie, Kickapoo, Iowa, Illinois, Winnebago, Miami, Mascouten, Chickasaw, Otoe, Quapaw, and others. These Indians were in a constant state of turmoil, fighting one another, migrating from one area to the next, moving up and down the river. Even the Sioux, now associated with the Great Plains, were once a river tribe and paddled fleets of war canoes on the upper Mississippi. These aborigines used a variety of names to describe the river that supplied them with food and acted as a great highway from one end of the continent to the other. They called it Messipi, Namosisipu, Nilco, Mico, Culatta, Okachitto, Olsimochitto, Sassagoula, Malabanchia; but it was the Algonkian name—Mississippi—which finally won out. French traders heard it from the Chippewa and the other northern tribes and carried it downstream with them, until this word, variously translated as the "Big Water" or "Father of Waters," became the accepted name from Montreal to Louisiana.

The early explorers found that many of the river tribes were relatively civilized. Far from being totally savage, they exhibited a high degree of social organization and had a so-

[4]

phisticated code of conduct. For example, they recognized the special protection afforded to any stranger who carried the calumet, or pipe of peace. Furthermore the tribes were seldom hostile. They usually regarded the white men as curiosities rather than enemies, and greeted the explorers with kindness. One of the earlier travel accounts by a European mentions the famous "wampum belt formula," a speech customarily delivered at a council to welcome an ambassador from a distant tribe. It ran: "Brothers, with this belt I open your ears that you may hear. I remove grief and sorrow from your hearts. I draw from your feet the thorns that have pierced them on your journey hither. I sweep the seats about the council fire that you may sit at ease. I wash your heads and bodies that you may be refreshed. I condole with you on the loss of your friends who have died. I wipe out any blood that may have been spilt between us."

This peaceable attitude on the part of the Indians, coupled with the absence of difficult cataracts or waterfalls, made the Mississippi an easy river to travel and explore by boat. Yet despite this, there is a gap of three centuries between the date when white men first saw the river and the time of the final discovery of the source in the little Minnesota lake. Of the several reasons for this lag, some are geographical but the important ones concern the explorers themselves and the policies they represented.

Among the geographical obstacles the first was the nature and position of the river's mouth. The Mississippi delta is awkward to find from the sea and dangerous to navigate. As a result the very existence of the "Father of Waters" was still a mystery to European mapmakers long after Spanish sailors had brought back a reasonably accurate description of the Gulf coast of North America. Only when the Spaniards began to probe inland did they discover the largest river in the continent, a river so big that when the Missouri and Ohio are included, it drains one-eighth of all North America. Indeed, it was only by chance that the main river was recognized as rising in upper Minnesota. If the white men had come overland from the Pacific rather than the Atlantic, they would have struck the headwaters of the Missouri in the Rocky Mountains, and this branch, rather than the shorter northern stream, would have been declared to be the main river. By a quirk of history the Spaniards withdrew and left the task of exploration to the French who were obliged to approach from their colonies on the St. Lawrence. This had two results: first, they believed that the nearest branch they encountered, the northern stream, was the main river; and second, their explorers were exposed to the geographical obstacle of greatest significance—the climate. Time and again the Europeans were caught off guard by the rigors of a continental American winter, when temperatures of thirty degrees below zero are not uncommon, the land is covered with deep snow, and the river icebound. The harshness of the winters was made all the more stunning by the remoteness of the Mississippi. The early explorers had to spend at least one summer traveling by foot and canoe to get within striking distance of the river, and even after the French-Canadian settlers had established outposts on the Great Lakes it was necessary for their "voyageurs" to winter on the shores of Lake Superior before crossing the watershed that separated them from the Father of Waters. The long, hard winters limited traveling time, increased costs, and deterred all but the brave and ignorant from winter journeys.

But the most important reasons for the delay in exploring the Mississippi were political. The river was controlled at various periods by the Spanish, French, British, and Americans. Each nation was usually more concerned with protecting its sovereignty than exploring the stream to its source. Thus, the first major French expedition turned back when it was halfway down the river because they were afraid of falling into the hands of the Spanish and being interned by the authorities. By the same token, neither the Spanish, French nor British held the Mississippi long enough for them to invest in costly expeditions of discovery. This was left to its eventual owners, the Americans, whose government was the first to spend substantial amounts of money on pure exploration. If international rivalries were not enough, it is remarkable how many of the explorers were also embroiled in quarrels with their own countrymen. The French, the most successful travelers along the river, were the worst culprits in this respect. Their explorers were constantly hampered by lawsuits of one sort or another, usually brought against them by vindictive rivals who were jealous of any commercial advantage that might accrue to the successful pioneer.

This obsession with the financial rewards of exploring the river is another peculiarity of the Mississippi's history. Unlike the Nile or Niger, the exploration of the Father of Waters was not carried out under the aegis of geographical societies or learned committees, but was achieved for the greater part by private persons who anticipated some sort of gain for themselves—gold, furs, or glory. In consequence, the river's exploration took place in a series of fits and starts, depending upon the activities of these opportunists. Otherwise the river was little used, because, in the words of Mark Twain, "nobody happened to want such a river; nobody needed it, nobody was curious about it, so . . . the Mississippi remained out of the market and undisturbed. When De Soto found it, he was not hunting for a river, and had no present occasion for one; consequently he did not value it or even take any particular notice of it." Of course this was far from the whole story, though there is a grain of truth in the humorist's version; there were many men on both sides of the Atlantic who dreamed about using the river's potential. From the very first days of discovery they envisaged a great heartland civilization served by ocean-going ships plying deep into the continent; the Mississippi would be an artery of commerce and perhaps might provide a water route to the Indies. These were far-reaching plans but they were based on conjecture. No one knew the exact course of the river and few of the dreamers were prepared to back their ideas with money or materiel. Once again the exploration was left to those individuals who were willing to take risks because they saw immediate profits.

These were the men who paddled along the river, encountered the tribes living on its banks, made treaties with their chieftains, and shared such native delicacies as fish fried in bear's oil and flavored with crushed blueberries.

Many of these early travelers never recorded their adventures. It is more than possible, for instance, that the first white men to reach the Mississippi from the northeast were not Joliet and Marquette, but a gang of illiterate voyageurs ranging beyond the outer limit of the French western frontier. There were many such wanderers who lived like gypsies, sharing the life of the Indian tribes. They did not bother to report their journeys to the authorities—many of their trips were illegal in the eyes of the colonial government—and it is unavoidable that the following chapters recount only the exploits of those travelers whose stories were written down by themselves or their contemporaries. Even so, some of their tales can be annoyingly scanty. However, one thing is certain: after the withdrawal of the Spanish, the exploration of the Mississippi, known or unknown, depended upon a vital tool—the lightweight Indian canoe.

The Spaniards never learned to use the birchbark canoe of the northland because their expeditions were limited to the lower river so they were familiar only with the dugout canoe of the southern tribes. These dugouts were impressive vessels; the largest, made from a single giant cottonwood trunk, had a three-foot beam and could carry more than fifty warriors, but for exploration purposes they did not rival the lighter bark canoe of the woodland tribes. The French were the first to discover the incredible versatility of the northern boat and use it to full advantage. Once they had adopted the native method of river travel, the entire Mississippi-Missouri-Ohio drainage system lay open to them and no account of the Mississippi explorers can ignore the importance of their vessels.

The bark canoe of the North American Indians offered the explorer unique advantages over plank-built European boats. The Indian vessel was a highly specialized design intended for use on the rivers and lakes of the interior. As such, it was light enough to be handled in the water by a single paddler who could carry it, if necessary, over forest portage trails. The canoe was also sufficiently maneuverable to steer through dangerous rapids, and at the same time the larger versions held up to a ton of cargo without drawing more than ten inches of water. As an added feature, certain versions of the bark canoe were so constructed that the traveler could beach his vessel at night, turn it upside down on trestles, and have a ready-made roof over his head.

Before the arrival of the white man the birch bark canoe was restricted to the upper Mississippi for the very good reason that the essential material for the hull was the outer bark of the paper birch (*Betula papyrifera*). This tree, its chalky white trunk marked with distinctive black blotches, was found only north of a line extending from Long Island to Washington State. Near the Mississippi it grew no farther south than Wisconsin, and though such barks as spruce, chestnut, hickory, and basswood could be used for making canoes in an emergency, only the paper birch developed large sheets of bark tough enough to withstand prolonged wear. In particular the upper trunk provided a canoe cover that did not flake or decay quickly. The Indians peeled the birch trees in late fall or early spring when the rising sap made their task easier and they could select the finest pieces, about three-sixteenths of an inch thick, to roll up in bundles and carry back to their villages. Freshly cut, the sheets of bark gave off an aromatic odor and were flexible enough to be wrapped over the canoe's framework of white cedarwood lathes which had been bent to shape in hot water. This frame was lashed together with rawhide thongs and the bark cover "sewn" into place with the pencil-thin roots of the black spruce (*Picea mariana*). The bark then dried to a cinnamon brown, retaining the desired shape. Paddles, ribs, thwarts, and headboards were cut out of cedar or spruce and the hull of the canoe was calked with spruce gum, the resin of black or white spruce which had been boiled or chewed until soft enough to smear

[9]

over the stitching holes and other cracks. The end product was a graceful, speedy craft which could be repaired with local materials en route and was ideal for hunters, traders, and explorers. The white newcomers proved the excellence of the native vessel by adopting it immediately, only adding a sail, whenever possible, and using steel rather than stone tools in its construction. Otherwise the shape and style of the canoe remained unchanged and it was the vessel which the river travelers chose to paddle, sail, portage, and pole from one end of the Mississippi to the other.

The efforts of these early white pioneers can be traced through the development of contemporary maps. The cartographers, nearly all of them working as royal appointees several thousand miles away in Europe, were confused by the reports that came back to them from North America. At first they were thrown off stride by the magnitude of the river—the Mississippi discharges eight times as much water as the Rhine—and were reluctant to credit the existence of such a gargantuan stream. But then, as more knowledge filtered back, they overcompensated in the opposite direction; an enormous waterway appeared on their maps, spreading its interconnecting channels from Florida to the Pacific. Along its banks were depicted swarms of strange beasts, including camels, ostriches, and even a giraffe. Compounding the confusion, the white explorers had almost as many names for the river as their Indian predecessors. The Mississippi was marked on Spanish maps as the "Rio Grande" or the River of the Holy Ghost; on French missionary maps it was the River of the Immaculate Conception; and elsewhere it was called the river "Buade ou Frontenac," the "Colbert," the "St. Louis," and the River of Louisiana. Not until 1684 could the eminent French mapmaker, Jean Baptiste Franquelin, unravel this confusion and draw the general outline of the Mississippi dominating the central valley. Even then he misplaced the delta almost into Mexico and it was customary for his successors to insert ornate cartouches which conveniently obliterated the unknown sources of both the Missouri and the Father of

Waters. By 1720 an English geographer was able to state that "The Mississippi springs from several lakes to the westward of Hudson's Bay and bending its course directly south falls through six channels into the Gulf of Mexico," though he was less informed about its overall course and concluded, rather lamely, that "it is reported 800 leagues long and very probably it may be much longer."

While these early maps can be a helpful index of the spread of knowledge about the Mississippi, they are useless when trying to determine who first discovered the river. In April 1495 Ferdinand and Isabella of Spain published a decree authorizing expeditions for discovery of "new isles and continents in the Indian Ocean" and two years later Amerigo Vespucci, a Florentine sailor in Spanish pay, is known to have been the pilot of a vessel that entered the Gulf of Mexico. Then, in 1519, the Spanish governor of Jamaica decided to send a fleet of four ships to explore for a "western passage" to Cathay. The expedition was entrusted to one Alonso Alvárez de Pineda, an experienced navigator, who searched along the Gulf coast for the mythical sea route to the Indies. In the course of this voyage he entered the mouth of a river which was described as "very large and very full." Here the Spaniards carried out repairs on their ships and Pineda's pilots made a chart of the coastline. This map was forwarded to Spain, showing that the Gulf "bendeth like a bow" and that a line drawn from Florida to Yucatán would "make the string to the bow." It might seem that Pineda had discovered the mouth of the Mississippi but for the fact that his fleet had sailed six leagues up the big river and found an "extensive town," friendly Indians, and forty native villages "covered with reeds." This flatly disagrees with all the later Spanish descriptions of the Mississippi delta which make it clear that not only was the mouth of the river impassable for ships, but the malarial marshland supported only a handful of aborigines.

Whether or not Pineda had discovered the Mississippi or, as is more probable, had sailed into Mobile Bay, the Spanish cartographers were unimpressed. Their maps merely showed a string of minor rivers draining into the Gulf and an occasional pear-shaped bay, utterly unlike the Mississippi delta. This coast they called the land of "Amichel" and declared it to be "too far from the Tropics" to contain gold. It was another nine years before a Spaniard went ashore to investigate, and even then the white men were there by accident.

It is difficult to imagine a more piratical figure than the Spanish general, Pánfilo de Narváez. He was a red-bearded, one-eyed scoundrel of low intelligence and amazing selfishness who went to the New World to grab a fortune for himself. In pursuing this goal he did not hesitate to betray his friends, break his word, or massacre unarmed natives. Unfortunately for his ambitions, Narváez was also incompetent to the point of stupidity, and few of his schemes bore fruit. On one ludicrous occasion he led a strong force into Mexico to arrest Cortés and steal his treasure, but his own troops deserted to the opposition and Pánfilo was soundly thrashed by the man he had come to capture. His greed undaunted, Narváez decided to tackle an easier foe and obtained a license to subdue the Indians of the Gulf coast. This expedition was an unqualified failure. A hurricane battered the ships; his army was mauled by the natives of Florida; Narváez lost touch with his supporting fleet; and the starving men slaughtered their cavalry mounts for food. Narváez was obliged to abandon the entire venture and lead his army back to the sea shore. There the Spaniards constructed five makeshift barges and attempted to follow the coast back to Mexico. At the first opportunity Narváez, who had taken care to select the best barge and the strongest oarsmen, ordered his crew to row ahead, abandoning the rest of his expedition to their fate. Narváez was never seen again, but four survivors from one of the other barges were shipwrecked and managed to walk back along the Texas shore to New Spain, turning up nearly eight years later. They told of a huge fresh-water current which had pushed their boat out to sea as they sailed westward. The current had been too strong for them to investigate closer inshore but there was speculation that this was the river which Pineda had mentioned. At any rate, the interest of the Spanish authorities was aroused, not so much by the big river, but by the survivors' report that there was gold in the interior of North America. The time had come for a full-scale invasion of "Amichel" by a competent commander; the man who led this invasion and who was the first to confirm the existence of the Mississippi was Hernando de Soto of Jerez.

2

Conquistador from Badajoz

HERNANDO DE SOTO, KNIGHT OF SANTIAGO AND HI-
dalgo of Badajoz, was among the most successful
men of his day and also one of its worst failures. He has been
awarded a niche in American history as the first white man
to set eyes on the Mississippi, but at the time he saw the river
he did not appreciate the importance of his discovery. His
whole life was a succession of contradictions. He managed to
combine cruelty with generosity, leadership with supreme
pig-headedness, ambition with self-sacrifice. To the modern
reader it is odd that he ever got as far as he did, and odder
still that he should have then failed so utterly. The course of
his extraordinary career, from the darling of the Spanish
aristocracy to a lonely broken-hearted death on the banks
of the river he discovered, unfolds like the plot in a Spanish
book of chivalry. De Soto himself would have approved of
the comparison, for he lived during the Golden Age of Spain
and died while pursuing his enchanted kingdom in the untouched vastnesses of the New World.

The year Columbus discovered the New World was also

the year of the surrender of Granada and the end of nearly eight centuries of almost continuous fighting to drive the Moor out of the Iberian peninsula. When the fighting petered out in Spain, a tough, experienced body of professional soldiers was left unemployed. Columbus presented them with a whole new continent for their ambitions and the Spanish men-at-arms flocked westward to try their luck in the Americas. These were the conquistadors, and Hernando de Soto's story is tightly interwoven with their achievements. The conquistadors enjoyed a brief but fantastic hour of glory. In less than fifty years what is now called Spanish America was overrun. In a dizzy streak of success the conquistadors seized Cuba, Panama, Venezuela, Mexico, Peru, Ecuador, Paraguay, and Chile.

Daring and reckless, the invaders marched across prairie, jungle, and mountain. Their tiny armies, seldom more than five hundred men, suffered from warfare, climate, and terrain; yet undaunted they often crowned the hardship as they rode in triumph through the Indian capitals they had come to conquer. The conquistadors were driven by a queer mixture of motives. Many were genuinely concerned, in the simplest possible way, with bringing Christianity to the benighted heathen. Others were professional adventurers, willing to launch out into the unknown, lured by the risks and dangers. Some had gone to America because they were persecuted in Spain. Their captains, De Soto included, had dreams of fame, of petty empires tucked away in the forgotten corners of the new continent. But first and foremost in the minds of everyone from arquebusier to "Gran General" was the hope that somewhere, perhaps only a day's march ahead, lay the treasure hoards of the natives where heaps of bullion would fill the marching packs of the army. Then the lucky ones would be able to leave the discomforts and the treacherous natives of the Americas, go back to Spain and buy houses, lands, and luxuries. The chance was worth taking because success in the New World was the only short cut to a life of ease in the Old World. It was the irony of the conquistadors' story that the rewards came first and not last; Peru and Mexico made millionaries of the successful captains; later, Florida and Chile were financial disasters. De Soto rode the crest of the wave and was destroyed in the empty years that followed.

The defeat of conquistador armies coincided with the spread of their activities north and south. In the beginning, in Central America, they achieved swift and total victory. Then, as they moved into South America and in the deserts of North America, native resistance stiffened. In Chile the Araucanians after thirteen years of subservience rose up to exterminate their Spanish overlords, and in the swamplands of the southern United States the local tribes stubbornly harassed the outer line of conquest. De Soto's career embraced almost every phase of this decline. As a subaltern he saw action in Panama; as a senior lieutenant he made a fortune in Peru; and as a general he was ground to a halt in North America.

Very little is known about De Soto's early life. He was born in Jerez de los Caballeros in the province of Badajoz. Thus, like Pizarro, Balboa, and Cortés, he came from the ancient kingdom of Estremadura. According to legend, he was a junior scion of one of the oldest and most distinguished families of Spain, but it is possible that his pure lineage may have been faked when the time came for him to enter the exclusive Order of Santiago. Whatever his background, De Soto's immediate family must have been short of money, for the young man's future was largely determined by his patron, Pedrarias Dávila, who paid for De Soto to travel to the New World and probably also paid for his education in Spain.

Pedrarias Dávila was a notorious figure. At the age of seventy-four he sailed to the Indies to assume the governorship of Panama, which was an important base for conquistador armies. Within a short time the old man's cruelty had shocked even his fellow colonists, who were seldom better than upper-class cutthroats. The ailing Pedrarias was a mean and grasping despot. He was brutal to the Indians, treating them as fierce children who needed a sound thrashing, and in his dealings with the Spanish settlers he was savagely unpredictable. They nicknamed him "furor Domini," the wrath of God, as he robbed, persecuted, and threatened the people under his authority. Among his other grisly deeds, he had his own son-in-law convicted of a trumped-up charge and then beheaded in his presence.

This was the man under whom De Soto came to the Indies, though it is not certain when the youth arrived in Panama with, according to one chronicler, "nought save his sword and shield." In 1520 we hear of De Soto officially. That year a small Spanish expeditionary army in Panama ventured too far inland, losing touch with its supporting fleet; the natives sallied forth from their mountain fortresses and encircled the rash invaders. A Spanish relief column was hastily dispatched from the nearest settlement to rescue the trapped army, and a hard-riding cavalry squad arrived in the nick of time. A single, bold cavalry charge took the native force in the flank and routed the Indians. Leading the charge was Hernando de Soto and his success that day established the pattern for his military career. He became, in fact, the dashing captain of horse. During future campaigns his specialty was to be the headlong cavalry charge delivered at the crucial moment against a surprised enemy, and time after time he was brilliantly successful. Very soon he was recognized as an outstanding field officer.

As a young cavalry officer De Soto was in his element. He was an impetuous man and did not care to become embroiled in the tortuous intrigues that flourished between the conquistador generals. De Soto remained loyal to his unsavory patron and refused to desert Pedrarias. Step by step he began to achieve rank and fortune. He formed a private alliance with two other gentlemen-adventurers—Captains Francisco Companon and Hernan Ponce de Leon. They agreed to pool their resources and all three of them prospered with an accumulation of slaves, land and booty. Then Companon died, leaving his portion to the two remaining partners. Ponce de Leon and De Soto decided to continue their association and use their capital to build two ships in Nicaragua. The vessels were probably intended for use in the slave trade, but as they lay on the stocks, there arrived in Nicaragua one Nicholas de Ribera, agent for Pizarro. He had come to raise support for a projected invasion of Peru.

Pizarro and his associates were desperate. They had assembled a bare minimum of ships and men for the Peruvian adventure, but they were still short-handed. Other expeditions had already stripped New Spain of battle-hardened soldiers and every day Pizarro's army was growing more despondent. There were reports that they would never penetrate the Peruvian highlands, men were deserting, and costs were mounting. Ponce de Leon and De Soto were a godsend; they were experienced captains and had men, money, and two brand-new ships for the voyage. Accordingly Ribera offered the two captains a junior partnership in the expedition and his offer was accepted. Almost seven years to the day before his own army sailed from Havana to Florida, Hernando de Soto found himself committed to Pizarro's attack on Peru, and his share in the fantastic success of that venture formed the basis of his Florida expedition.

The collapse of the Inca empire was an act of astonishing swiftness. Caught on the wrong foot by the ruthless speed of the Spanish forces as they struck inland from their beachhead, and hampered by a civil war,[1] the Supreme Inca put up little resistance. De Soto and his cavalry led the invaders, probing, scouting, and patrolling. He was among the first to cross the dizzying wickerwork bridges which spanned the Andean gorges, and to discover the great imperial road network along which the native troops moved to control the Inca's kingdom. Finally, on that tense day when the ponderous native army surrounded Pizarro's handful in the town of Caxamarca, it was De Soto who was sent out as the Spanish emissary. Galloping toward Atahualpa, the Supreme Inca who sat on a portable throne in front of his vast army, De Soto gave an

[1]Cortés had been lucky enough to encounter the same conditions in Mexico.

unabashed display of his horsemanship, which the chronicler has recorded:

"Observing that Atahualpa looked with some interest on the fiery steed that stood before him, champing the bit and pawing the ground with the natural impatience of a war-horse, the Spaniard gave him the rein, and striking his iron heel into his side, dashed furiously over the plain, then, wheeling him round and round, showed off all the movements of his charger and his own excellent skill as a rider. Suddenly checking him in full career, he brought the animal almost on his haunches, so near the Inca that some of the foam that flecked on his horse's sides was thrown on the royal garments."

De Soto's mission was successful. The Supreme Inca ventured into Caxamarca, was captured, and used to extort a ransom from his people. The remainder of the Peruvian campaign then followed the classic conquistador pattern. Atahualpa was murdered, a puppet ruler was installed, and, while rebel armies were annihilated, the pillaging went forward. The invaders looted temples and treasure hoards for gold, silver, and gems; their rewards were unbelievable—at one stage the cavalry shod their mounts with silver horseshoes because iron was scarcer than bullion. Spanish priests arrived to spread the good word to the bewildered natives that Christianity had come to save their heathen souls and the capital city was redesigned as a Spanish town. As usual the division of the spoils led to bitter quarrels among the victors and for a while it was De Soto's job to keep the peace. Eventually, the incessant squabbling became too much for him and he decided to get out of the entire Peruvian affair while he could, taking his share of the profits with him. Besides, he already had plans for an expedition of his own and resented being junior to Pizarro. De Soto's booty was loaded onto carts and dragged down to the coast and in December 1535 he sailed back to Panama. There he stayed long enough to invest some of his wealth by buying land and then left for Spain.

The voyage home almost cost De Soto all he had so recently gained. One of the fleet, carrying a portion of his valuables, ran aground on Bimini point in the treacherous Bahama channel and went down with its cargo. The man responsible for the near-disaster was Luis de Moscoso, a veteran officer of the Peruvian campaign whom De Soto had placed in charge of his loot. Moscoso was rescued and De Soto in an act of typical generosity forgave him, even going so far as to reinstate Moscoso as chief lieutenant of the forthcoming Florida expedition. Dividing his spoils between several ships in the fleet had been one of De Soto's rare acts of prudence and it paid off. Much later, the easygoing Moscoso redeemed himself when he proved to be the unexpected savior who led the survivors of the Florida army back to civilization.

Despite the loss of one of his vessels, De Soto arrived back in Spain a very rich man—rich enough to be drawn into the royal orbit where the King himself had no hesitation in borrowing money from the highly successful adventurer. De Soto's fortune was estimated at no less than 180,000 cruzados, not counting his properties in the Americas, and was probably a lot more. In Spain the dashing and good-looking Hernando de Soto was the lion of society. He was a success story personified; the adventurous youth who had sailed to new lands to seek his fortune, returning as a captain of cavalry, wealthy and successful. About him clung his retinue, nearly all veterans from Peru—Juan de Anasco of Seville, Luis Moscoso de Alvarado, Nuno de Tobar, and Rodrigues Lobillo. They had all fought in the squalor and discomfort of the Americas, and now they had come back rich with plunder and eager to taste the fruits of success. They moved as new constellations through the glittering luxury of the imperial court. Hovering in attendance were panderers, favorites, and flunkies. Immediately upon his return, De Soto hired a majordomo, a grand master of ceremonies, pages, equerry, chamberlain, footmen, and a whole host of lesser retainers. The entire entourage was specially fitted out in matching livery. This was a homecoming in a grand manner.

Hernando de Soto's ambition was far from satisfied. He

was rich enough to live at ease for the rest of his life, but he sought power and that meant he wanted the ultimate crown of glory for the conquistador—an independent government for himself somewhere in the New World. Riches and prestige were not enough, power was the final goal; power which he could wield in a far-off land where the King's writ was out of date and meaningless by the time a galleon had brought it to the foreign shores, three thousand miles and three months at sea away from the Council of the Indies who were supposed to rule the colonies in the King's name. This was what Cortés, Balboa, Pizarro, Guzman, and the others had done. Now it was De Soto's turn.

His first move was to marry Isabel de Bobadilla, daughter of Pedrarias, his old benefactor. Through his wife De Soto acquired the sinews of strength for an ambitious conquistador —more wealth and a network of family alliances that spun a web of supporting partisans throughout the provinces of New Spain. Then De Soto applied to the Spanish Court, asking for the governorship of virgin territory in what is now Ecuador and Colombia, the land to the north of Francisco Pizarro's fief. But the Court had other plans for this region and probably feared that if De Soto were allowed to return to South America he would form an alliance with Pizarro and their combined provinces would break away from the Spanish crown. Instead the authorities produced a counteroffer. They suggested that De Soto govern the little-known and as yet unconquered lands in North America bordering the Gulf of Mexico, the whole area being vaguely described as "Florida."[2] De Soto accepted, and a formal agreement between him and the King was drawn up on April 20, 1537.

The royal license giving De Soto legal authority to strike out northward from New Spain was the product of many years of Spanish colonial experience. It catered simultaneously to the ambitions of the conquistador and the suspicions of the King. The royal advisers knew that they had to give the hopeful conquistador enough freedom to let him reap a

[2] Like California this name was taken from a book of Chivalry.

profit from his investment of men and money, but at the same time they had to place sufficient curbs on his authority to stop him from declaring his independence from Spain once he was successful. The Council of the Indies was less troubled about its own right, legal or moral, to hand out lands which did not belong to them; by papal bull, Spain had been given the heathen or unoccupied lands beyond a line running from pole to pole through a point a hundred leagues west of the Cape Verde Islands. Also the system of licensed conquest by semi-private armies was admirably cheap; if the hopeful licensee managed to conquer a heathen land, so much the better. If he and his men lost their lives on a fruitless adventure, then Spain was no worse off than before.

De Soto was not the first to hold the Florida license. Before him, Pánfilo de Narváez, Juan Ponce de Leon, and Lucas de Ayllon had tried and failed. Narváez's fate has already been mentioned; Ponce de Leon gave up in disgust; and Ayllon's colony vanished without a trace on the inhospitable coastland of Georgia. Now Hernando de Soto was given his chance. The terms of the charter were precise: He was obliged to furnish at least five hundred men, complete with "the necessary arms, horses, munitions, and military stores"; the expedition had to set out within one year of the signing of the license; it must have a minimum of eighteen months supplies; and all expenses were to be paid by De Soto, the Spanish government specifically absolving itself from any financial responsibility in the venture. For his reward, De Soto was immediately made governor of Cuba, which was to be the base for his conquest of North America, and once he had conquered "Florida," he would also become governor, captain general, and adelantado of any two hundred leagues of the coast he might care to select. In his fief he was permitted to build three harbours, appoint officers, and claim for his personal possession twelve square leagues of land, provided it did not include the chief town or a seaport (the Spanish government was taking precautions against a breakaway self-sufficient kingdom). Furthermore, the successful conqueror of

[22]

Florida would receive a lifetime annuity of 2,000 ducats; though this, of course, was to be paid out of income from the colony, so that the Crown did not have to reach into its own pocket. In return the governor of Florida promised to support any priests the Crown sent out to him; he would meet every additional expense of the adventure and swore he had no financial claim on the Court of Spain. He would "conquer and populate," and the settlers would not have to pay taxes for the first ten years.

It was all very clear, precise, and sensible. The only drawback was that De Soto had to overrun a virtually unknown country, defeat its natives whoever they might be, and with a handful of men-at-arms hold the land for Spain and the Emperor.

Naturally the Crown did best out of the arrangements. In exchange for the royal license, the treasury would receive one-fifth of all gold plundered, bartered or mined; one-fifth of all other output from the mines; one-fifth of all "silver, stones, pearls and other things" won in battle; one-fifth of ransom money from captured chiefs; and one-half of all buried treasure. If anyone tried to cheat the Crown by hiding his loot, his profits would be confiscated by the exchequer and half the remaining property seized. Finally, if De Soto deliberately failed to comply with any of the conditions in his license, he would be punished under the charge of high treason.

The Crown could not lose. If De Soto was successful, the King would gain a new colony, new subjects, and a fresh supply of bullion to pour into the royal coffers. If De Soto failed, the Court would merely sympathize with his widow, comment on the sad loss of so brave and loyal a subject, and promptly issue the Florida license to somebody else.

Unlike many other Spanish generals, Columbus and Pizarro included, Hernando de Soto had not the slightest difficulty in raising the five hundred men which his license stipulated. Everything was in his favour and the chances for success too great. Here was an illustrious, rich, and experienced commander; no callow youth or groping amateur, but a captain who had already fought and conquered in central and south America. He promised to pay well and spare no expense in equipping his expedition. Best of all, there were rumors of fabulous riches in the lands to the north of New Spain. This Florida expedition was a logical step in the right direction: first, there had been Mexico of the Plumed Serpent in the center; then Peru of the Inca in the south; now surely the greatest prize lay to the north where no Spaniard had yet penetrated. Somewhere in the heart of the unknown land of North America bold conquistadors would find immense wealth. Was it not strange that De Soto, already so rich, should want to risk his neck again? He must surely have heard some definite news of a Golconda, perhaps from Cabeza de Vaca, who had been the treasurer of Narváez's unsuccessful trip and one of the four survivors who had emerged from the interior tantalizingly close-mouthed about their experiences in North America. It was reported that but for a squabble over his contract, de Vaca would have joined up with De Soto, and as it was he advised several of his cousins, including Baltazar de Gallegos and Cristobal de Espindola, to go along on the new venture. (Why Cabeza de Vaca did this will never be known; he had suffered nothing but misery and poverty as he walked from a shipwreck on the Texas coast to Mexico.) This combination of rumor, experience, optimism, and the spirit of adventure conjured up a giant mirage of certain success. Hidalgo and peasant flocked to De Soto's recruiting officers.

On the first day of registration 140 men signed up. The Marquis of Astoza was so attracted by what he heard about the chances for success that he sent along his brother Don Antonio Osorio and two other kinsmen. Many of De Soto's former comrades came out of retirement to join up once again. Some, like Moscoso, had already squandered their Peruvian spoils and wanted more; others had grown tired of the easy life and looked again for adventure in the unknown

west. Artisans abandoned their shops and farmers sold their
olive fields. Among the eager troops were three notaries, six
tailors, a seaman, a farrier, a stocking maker, a shoemaker, a
calker, and a sword cutler.[3] It was just as well that they were
signed on; two years later when the Florida army was isolated
and living off a hostile land, these artisans taught the proud
hildagos how to improvise badly needed equipment. Most of
the recruits came from De Soto's own province, Badajoz,
which had long been famous for providing conquistadors, but
nearly every Spanish province was represented. There was
also an international group—at least nineteen Portuguese
from across the border, two Genoese, a Greek engineer, four
"dark men" who were probably Berbers from North Africa,
one of whom finished up by running off with a Red Indian
princess, and even an Englishman who insisted on keeping his
longbow instead of adopting the Spanish crossbow. One
wonders how this lonely archer fared against the Seminoles of
the Florida swamps who used a similar weapon and outranged
the crossbows.

Still the recruits came in. Cavaliers in fine Milan plate
armor brought their horses, stewards, chamberlains, and
pages, as well as cases of delicacies and fine wines. There were
armorers and cooks, halberdiers and arquebusiers, lancers and
crossbowmen, quartermasters and secretaries. The Florida expedition resembled a medieval crusade preparing to depart for
the Holy Land; they had the same fervor and mystic faith in
their success. Twelve priests, including four friars, came to
convert the defeated heathen, and every detail of European
civilization was taken along to equip the travelers. Of course
it was better to pick up the bulky or perishable supplies when
the expedition visited Cuba, but there were many items that
could only be obtained in Spain, not least of which were
237 horses for shipment, including De Soto's favorite charger.
Most of the animals were cavalry mounts though there were

[3] Judging from these occupations, De Soto's expedition included
several Jews who wanted to leave Spain in order to escape the In-
quisition.

one or two pack horses. A number of specially selected cattle were also embarked for delivery to the Cuban settlers, and more important, a pack of fighting dogs was trained for the coming campaign. At an early stage in their American wars, the conquistadors had learned that nothing was more terrifying to the Indians than these vicious war hounds which the white men used to track down runaway slaves or to tear recalcitrant Indians to pieces.

The quartermasters busily checked in tents and weapons; blacksmiths' and carpenters' tools; spare bars of iron; kegs of nails; wine, bread and "twenty-five hundred shoulders of bacon"; horseshoes and farriers' supplies; beads, metal bells, knives, and looking glasses for the Indian trade; salt and spices; water barrels and shackles for prisoners. There were extra bowstrings for the archers and festoons of spare harness for the cavalry; bundles of pikeshafts and swordblades; cooking oil and garlic. The list was long as it was varied; once the army had landed in Florida, its contact with the supporting fleet was problematical and they had to provide for at least eighteen months of independent operations in the interior of the country. Quite what they would find, no one knew. It was best to be prepared. The Army of Florida was the youngest, the best equipped, and the most professional ever to sail from Spain to "conquer and populate" lands in the New World. Only half the 622 warriors were to return.

De Soto's fleet crossed San Lucar bar on Sunday morning April 7, 1538. It was a brave show. Seven vessels had been hired for the transport of the army and they joined a fleet of twenty sail bound for Mexico. De Soto himself, newly created a knight of Santiago, led the way aboard his flagship, the *San Cristobal*. Behind him wallowed the rest of the fleet— tubby "galeons," high-decked and square-rigged; sleeker, more heavily armed caravels, the true ocean-going vessels of the Spanish explorers; low-built brigantines; and, almost lost among the waves, tiny pinnaces which would later be used for searching out coastal inlets and sounding the way for the bigger ships.

The transatlantic voyage was a gay holiday. The weather held clear and the fleet stayed close together. Captains and noblemen maintained all the elegance of life ashore; they paid courtesy calls from one vessel to another and gave dinners and graceful luncheons. None of the niceties were overlooked. Precedence was observed, compliments were passed from ship to ship, and the hidalgos dressed in their best finery. Occasionally De Soto called together his lieutenants for portentous conferences on tactics, logistics, and battle plans. The entire company was buoyant with expectation and optimism. The great adventure was under way and no obstacles could stop the conquistadors.

Cuba was reached by early June and there De Soto took possession of his governorship. He toured the island, exercised his troops, installed his wife in Havana as his personal representative, and appointed a lieutenant-governor. But this was all incidental to the main quest; Cuba was the jumping-off point for Florida and was to be turned into the supply base for the expedition. He dispatched a squadron of ships to find a suitable landing place on the Florida coast and to bring back native hostages to use as guides and interpreters. A commissary was established in Cuba; crops were reserved for future supply fleets; and cattle were turned out on newly acquired grazing land. De Soto's money seemed inexhaustible and, as this expedition was his heart's desire, he spent it like water. The storeships took on "2,500 hanegas of maize," 500 quintals of cassava, cloaks, coats, doublets, breeches, stockings, footware of all kinds from half boots to sandals, cuirasses, shields, helmets, sails, rigging, pitch tallow, ropes, baskets, crates, anchors, cable, "much iron and steel," spades, mattocks and pincers—all "things necessary for settlement." De Soto had scoured Spain for his supplies and now he scoured Cuba in the same grand manner. He even took aboard a herd of swine which, by a stroke of genius, were to form the army's mobile larder, following the line of march all the way to the Mississippi and beyond. Finally De Soto drew up his will, reaffirmed his partnership with Ponce de Leon, said good-bye to his wife, and set sail for Florida. Isabel de Bobadilla did not see her husband again.

Everything continued to go well, far better, in fact, than De Soto had any right to expect. On May 30, 1539 the army —horses, dogs, pigs, and men—began going ashore at Tampa Bay on the coast of the Florida peninsula. The disembarkation was unopposed and there was no sign of the natives, who, incidentally, had seen Narváez and his expedition come ashore in the same businesslike fashion eleven years before and flee a few months later in complete confusion. Once the landing was over, the main army camped on the pleasant beach while patrols went out to make contact with the wary Indians.

The venture still had the air of a holiday. The young cavaliers were enchanted by the beauty of the scene—the dazzling blue of sea and sky, the white curve of the sand leading up to the woods of cypress, live oak, and ash. Tents and pennons rippled in the breeze, horses were exercised on the beach to shake off the effects of the voyage. It was good to leave behind the stuffiness of the overcrowded ships and breathe the fresh air of the riviera.

The first patrols, probing inland, also succumbed to the holiday mood. Small groups of lancers rode off, the sand spurting beneath the hoofs of the chargers, to hunt in the woods for Indian or deer—it did not matter which. A foot patrol of forty soldiers marched inland to seize some natives to use as hostages and guides, because the captives brought back to Cuba by the scouting ships could not find their bearings and were sullenly unhelpful. The halberdiers clumped off in their hot armor and disappeared into the bush while the army waited impatiently and the young gallants itched to ride into battle against the natives and cover themselves with glory.

Soon it was clear that contact had been made with the Indians. Columns of smoke rising up over the dense green of the forest signaled that the natives were passing the alert from village to village. Then the lancers returned to report that the beautiful woodland was in fact hopeless country for cavalry maneuvers. The forest was a maze of ponds and marshes, separated by impassable undergrowth. The horses became entangled in thickets or sank up to their haunches in quagmires, cutting their legs on hidden snags. The silence of the swamps was unearthly, a half-lit gloom made all the more garish by long skeins of moss dripping from the branches of dead trees. Through these unnatural surroundings the patrols had forced their unwilling mounts. Constant plunging through scum-covered ponds and muddy sloughs took the heart out of the animals and they were soon reduced to a quaking, unreasonable stubbornness. The lancers were reluctant to dismount; their arms and useless weapons weighed them down and every step in slime or underbrush required a fresh effort. Luckily there were occasional Indian trails which followed dry ground, and on these footpaths the cavalry could improve their pace. But the trails were too narrow for more than a pair of lancers to ride abreast and this crippled their effectiveness; the massed charge, the favorite conquistador attack, would be out of the question in Florida. But that was not all. The patrol had surprised a small party of natives. Two of the Indians had been spitted on lances before the others collected their wits and fled into the woods where they had begun shooting arrows at their attackers from the shelter of the trees. By the time the patrol regained the safety of the open beach, the lurking savages had managed to kill two horses and wound several others. This was serious, for horses were irreplaceable and in the days to come the Spanish veterans knew from experience that they would depend on their cavalry to outmaneuver and frighten the natives.

When the foot patrol returned with two women prisoners, it was evident that the infantry had fared little better than the horsemen. Using an Indian trail, the halberdiers had reached an Indian village and seized the two women without difficulty. On the way back to camp their march had been haunted by savages, nine of them, a mere handful against forty trained pikemen, the best in Europe. However, there had been no contest. The Indians refused to face a pitched battle and instead had slipped from tree to tree, half-hidden and almost impossible targets. Arquebus and crossbow were outmatched by the Indian bows. The Spanish weapons were caught up in the undergrowth and there was no time to take careful aim at the flitting shapes of the natives. In return the Indians maintained a running fire of long, deadly arrows which hissed out of thickets, bushes, or from behind trees. The patrol had been lucky to fight its way back to camp with only one man killed and three or four others wounded. It was a stiff price to pay for two snarling, spitting women who would be unreliable as guides.

These two somber reports brought back by the patrols took the edge from the high spirits of the Spanish army. Their gaiety never really returned. The optimistic conquistadors did not know it then, but the next four years would provide an almost daily repetition of this futile punishment, as ambush followed ambush and the invading army was raked from end to end by the stinging hit-and-run attacks of the natives. Half the carefree cavaliers would leave their bones to whiten in "Tierra Florida"—the land of flowers.

The Spaniards were sobered, but not unduly alarmed. The veterans who had fought in Mexico and South America knew perfectly well that the natives usually put up stout resistance at the start of a campaign, culminating in a major battle. On previous occasions this head-on clash had been a disaster for the native forces. The foreigners' horses—completely unknown until then to the aborigines and often believed to be flesh-eating monsters—threw the vast native army into confusion. A shrewd cavalry charge delivered with tremendous punch turned this confusion into utter panic. The "men in steel," with their deadly metal weapons and screaming their battle cry "Santiago", the disciplined rush of the halberdiers accompanied by the metallic whir and thud of the crossbow bolts, the futility of blows ringing off steel cuirass and helm, and, above all, the fanatical crusading confidence of the invader—all these struck terror into the native warriors. They abandoned their leader, scattered and ran, while the Spanish cavalry dashed blithely among the fugitives, cutting them down as a small boy slashes at thistles.

Sooner or later De Soto's veterans anticipated just this kind of total victory. For the moment their experience told them that they must move inexorably forward, ignoring the pin-prick attacks of the guerrillas. Native guides, friendly or under torture, would eventually lead the invaders to the Indian capital and there the cacique, or chief, would mass his forces to defend the royal treasury. Accordingly, the Spanish army began to march inland, leaving a small force to hold the beachhead.

Almost at once De Soto had a tremendous stroke of luck, possibly the only time that good fortune really helped his Florida expedition. An advance patrol of cavalry came across a band of Indians in a clearing along one of the forest trails. Without pausing to consider why the Indians were exposing themselves in the open, the horsemen leveled their lances and charged. Their hasty belligerence almost cost the life of the most valuable member of the whole trip. The Indians fled into the trees, leaving one man wounded on the ground and another standing there apparently in a state of shock. A trooper was just poised to run the savage through, when the "Indian" fell to his knees, made the sign of the cross, and with difficulty cried out in halting Spanish, "Sevilla! Sevilla!" The effect of his strangled words was electrifying. The lancers dropped their weapons and clustered round the naked man, who explained that he was Juan Ortiz, a native of Seville. He had come to Florida with Narváez's expedition and had been captured by the natives. After being badly treated by the Indians, he escaped to join a friendly chief and had survived by "going native." He had been on his way to the Spanish camp with a party of friends, when the lancers had attacked them.

Juan Ortiz was a heaven-sent bonus for De Soto. The general was bewildered by the mysterious savages and the dense woodland. His Indian guides were either ignorant or surly and he could not trust them. The army had been blindly groping its way forward through the maze of swamps and forests. Now De Soto had the services of Ortiz, a reliable, intelligent guide, who spoke the local dialect fluently, knew the Indian customs, and could provide information on the politics and geography of the land. Ortiz was given the very best treatment. He was appointed to De Soto's staff, fed, and given communion by the priests. Because he was uncomfortable in the close-fitting Spanish clothes after eleven years of nakedness, he went around camp dressed in a long, loose linen wrap. In the coming days he was to act as De Soto's eyes and ears in the search for gold.

The army now marched forward with more confidence. Through Ortiz, De Soto managed to establish contact with Mococo, the friendly Indian chief who had looked after the marooned Spaniard. A peace treaty was arranged and the Indians agreed to supply the invaders with maize and guides. But Mococo did not possess any gold and it was necessary to send a squadron of cavalry to seek out the neighboring tribes deep in the forest. De Soto entrusted this raiding party to his oldest hidalgo, Vasco Porcallo de Figueroa. The fat Porcallo was a standing joke among the army. He was one of the few old men on the trip and built like a barrel of lard. He had joined the expedition at Cuba where he helped supply the army with victuals on the condition that he could recoup his investment by enslaving Indian prisoners in Florida and shipping them back to work on his Cuban estates. The younger officers in De Soto's expedition made fun of the obese cavalier who preferred slaves to gold and glory; Porcallo had put up with their banter, even when his first cavalry sortie ended up in a marsh and its portly leader had fallen headlong into the slime. His return to camp had been greeted with howls of mirth as the crestfallen knight had ridden in, covered from helm to boot with mud and weed. But it was not so amusing when his official raiding party failed to find any Indians to enslave. After a long, hot ride his forty troopers compelled a native to lead them to his village, but the guide succeeded in warning the tribe, which fled. The patrol rode into an empty village and in his rage Porcallo had the treacherous native torn to pieces by the war dogs. Then the patrol rode back to the main camp where Porcallo and De Soto had a bitter argument—De Soto was angry with Porcallo because he had failed to find gold; Porcallo was upset because he hadn't found slaves. The upshot of the quarrel was that Porcallo withdrew from the expedition. His baggage was taken back to the coast and he sailed to Cuba with the fleet, which was returning to the island to refit.

By now the Spanish had worn Mococo's hospitality thin. The Indian chief realized that the sooner the Spanish army left, the better it would be for him and his tribe. He therefore employed a simple ruse which De Soto was to encounter again and again: Mococo informed the Spanish general that although he himself did not have any gold, another tribe some distance away possessed legendary stores of bullion and gems. Naturally it would take several weeks' march to reach this glittering prize, but he, Mococo, would gladly provide guides for the first part of the journey. These guides could lead De Soto to the limits of their tribal territory and then hand him on to Indians from the neighboring tribe.

It was a childishly naïve strategem, but it always worked. One chief after another used the same trick to rid himself of the Spanish army, preferably diverting the unwelcome invaders into the lands of a tribal enemy. The Spaniards were a menace. Their priests insisted on lecturing the simple villagers; their soldiers always demanded porters and servants; and, worst of all, they ate like locusts so that if they were not encouraged to leave, there would be nothing left in the granaries for winter.

Of course De Soto knew exactly what the Indian chiefs were plotting. Yet he had no choice but to move on. He could not afford to exhaust his men in fruitless holding operations and he was equally worried by shortages of food. The native economy could support his invading army for a limited length of time only. As soon as the local stocks of maize were eaten, the Spanish were compelled to move on. They assembled a marching supply of food, packed up their belongings, and forced the local cacique to provide a small army of porters. Then the expedition snaked off through the woods, a long file of cavalry, halberdiers, crossbowmen, arquebusiers, retainers, camp followers (including one or two women), natives, porters, and livestock. At the head of the column small mounted parties fanned out to select the route, to probe for ambushes, to forage and, always, to search diligently for the slightest trace of gold or silver. The expedition was an enormous questing centipede, groping forward, feeling a path around obstacles, stopping for food and rest. It marched deeper and deeper into the blanket of primeval forest which covered the southern United States, up the Florida peninsula, and toward what is now the state of Georgia.

The cavalry was always the busiest. Besides scouting ahead, the lancers galloped up and down the long-drawn-out line of march trying to control the unwieldy mass of porters and footmen. The horsemen had to be everywhere at once. They provided the mobile reserve in case of attack; they acted as couriers, carrying messages between the various captains; and they were allotted the undignified role of swineherds. The porkers which De Soto had brought from Cuba were already proving a huge success. The pigs thrived and there were now more than three hundred of them, happily grubbing for roots and nuts on the forest floor. Several had been stolen by the Indians, drowned while crossing rivers, or strayed off into the forest, but the bulk of the herd was in fine fettle and squealing families of piglets more than made up for the losses. De Soto attached great importance to the swine; indeed he was obsessed with their welfare and refused to allow his soldiers to eat them. The pigs were to be preserved as a mobile larder against hard times and the cursing troopers were ordered to chase the grunting herd along the line of march, taking care not to lose a single animal.

The Spanish men-at-arms learned to adapt themselves to the strange conditions of the mainland. When it became apparent that there would be a great deal of marching before they reached their goal, the soldiers had abandoned such heavy equipment as mattocks and spare armor, and the expedition's trail was dotted with caches of materiel which had been buried for future use. Most of the heavy labor and transport was handled by the gangs of Indian porters who were either captives or coerced from local chiefs. The manacles which De Soto had brought from Spain were used on the more unruly porters, but despite this precaution a steady trickle of fugitives vanished into the bush each night. As the army moved forward the Spaniards noticed that they had less and less trouble from their slave labor; it was evident that once a captive Indian was taken outside his tribal territory he was reluctant to escape, preferring to stay with the Spanish army rather than run the risk of falling into the hands of a hostile tribe. Only the bravest Indians were prepared to face unknown country, unfriendly natives who did not speak his dialect, and the inevitable pursuit by bloodhounds and cavalry. If the fugitive was caught, he was thrown to the dogs and torn to pieces by the pack as an example to his fellows.

The Spaniards never quite grasped the extent of Indian bravery and tribal loyalty. One guide after another coolly led the invaders into swamps or ambushes, even though it was suicide for the man concerned. Even the smallest tribes put up a fight. They burned their crops and villages to the ground in a scorched-earth policy, cut off and killed isolated dispatch riders, set ambushes, and hid their food supplies. Any solitary Spaniard wandering too near the trees was liable to collect an arrow in the back, and at night the bushes around the bivouac rustled with hidden snipers. In the morning it was not uncommon to find the headless body of a Spanish soldier dangling from a tree in full view of the camp.

The Indians were unlike any enemy that the conquistadors had experienced in the New World. It was impossible either to force them into an open fight or to conclude a lasting peace treaty with their caciques. The steel-clad might of the Spanish veterans had run into the one obstacle it could not crush—guerrilla warfare conducted by skilled archers.

The Indians chose to stay within the shelter of their forests and there was nothing the Spanish cavalry could to do dislodge them. The pikemen were too slow and the crossbowmen were helpless. All this would not have been fatal if the invading army could have marched through the country like a Roman "tortoise" protected by its defensive armor. But this was impossible; the native weapons were too powerful. The Indian archers used a crude composite bow which the Spanish found difficult to bend. These bows discharged arrows with terrific force and considerable accuracy. In one experiment De Soto watched an Indian warrior put an arrow clean through a plate of Milan steel hung up in a tree eighty feet away. When a second plate was put up behind the first, the Indian put his next arrow through both pieces of armor. As few of the conquistadors wore really good armor and many of the foot soldiers threw away their heavier defensive equipment while on the long, hot marches, it was not surprising that after a skirmish the Spanish dead were sometimes found transfixed from front to back by a three-foot arrow tipped with bone, flint, or even the needle-sharp claw of a crab. However, the Spaniards found that even the best armor was of little use against the deadliest version of Indian arrow—a simple cane shaft sharpened, and the tip hardened over a fire. When one of these scored a direct hit on chain mail, the first six inches shattered into splinters that penetrated the interstices of the mail and left an ugly festering wound that healed far more slowly than any sword cut. To protect themselves against these projectiles, the Spanish adopted the native armor of loose quilted jackets stuffed with cotton padding—an ominous trend when the "civilized" invaders were compelled to use native weaponry.

The Spanish were resourceful in other ways as well. After one or two false starts and several accidental poisonings they discovered which herbs they could use for cooking, and they learned that it was easier to eat roasted maize than waste time grinding the kernels for flour. For some time they hunted deer, but these were hard to find and so the troops took to eating opossum, acquiring a taste for the "little dogs which do not bark." Swamps, marshes, and rivers were the worst problems. They delayed and exhausted the army, which often spent whole days wading chest-deep through water. Fortunately one of the Genoese volunteers and two Cuban half-breeds were engineers and knew how to make bridges and causeways. With local timber and ropes specially brought for the purpose, the vanguard went ahead to prepare a road for the main army across the worst obstacles. At the shallower rivers the horsemen would ride their mounts into the stream and form a long line from bank to bank. Then the footmen would scramble across, clinging to stirrups, girth bands, and manes. Once or twice crude rafts were made and floated across, or a block-and-tackle arrangement reeled in the less willing animals to the opposite bank.

As the Spaniards pushed northward, De Soto found himself more and more isolated. His line of communication with Tampa became too tenuous and had to be abandoned; the forests seemed interminable; and, to make matters worse, Ortiz was losing contact with the natives. His knowledge was limited to the tribe he had lived with and now it was increasingly difficult for him to interpret. He had to work through a long chain of translators, each of whom spoke only one or two regional dialects. By the time the information had been passed along the line to Ortiz, the result was scarcely intelligible. De Soto was increasingly forced to rely on guesswork to determine his route.

Near the Suwannee River in northern Florida, De Soto finally encountered the stand-up fight he had been hoping for. A band of some four hundred Indian warriors tried to rescue their chief who was a hostage in the Spanish camp. They asked for a parley on open ground and planted an ambush, concealing their weapons in the long swamp grass. De Soto was too experienced a campaigner to be taken in by their offer and decided to spring the trap. Stationing his cavalry in the cover of the surrounding woods, he and several attendants walked out toward the waiting Indians. It was a characteristically brave maneuver which paid off. Moscosco, hidden among the trees, waited until he saw the savages closing in behind his commander. Then he ordered the attack and his lancers poured out of the wood, screaming their battle cry. The Indians were caught in their own ambush and could not withstand the full-blooded impact of the horsemen. De Soto swung into the saddle of a spare charger and led the slaughter. Few of the half-naked savages had time to grab their weapons; they scattered and fled for the woods with the cavalry at their heels. Most escaped safely but some were cut down and a few took refuge by throwing themselves into two small lakes nearby. There they swam out of crossbow range and hurled insults at the white men. De Soto saw his opportunity to teach the enemy a lesson and stationed guards around the shores. All night long the sentries picked off the Indians as they tried to swim to the bank, using lily pads for camouflage. Next morning twelve exhausted Indians were still treading water defiantly. De Soto ordered his best swimmers to fish them out and had them put in chains. De Soto had proved his point—the invaders were infinitely superior in open battle. Unfortunately for the Spanish this was the only occasion in which De Soto was able to show his flair and courage as a field commander.

Though they had been defeated and captured, the Indians refused to give up the struggle. The Spaniards had scarcely finished celebrating the victory of the lakes when their slave gangs rose up in revolt. The camp was thrown into an uproar. Howling porters rushed about bludgeoning their masters with stools, pots, pans, and firebrands. De Soto himself was attacked in his tent and a blow in the face knocked out several teeth before his bodyguard rushed in to the rescue. But once again the natives did not stand a chance. As soon as the Spanish had collected their wits, they grimly settled down to scotching the insurrection. Those Indians who had not fled were disarmed or put to the sword. Only one man lasted any length of time. He had managed to seize a lance and take refuge in a grain loft. There he made a last-ditch stand, fend-ing off all attackers, until a well-aimed Spanish battle-ax finally brought him tumbling to the ground. When order had been restored, a grim-faced De Soto ordered the execution of all surviving rebels.

On September 3 the army resumed its northward march. It was time for De Soto to find winter quarters for his expedition, and fortunately near modern Tallahassee the country began to improve. The woods thinned out and there were many more villages surrounded by fields of maize. The inhabitants had all fled but they left behind the contents of their "barbacoas"—elevated grain bins—and the standing crops. The Spanish soldiers harvested beans, pumpkins, walnuts, and plums until there was enough food for winter, and then began building a fortified camp. A cavalry patrol reported that the Gulf coast was only eight leagues away. On the beach they had found the last traces of Narváez's departure: crosses carved on trees, mangers hollowed from tree trunks, and the skulls of horses. It seemed a good moment to consolidate his forces, so De Soto ordered up the men from the base camp at Tampa and his supply fleet arrived with fresh supplies. When these had been landed, the general sent his ships back to Cuba except for one caravel which was dispatched westward to follow the coast until a good natural harbor was found.

The caravel returned in February after the army had spent a miserable winter under daily harassment from the natives. Now there was good news to cheer them. The exploring ship had located an excellent harbor in Pensacola Bay, and it was arranged that her captain would return there with the supply fleet the following autumn to greet the expeditionary force after its second summer in the field. To add to the general feeling of well-being in the Spanish camp, a native prisoner revealed that he came from a land far to the east which was ruled by a woman. His queen received tribute of furs and gold from all the surrounding tribes. To convince his audience, the native even demonstrated how the yellow metal was dug from the ground, melted and refined. The Spanish soldiers were elated; the captive's story sounded just like a description of another fabulous Mexico or Peru. They could hardly wait to invade this promised land. Swayed by the eagerness of his men, De Soto ordered the evacuation of their winter quarters and on March 3, 1540, the army of Florida began its march into the pinelands of Georgia.

It was a miserable journey. The Spanish were being lured deeper into the heart of the great North American land mass. The glittering prize of gold always seemed to elude them by one day's journey—so they struggled on, mesmerized by hope. They were marching through the trackless southern forests which even the Indians shunned. Food ran out, porters starved to death or were sent back to lessen the number of mouths to feed, men-at-arms staggered forward with their extra load of equipment, horses died. De Soto ordered some of the hogs to be killed, but the issue of half a pound per man did not ease the situation. The usual food ration was a handful of parched grain each day. The advance guard wore itself out hacking a path through the trees, river after river was flooded, and only the unquenchable optimism of the conquistadors kept them moving forward.

It was all to no avail. The army emerged from the forests into the land of the Creek Indians. The countryside was green and fertile, but the Spaniards were not there to colonize, they wanted precious metal. It was obvious that they would not find it among the grass huts of the Creeks, whose most valued belongings were skeins of pipe weed and beautifully decorated straw baskets.

Near the northern border of Georgia the army found its tribute-collecting queen, the "Princess of Cofitachequi." But she was a sad disappointment. Her "gold" turned out to be burnished copper and her slabs of silver were sheets of mica. The only booty was a heap of river pearls extracted from fresh-water mussels, but most of these were ruined by boring or discolored in the fire. The Spaniards collected 350 pounds of the pearls and left in disgust. According to legend one of the Berbers stayed behind to marry the princess and rule as lord of Cofitachequi.

Through the southern part of South Carolina, into North Carolina, Tennessee, and northern Alabama, De Soto led his army, during the summer of 1540. Marching and counter-marching, they quartered the land ruthlessly, following up every rumor of gold. Their spirits rose as they climbed the Appalachians for they were reminded of the uplands of Peru and Mexico, but they found nothing. The soldiers suffered the cold nights of the Blue Ridge Mountains and were battered by hailstorms. The Indians stayed out of their way, leaving mute offerings of food, deerskins, and feathered cloaks in the path of the ferocious invaders. The Spanish were not interested. The unending countryside seemed a cruel joke, beckoning them on. One mountain ridge after another had to be climbed; each river looked the same as the previous one they had forded, and the maps which the sixteenth-century geographers pieced together from the expedition's diaries reveal the extent of their confusion: the southeastern United States is misshapen and embellished with a random scattering of Indian villages, mountains and rivers. Even the Tennessee is mistakenly believed to be the Mississippi and labeled as "the great river from which we (the army of Florida) took our departure."

With the decline in their hopes, Spanish discipline began to sag. The cavalry had little to complain about, riding with moderate comfort in their high Moorish saddles. It was the foot soldiers who began to grumble. They bore the brunt of the hardships. It was their job to carry the bulk of the equipment, hack the paths, and erect the bridges. At river crossings they were compelled to wade through the icy water, holding crossbow and arquebus out of the stream, and to add insult to injury, they were the worst fed. The cavalry did the foraging, and when they returned to camp there was little food left for the half-starving infantry. De Soto of course was a cavalryman at heart and in this age-old rivalry he failed to look after his men. One by one the foot soldiers began to desert, slipping away at night to seek an oblivious life of ease among the natives. De Soto was obliged to post sentries at night to guard against desertions and to place a cavalry squad at the rear of his column to round up stragglers.

De Soto could not allow his army to linger and rest. The native economy was so delicately balanced that the arrival of his army wiped out local food reserves. He was forced to keep on the move, swinging in a great loop across the mountains and then heading southward through Alabama toward the coast. The end of August saw the expedition marching briskly in the direction of their proposed rendezvous with the supply fleet at Pensacola Bay. There they would pick up replacements and supplies; it was enough to encourage the men and make them travel faster. By now the army had evolved an effective technique for dealing with the natives: at each village a show of force persuaded the Indian chief to cooperate in providing food, shelter, and porters. If the soldiers needed women, the gift of a few mirrors, combs, and other trinkets was considered a fair trade. Before the expedition left the settlement, De Soto would arrest the chief and take him along as a hostage to prevent a revolt in the rear of his line of march. It was a callous policy which, sooner or later, would anger a warlike tribe.

The Indians who struck back at the Spanish were the Choctaws of south central Alabama. De Soto entered their territory early in October and was greeted by their paramount chief Tuscaloosa, the "Black Warrior." If De Soto had known the fierce reputation of the Choctaws, he might have advanced with a little more caution. As it was, he agreed to meet Tuscaloosa in the central square of the village of Athahachi. It was an impressive meeting; the Spanish general clad in armor on his charger and the Indian chief seated on a pile of cushions, wearing a full-length mantle of feathers. Tuscaloosa greeted De Soto warily but seemed willing to let the Spanish cross his lands. De Soto responded in his usual high-handed style. He accepted the offer and ordered his halberdiers to seize Tuscaloosa and take him with the column. It was a fatal mistake; Tuscaloosa managed to send runners to his war chiefs, summoning them to his capital at Mobila where they were to ambush the Spanish.

When Tuscaloosa told him that Mobila held ample supplies of food, De Soto decided to march on the capital. He was moving straight into the trap and to make matters worse he allowed his troops to disperse and forage. When the main column reached the town, De Soto was accompanied by fifteen troopers and a huge, surly mob of slaves, hostages, and prisoners. Despite the warnings of a Spanish spy who told De Soto that Mobila was swarming with Choctaw warriors, the stiff-necked general decided to enter the town with Tuscaloosa at his side. As the handful of Spaniards passed through the gates, their attention was diverted by a team of dancing girls stationed there as decoys. Then Tuscaloosa signaled his braves to attack and they rushed out from the houses. De Soto and his companions were hard pressed. Fighting desperately, they backed toward the gate with blows ringing off their armor. Five of the white men were cut to pieces protecting their general, and if De Soto's secretary, Roderigo Ranjel, and a lone cavalier had not suddenly charged into the fray, De Soto would certainly have been killed.

De Soto's life was saved but his negligence was still to prove the ruin of his expedition. During the skirmish in the town, the Indians in the baggage train had seized their opportunity to escape. They broke ranks and streamed into Mobila, taking with them all the Spanish supplies including the spare weapons, sacraments, tents, pearls, and gunpowder. By the time the main body of the Spanish army arrived, the situation was desperate. They had only their weapons, while on the other side of Mobila's palisades lay all the equipment they needed to survive the march down to the coast. Already the ramparts were lined with newly liberated slaves, jeering and holding up their booty to mock the white men.

For De Soto there was no alternative: he had to capture Mobila and regain his equipment. The siege lasted all day and was a blood bath. The Spanish infantry desperately hurled themselves against the palisades, hacking at the logs with axes. Each time they were beaten back by the fanatical Choctaw. Finally De Soto had to fire the town, risking his equipment in the conflagration. Mobila was built of wood and straw so it

burned like a tinderbox. But with the flames behind them and
the halberdiers in front, the Choctaw warriors refused to surrender. They stubbornly resisted the armored Spanish attack
and inflicted heavy casualties—De Soto himself received an
arrow in the rump and spent the rest of the battle standing in
his stirrups, while Nuno Tobar was amazed to see an arrow
pierce his lance shaft and stay there like a cross-piece for the
remainder of the battle. As the day progressed, it became
clear that the Spanish would never recover their equipment;
it was all being destroyed in the flames. The siege became a
massacre but still the Choctaw kept up the fight. Not until
their last warrior hanged himself from the ramparts with his
own bowstring did the fighting stop, and by then there was
very little left of the town.

The battle was a total military victory for the Spanish but
it was a victory they could not afford. In addition to losing
their matériel, they had 22 dead and 148 wounded; among the
latter the surgeons counted 688 arrow wounds. Included
in the dead were Don Carlos, De Soto's brother-in-law, and
his nephew, Francisco de Soto. Hardly a soldier had come
through unscathed; they were burned, hungry, and exhausted. De Soto had put himself in an impossible tactical
position and paid the price for his stupidity. By rights, his
Florida expedition was finished. They should all limp to the
coast, rendezvous with the ships, and go home.

But that was not De Soto's style. He had plotted, worked,
and risked so much for this venture that he was not willing to
abandon his dream. He was stubbornly convinced that somewhere in Tierra Florida he would build his empire, and he
was too proud to return to Spain in failure. So when a messenger secretly arrived from the coast to report that the supply fleet was waiting, De Soto suppressed the news. Instead he
ordered his army to march directly inland away from the
ships, for fear that the men would desert and sail home. By
sheer force of character De Soto led his men from their obvious salvation and took them, ill-equipped and battered, into
the interior for three more years of fighting. The army

dressed its wounds with fat from the Choctaw dead and grimly set off toward the northwest, marching between the Tombigbee and Alabama rivers. The fleet waited in vain to provide them with fresh supplies and then sailed back to Cuba, not knowing what had become of the Florida expedition.

The siege of Mobila changed De Soto and changed his army. After the disaster the general lost his flamboyance; he became morose and spent more time alone, brooding over his plans. With the loss of their baggage, the army took on the appearance of a gang of buccaneers. There was no more need for porters as they possessed only what they stood up in. Yet they did not complain. Their earlier craze for gold was replaced by a strange crusading spirit, a feeling that they had embarked on a Christian quest which required penitence and sacrifice.

At first the natives stayed clear of this wild-eyed rabble of men; they had been shaken by the ferocity of Mobila and did not wish to tackle the Spanish again. But as De Soto moved toward the northern part of what is now the state of Mississippi, his route took him into the territory of the Chickasaw Indians, who had never yet seen a white man and were famous for their valor. The Chickasaw resented the intrusion of De Soto's army and his constant demands for food, blankets, and furs. They planned an attack and waited their opportunity. De Soto, however, was a chastened leader; he was more cautious and more watchful. It was the easygoing Luis de Moscoso who gave the Chickasaw their chance. Moscoso was Master of the Camp and responsible for the posting of sentries. On the night of Thursday, March 3, 1541, he neglected to set a trustworthy guard around the Spanish bivouac. Several hundred Chickasaw warriors succeeded in creeping within range of the camp, each carrying his weapon and a firebrand concealed in an earthenware pot. It is said that each Indian also carried three ropes—one for a Christian, one for a horse, and one for a pig. The fire attack was a complete surprise. Within minutes the camp was in flames while the dazed soldiers fumbled with breastplates and helmets. The sparks set alight the pigsty and the squealing of porkers added to the pandemonium as almost three hundred pigs roasted to death. Only the piglets managed to wriggle through the bars; the air smelled of roast pork while, according to one account, the bacon grease flowed out over the ground. Almost single-handed De Soto saved his army. Buckling on his armor he was first into the fight and rallied his men. The horses broke loose and the thunder of their stampede terrified the Chickasaw, who fled. The Spanish were left to battle the flames.

When the fire was extinguished, De Soto saw the smoldering debris of his army of Florida. It was a worse disaster than Mobila. A dozen Spaniards had been killed or burned to death, fifty or sixty horses had been lost, and the last surviving woman member of the expedition was dead. The real damage was to the weapons and clothing. Almost every shred of the soldiers' blankets and garments had been burned, most of the men were naked, and there was nothing to protect them from the cold nights. Nearly all the metal weapons had been ruined, losing their temper in the inferno, and all the saddlery was wrecked. Everything wooden was now a charred mass—saddles, lance shafts, ax and pike handles. The Chickasaw had not lost a single warrior.

Under these appalling conditions the Spanish army was at its best. Their resilience was extraordinary. Luckily a heavy shower of rain broke up a second Chickasaw attack, wetting bowstrings and rendering their weapons useless. The Spanish used the respite to full advantage. Working furiously for the next two weeks, they rigged up a crude forge, using rough bellows made from bearskins and musket barrels, and retempered sword blades, crossbows, pike heads, and armor. They salvaged every scrap of metal from the cinders and cut lance shafts from the nearest grove of trees. The runaway horses were rounded up and equipped with harness made from twisted grass ropes. The men scavenged for skins and grass mats, making sleeping bags and kilts to ward off the cold. By the time the Chickasaw returned to the attack, the Spaniards were in fighting trim and easily defeated their enemy.

Although Moscoso was demoted for his negligence, there was little time for recriminations. De Soto realized that it was essential to leave Chickasaw territory before his command was wiped out by this warrior tribe. Accordingly the army of Florida gathered together its home-made gear and moved westward through the northern part of the state of Mississippi as fast as their wounds and burns would allow.

3

The "Rio Grande"

IN EARLY MAY, DE SOTO'S WESTWARD PATH BROUGHT
him through forest and swamp lands to the province of
Quizquiz, held at that time by Indians of the Alabama tribe.
Pushing forward through a succession of small villages, the
army came within sight of a huge river, bigger by far than
any river ever seen before in Europe or Mexico. The date
was Sunday, May 8, 1541, and the army had been in the
field for two years. The river was the Mississippi.

Much has been made of the historic moment when De
Soto and his men first looked upon the greatest river in North
America, until then known to Europeans only as a dim and
shadowy mystery. Paintings, murals, statuary, and poems
have commemorated the event. Very few pay any attention
to the realities of the scene. What is probably the most famous painting of all shows De Soto, gorgeously plumed with
flaunting ostrich feathers, clad in a shining suit of jousting
armor, astride a leggy, prancing steed. Clustering around their
lord are his innumerable soldiers, sturdy, strong and crisp in
gleaming steel. Happy-looking Indians in feather crowns,
robust Negroes in panther skins, cedars, cypresses, and flow-

ering azaleas complete the picture. Above them proudly flies
the flag of Castile, and there, before the eyes of the conquistadors, flows the mighty river, almost lost in the depths of a
stupendous gorge.

The arrival of the exploring Europeans on the banks of
the Mississippi was indeed a historic moment, but the actual
circumstances were vastly different from the popular picture.
The river, in fact, was hidden by a thick, dank forest, probably cypress and oak. Straggling in untidy batches through the
willow thickets of the soggy river bottoms, the Spaniards
found themselves looking across a huge expanse of water,
flowing from right to left across their line of march. To the
Spanish soldiers the Mississippi was, at first, like any other
large lowland river—broad, flat, and turbid. Later the Father
of Waters was to be the lifeline that saved the bulk of the
army, but at first glimpse its only real distinction was its
immense size—the army's chroniclers immediately called the
river the "Rio Grande." The sheer width of so large a body
of flowing water has always staggered the European observer;
and it must have been all the more huge to De Soto's men,
most of whom came from the arid Iberian peninsula, where
such monstrous rivers are geographical impossibilities. Before
them the Spaniards saw a dirty chocolate-brown flood of
water, some two miles wide, pouring steadily and rapidly to
the south. In the current floated dead trees of every size, from
forest giants to twigs, all of them twisting and gyrating in
gurgling circles as the floodwater carried the debris of a continent down to the sea. The current ran strongly with quirk-
ish humor, ripping, sucking, and gnawing at the soft black
earth of the alluvial bank. Without warning a slice of the
bank would quietly slip down into the water with a soft hiss
and a spatter of pebbles. For a moment the waters riffle and
color with tons of earth, then they close back to slide on
seaward, unchanged and indistinguishable. A tall tree that has
grown untouched for a century falls with a sudden splash as
the river eats under the roots. The tree, wallowing in a brief
surge of foam, hangs a moment or two, fighting the pull of

the stream which piles a sleek hump of pressure against the obstacle. Then, as the roots finally release their grip, the great tree swings slowly away and out into the current, gradually accelerating to join the anonymous flotsam of the great river. Out on the warm surface of the water, small whirlpools and spiraling upcurrents break the brown flood into constant streaks, whorls, and circles. In a breeze the river glitters with bright flecks, and in a storm thousand upon thousands of short, ugly waves tumble and thrash in a wicked criss-cross jumble.

Gazing across at the far bank, a low distant line of thick forest green, De Soto and his men could not appreciate the significance of their find. Undoubtedly it was the giant river they had heard rumored in Spain and Cuba, from Indian tales and from their guides. But America was known as a land of wonders and somewhere in the interior there might be other rivers, even bigger; at best the "Rio Grande" could lead them to some rich tribe of valley Indians abounding in precious metals and gems. The Mississippi was, first and foremost, a tiresome obstacle to their march; it meant building ferry boats and that would delay the army. No one in the hard-bitten band of adventurers realized that the fame of their expedition would rest in part upon their discovery of the Mississippi and that several of them, De Soto included, would find a graveyard in its muddy depths.

The Spanish army was indeed a remarkable sight, but not for its pomp and splendor; De Soto, lean and unkempt, sitting loose in the short stirrups of his high wooden saddle, his horse scrawny and jaded; the gaunt soldiers, hollow-cheeked and unshaven. Most of the men were dressed in ponchos and kilts of dried grass, though a few luckier ones could boast padded cotton surcoats or rough breeches made from animal skins, bald with wear. The priests had lost all their vestments and now were dressed like the other men, only a crude cross daubed with ocher on their buckskins set them apart. There were hungry, exhausted Indian porters stooped under their loads, ungainly wicker panniers and sacks of corn and nuts;

here and there were war dogs, fierce and lean after months of ill-treatment and semistarvation, scarred from battles and distempered through neglect. There was not a single piece of shining armor to be seen anywhere; cuirasses, helms, morions, arquebuses, and swords were dented or rusted, home-made lance shafts crooked, saddle frames crude and ugly. Yet this was a unique army. Hounded by bad luck, it had lived and fought for twenty-three months across thousands of miles of hostile territory. It had survived two major disasters that by rights should have broken its back and sent it packing for civilization. With machete and ax the invaders had hacked out trails for horse and foot through territory so harsh that the Indians had left it untrodden. A lone Spanish expedition had ranged more widely than the fiercest war party had dreamed of, farther even than the Spanish authorities in Madrid had imagined possible; all this without reinforcements or extra supplies from its base in Cuba. Every inch of the long road had been covered by foot soldiers encumbered with the clumsy weapons of their day. They had met and defeated army after army sent out by the opposing natives, not by superiority of weapons, for steel equipment and horses did not make up for the gross lack of numbers, but by courage and persistence. By the time the Florida expedition reached the bank of the Mississippi it was a hardened, compact band, which had learned to live off the land without faltering. Cut off from all contact with the world it came from, it marched forward in the finest blood-and-guts style, searching the country for plunder, led by a stern general whose character had been tempered by a succession of black disasters that followed an earlier history of dashing success.

De Soto now ordered his patrols to scout upstream until they found a suitable place to build ferry barges. Building, protecting, and operating these craft would be a delicate operation, for the river Indians were well organized and hostile. Near Sunflower Landing in the present state of Mississippi a site was selected where the river, instead of eroding the bank, had built up a firm sand bar. As it was on the inside of a meander bend, there was slack water into which the barges could be launched, and behind the sand bar the river bank rose steeply to a height of some twenty-five feet. Here De Soto posted his crossbowmen so that they had a clear field of fire overlooking the landing and could protect his carpenters as they worked on the boats. On May 21 the troops began felling trees and hauling them to the river, where amateur boatbuilders cut the timber into ribs, frames, and planks. The blacksmiths set up their home-made equipment once again and forged nails and spikes from scrap metal that had once been the army's spare weapons and armor. It was hard work and the men cursed the muggy heat of the river valley. They were suffering from malnutrition and salt deficiency, so their work progressed slowly as they toiled away with makeshift tools.

De Soto was unable to put all his men to work on the barges; he still needed foraging parties and guards. Food was a minor problem as the men quickly discovered that the "Rio Grande" swarmed with edible, if outlandish, fish which they could catch with crude nets and lines. On the other hand De Soto had to regard the local Indians with suspicion. Soon after the Spanish began operations on the sand bar, the Indians of the far bank sent across an armada of about two hundred war canoes. They were impressive vessels, huge dugouts manned by a double rank of paddlers, all moving in time to the commands of a captain in the stern. Archers stood in the bow of each canoe and the whole fleet was controlled by a chief who sat on cushions under an awning in the lead vessel. The Indians were probably arriving to investigate the presence of these curious white men, but De Soto, seeing their feathered headdresses and painted bodies, ordered his crossbowmen to warn them off. The Spanish archers opened fire as soon as the native armada came within bowshot, and the Indians received the salvo with dignified composure. The fleet put about in an orderly maneuver and not a single paddler broke rhythm, even when a crossbow bolt struck down the man next to him. Every day thereafter the Indian armada put in an appearance at three o'clock in the afternoon and stood off at long range, firing arrows at the boatbuilders. No one was hurt but the construction of the barges was delayed and everyone in the army worried about the crossing.

After twenty-eight days of feverish activity De Soto had four barges ready for the water. He was deeply concerned about the dangers of the crossing. If the disciplined Indian war fleet caught his boats in midstream, the Spanish would be annihilated. The men-at-arms rowing the unwieldy barges would be hampered by their cargo of horsemen and at the mercy of the faster Indian dugouts, who would pick off the Spaniards one by one. Accordingly De Soto decided to link his boats together and try a dawn crossing, hoping to take the Indians by surprise. On June 18, three hours before daylight, the soldiers manhandled the barges into the water and towed them upstream for about a mile. There the boats were tied in line ahead with cables and in each of the three rear vessels De Soto placed four picked lancers, their horses, and a covering force of crossbowmen. The lead barge was packed with heavily armored Spanish footmen; their job was to row the string of boats across the river, regardless of Indian attack.

The crossing was a complete success. The Indians had no idea that the Spanish were ready to make their attempt and failed to post lookouts. Using the four-mile-an-hour current to the best advantage the Spanish oarsmen towed the convoy across the Mississippi without encountering a single hostile canoe. When they were two stones' throw from the opposite bank the twelve lancers spurred their horses off the boats and went charging up through the shallows. In the dawn light the surprise was devastating. A handful of Indians who were supposed to be guarding the beach were caught unawares and fled without contesting the landing. De Soto had secured his beachhead without losing a man.

While the advance party established and held a defense perimeter, the ferries shuttled back and forth with the remainder of the expedition. By noon De Soto had taken off his last soldier and the entire army of Florida was safely on the far side of the Mississippi and ready to advance.

As soon as his forces had regrouped, De Soto decided to

move upstream against the "civilized" Indians whose highly organized war fleet indicated that they might be a rich and sophisticated tribe. It was De Soto's intention to attack the tribe from both the landward and river approaches, so he retained the four barges. While the cavalry and crossbowmen advanced along the bank, the bulk of the pikemen worked the boats upstream, keeping close to the bank in order to avoid the Mississippi's current. By splitting his army, De Soto made a tactical mistake: frequently the land party was obliged to detour away from the river to avoid sloughs, and the native archers took their chance to slip between the two halves of the Spanish expedition. The pikemen in the boats found themselves exposed to snipers firing down on them from the high bank and the boat crews began to take losses. After a few miles of this dangerous progress De Soto was forced to order his boats into the bank where they were beached and knocked apart. It was a hard decision to make, expecially after the labor that had gone into the construction of the vessels, but De Soto had become an exceptionally frugal commander. The days of lavish outfitting were long since past and every iron spike and metal nail in the barges had to be salvaged.

The army, now entirely on land, advanced through the worst country imaginable—the Mississippi bottomlands. The river, shifting its channel back and forth over the years, had left a waterlogged maze of swamps, ponds, oxbow lakes, and mud flats. The Indians seldom traveled through these stagnant areas except in their dugout canoes, while the Spanish in their ignorance tried to push straight through. Almost immediately they came to grief and became hopelessly bogged down. On June 22 the army spent the entire day, from dawn to sundown, splashing through water from ankle to waist deep. Before long De Soto was disgusted with this turtle-like progress, and he led his force away from the Mississippi until they climbed to firmer ground on the inland bluffs.

The drier uplands were thickly settled by a tribe of Casqui Indians, and when the Spaniards were some seven miles away from the river they found themselves marching within sight of three or four villages at the same time. The Casqui were enemies of the riparian tribes and welcomed the Spanish as allies against their traditional foes. By now De Soto knew that his expedition was too weak to rebuff offers of friendship and, for once, he treated the natives civilly. At the same time he was wary of any repetition of the Chickasaw fire raid and insisted on setting up camp some distance from the nearest Indian villages. This did not deter the Casqui from clamoring for his protection which the superstitious aborigines associated with the sign of the cross. They demanded to be baptized so that they too would enjoy the same magical properties of this mysterious symbol which they believed would deflect the arrows of any enemy. De Soto obliged by turning loose his priests on the tribe.

Up to this point in his campaign De Soto had done very little to fulfill those conditions of his royal license which called for the conversion of the heathen. The army had been too hurried or the natives too hostile for any missionary work on the part of the invaders. The eagerness of the Casqui provided De Soto with a good opportunity to try his hand at spreading the Faith and the general himself took time from his other duties to preach a sermon to the assembled Casqui. His exposition of the nature of Christianity was a qualified success. Struggling through the interpreter's translation of De Soto's text, the Casqui showed their eagerness to please the "Gran General" by bowing down with great gusto in front of a large wooden cross erected for their instruction. But at the same time they found it simpler to regard the white-skinned commander as a child of their Sun God and insisted on bringing forth their maimed and crippled for De Soto to heal. They even suggested that the Spanish leader invoke his Father to put an end to the drought which was parching their crops. Luckily for De Soto a heavy thunder shower soon afterward enhanced his reputation.

On June 26 the combined Indian and Spanish forces began their advance. Their target, De Soto learned, was the Quapaw tribe, which had its capital at a strongly fortified village on a backwater of the Mississippi. Unfortunately for the Spanish, it became quite clear as they advanced into Quapaw territory that the "armada tribe" was not as prosperous as they had hoped. The chief was no more than a local ruler and there was no gold in his village. Indeed, the Quapaw capital was superbly defended by a natural moat which would provide the inhabitants with fish in time of siege. De Soto had no intention of throwing away lives in a useless and difficult attack, so he concluded a peace treaty without delay. The Casqui were not unduly sorry—they had seen that the Quapaw were also painting the magic cross on their shields— and after stripping the village of booty, De Soto's allies quietly decamped. The Spanish stayed behind with their new hosts and De Soto sealed his treaty agreement by accepting two Quapaw princesses as concubines. One of the girls, according to an eyewitness, was "well porportioned, tall of body and well fleshed, in her shape and face she looked a lady of high rank," but her sister was merely "strongly made." These bigamous arrangements aroused little comment from the Spanish soldiery; most of them had already formed private liaisons with native women and their commander's political maneuverings were obviously in their own interests.

At this stage in his wanderings De Soto must have realized that the crossing of the Mississippi was a significant turning-point for the army of Florida. The river was both a geographical division and a psychological dividing line. For two years his troops had searched the country to the east of the "Rio Grande" and failed to find any worthwhile booty. The actual crossing of the river had been difficult and risky; so there was little point in going back to the other side. From now on his army must scour the western lands, the unknown regions which lay between the Mississippi and the Spanish colonies in New Spain somewhere to the southwest. There could be no return to Tampa; he had to lead his tattered expedition westward.

The story of those months in Arkansas and Louisiana from July 1541 to March 1542 repeats the history of the previous two years. The Spaniards trudged forward, chasing one rumor after another. They sent cavalry patrols in all directions, hoping to find the elusive treasure troves, and they refused to admit that Florida was barren. It was a brave but useless effort. The Spanish saw bison and met tepee-dwelling nomads who were always poor and usually hostile; occasionally the tribes had interesting customs—one band near the Ouachita River fought with pikes in the Spanish fashion—but there was never any loot. The conquistadors marched countless miles over broken terrain, fought their way out of ambushes, and struggled to survive in the harsh countryside. This constant grind wore down both horses and men. The irreplaceable cavalry mounts were nursed with the greatest care but several of them died, and a handful of men succumbed to strange illnesses for which there were no known cures. Physical strain, poor food, disease, and warfare gradually whittled away the army of Florida. The conquistadors were remarkably tough and resilient but there was a limit to their endurance; once again soldiers began to desert, including some of the nobly born officers, but this time De Soto was too tired and dispirited to do anything about it.

They spent the winter of 1541–42 at a village called Utiangue, near the junction of the Canadian and Arkansas rivers. It was a cold winter but the men made themselves comfortable enough, snaring rabbits for food and using buffalo robes, obtained from the Indians, as blankets. De Soto, in contrast to his Tallahassee days, was taking no chances. He built an impregnable stockade and cleared away the surrounding underbrush so that the natives could not launch any more sneak attacks. It was here that Juan Ortiz, the Florida castaway, finally died, leaving De Soto without a reliable interpreter of any kind. Ortiz's death brought home to De Soto his terrible isolation. For month after month the general had been leading his men on a wild goose chase, searching for mythical cities of gold which had no more substance than the wild rumors brought back by Cabeza de Vaca from the Narváez expedition. His army had proved that it could still travel across the endless continent, but it was desperately short of equipment. There was not a trained geographer, mapmaker, or navigator in the entire group. If they continued west they might reach Mexico or they might perish in the Texas deserts which the Indians had told him about. There was still a chance that if he marched to the Gulf coast he could built boats or follow the shore line until he came to a Spanish settlement.

Brooding over the alternatives, De Soto began to show the strain of his position. His officers noticed that the general spent more and more time by himself and that he was increasingly subject to fits of black depression. On several occasions this moodiness burst into anger and De Soto publicly upbraided officers who neglected their duty. Yet no one dared challenge their leader's authority. After two and a half years De Soto's personality still dominated his men; he had paid most of the costs of the venture and the army of Florida was still his to command. The grizzled conquitadors waited for their general's orders and wondered what he would decide.

At the beginning of March, 1542 De Soto made up his mind. The army would strike for the coast and try to contact their supply base in Cuba. A small barge might be able to get through to the island and bring back a supporting fleet. The expedition broke camp and set out southeast through Louisiana. They were heading back toward the Mississippi which they hoped to reach near its mouth. Though he did not know it, De Soto was in retreat. He was still determind to "conquer and settle" Florida, but he had lost his bearings; the Spaniards were not marching toward the sea, they were well to the north of their destination. The weather continued cold and rainy, and the terrain did not improve. The Spaniards were kept on their feet by the thought that they would find salvation on the shores of the Gulf coast. It was a cruel disappointment when they came within sight of the "Rio Grande" and learned from the local chief that he had never heard of the ocean. In reality the expedition was three hundred miles in a straight line from the Gulf and even farther by the winding river route.

De Soto refused to believe that he had gone so badly astray. He sent a squad of the fittest cavalrymen under Juan de Anasco to follow the river bank downstream, scouting a path to the ocean. It was a hopeless gesture. Anasco came back to report total failure. His patrol had spent eight days groping through the bottomlands and had advanced a mere fifty miles. The swamps, canebrakes, and forest were equally impenetrable. There were no trails, Indians, settlements, and there certainly was no overland path to the sea. De Soto's escape route was yet another myth.

One suspects that at this moment De Soto's stubborn nature finally collapsed. He had invested his fortune and his own life in the Florida expedition. For three years he had not spared himself; he had carried the entire burden of command and shared the hardships of the most humble men-at-arms. Now when he sought to find an escape from his predicament, it was denied. His force was reduced to about three hundred effective men and only forty horses, many of whom were lame after going unshod for a whole year due to a shortage of metal. Faced with Anasco's gloomy report, De Soto lashed out in anger. The Indians of the area, Guachoya of the river, sensed the Spanish despair and sent messengers to taunt the invaders. In a rage, De Soto ordered his troops to teach the Indians a lesson that could make them respect the white men and leave the Spanish camp alone. His officers, already harassed and nervous, exceeded their instructions. That night a raiding column, reinforced by friendly Indians, attacked the nearest Guachoya village and a massacre ensued. Most of the villagers managed to flee into the woods but the remainder were slaughtered. It was the worst blot on De Soto's record, and in later years his enemies in Spain used it to discredit his memory. At the time, it hardly seemed to matter; De Soto was sick with fever, and after reprimanding the officers who led the massacre, he withdrew into his tent.

The army knew that their general was dying. The fetid air of the Mississippi was conducive to fevers and De Soto may well have caught malaria. Whatever the reason for his illness, the conquistador scarcely resisted the ravages of the disease. He seems almost to have welcomed it. His secretary, Roderigo Ranjel, was called upon to draw up his will and because of a lack of paper this was done in a compressed cipher.

On the third day of the fever, the priests were summoned and De Soto reconciled himself to death. His last act was to assemble his officers by his bedside and ask them to choose a new leader. But so great was their respect for the dying man that the hidalgos asked De Soto to appoint his own successor. To their surprise he selected his disgraced lieutenant, the easygoing Luis de Moscoso. The next day, according to the chronicler, "departed from this life the magnanimous, the intrepid, the virtuous Captain, Don Hernando De Soto."

De Soto's death posed an immediate and macabre problem for the new commander. The superstitious natives had believed that the white general was a demigod; the aborigine chiefs often claimed to be divine and the invincible De Soto had fitted neatly into the same pattern. Moscoso was worried that if the Indians discovered that De Soto had died a mortal's death, they would lose their awe of the Spanish and launch an attack on the camp. To avoid this danger, De Soto's corpse was stealthily buried in the loose soil at the main entrance to the Spanish camp, where his grave would be obliterated by the constant trampling of men and horses. However, this stratagem did not deceive the Indians, who quickly noticed the freshly turned earth and began asking pointed questions about the absence of the general. Fearing that the natives might dig up and perhaps mutilate the corpse, Moscoso had De Soto's body disinterred by night and carried down to the river. There it was wrapped in a shroud and weighted with sand. Then the burial squad paddled a dugout canoe to the middle of the river and dumped their former commander's body into the muddy depths of the Mississippi. It was a strange burial ground for a knight of Santiago who had already set aside ample funds for his own marble tomb in the church vault at Jerez de los Caballeros.

Attention now centers on the man De Soto had picked to

succeed him—his countryman, former comrade-in-arms and friend, Luis Moscoso de Alvarado. At first glance Moscoso seems an odd choice. Although he was one of the most experienced officers in the army and had fought with Pizarro in Peru, Moscoso was also the man responsible for the disastrous Chickasaw fire attack. His negligence on that occasion had crippled the army, and quite rightly De Soto had demoted him in disgrace, promoting Baltasar de Gallegos to fill the post of master of camp. Now Gallegos seemed to be the obvious choice to take over command. He was nobly born, resourceful, efficient and experienced. Throughout the Florida campaign he had held the positions of chief constable and captain of infantry, and had always discharged his duties with credit. After his promotion he had also proved to be a valuable second-in-command. It is not entirely clear why De Soto passed him over. Possibly he feared that Gallegos would commit the same blunders as his former general—the two men were strikingly similar—or perhaps De Soto foresaw that the ambitious hidalgo would cause dissention among the other officers. In this respect Moscoso's placid nature counted in his favor. The even-tempered Luis was popular with both men and officers. He had joined the expedition in order to recoup his squandered Peruvian fortune, and when he saw that the new venture would not make a profit he had consistently advocated returning home. Furthermore, he had shown an uncanny instinct for survival, having weathered shipwreck, disgrace, defeat, and illness. By choosing Moscoso as his successor, De Soto made sure that the Florida expedition would eventually head for home.

The first few days of Moscoso's command revealed the difference in character of the new regime. Moscoso made it clear that he did not intend to follow De Soto's harsh policies. Symbolically he ordered the sale of the herd of pigs which De Soto had so carefully kept in reserve. The troops obeyed with glee and held an enormous feast of roast pork. De Soto's personal belongings were also put up for auction, his five slaves and three horses fetching approximately two to three thousand cruzados each, a poor showing for a man who had once dazzled the Court of Spain with his opulence. The money was set aside for Dona Isabella, the general's widow, but there was some doubt about the income because the army did not possess any Spanish currency and most of the purchases were made with promissory notes. According to one account, it was remarkable how little was bought by those men who owned property in Spain which could be attached, while those who had nothing to lose spent freely.

Because the Indians were still curious about De Soto's whereabouts, they were fobbed off with the lame excuse that the general had ascended into the sky to consult his Father, and would be returning shortly. This failed to satisfy the natives, and it was obvious that if the Spanish lingered they would be attacked once more. Moscoso knew he had to extricate his army and that he had three alternatives: he could cross the Mississippi and return eastward the way the army had come, risking the vengeance of those tribes which De Soto had antagonized; he could build boats and float down the river to the Gulf, then coast along to New Spain; or he could try to reach Mexico overland. Typically he asked for a consensus from his officers. None of them wanted to try the long, hard march back to Tampa and they were equally afraid of the river trip, remembering that Narváez's expedition had drowned while attempting to flee the country in home-made boats. There was no choice but to try to march overland to Mexico. To forestall arguments, Moscoso cunningly drew up a document which stated the consensus and made all his officers sign their agreement.

On June 5 the army set out on their futile trek. They did not have the least idea of the distances or deserts that lay between them and the nearest Spanish settlement. If they had known, they certainly would not have attempted the journey. As it was, they needed little encouragement to push ahead with all speed, anticipating that they would reach Mexico in a few weeks and possibly pick up some booty as well. By now they had evolved a lean and efficient routine for travel; they carried almost no supplies, raided Indian villages for food, and brushed aside opposition without waiting to parley. By keeping on the move they escaped full-scale tribal attacks and wriggled through unscathed. Moscoso handled the march competently. Stupid or treacherous guides were thrown to the dogs, and hostile Indian villages were set on fire. Moscoso knew precisely what he was doing and had no scruples about the conduct of his advance. There was no reason why the expedition should not have reached Mexico without the loss of a man had it not been for the acute food shortage. Moving west, the army passed out of fertile, well-populated regions into the edges of the desert country. As the land became parched, the native villages dwindled in size and were less frequent. The Spanish gradually outstripped their means of supply and found themselves facing starvation. They kept pushing forward, hoping for the conditions to change, but it became obvious that they had reached the limit of their capability. The sterile deserts had stopped them and they would have to turn back. It was an inevitable decision which Moscoso had to make, even though some of his more hotheaded juniors were excitedly demanding to press onward; they had found bits of turquoise and finely woven shawls which were probably articles of trade from the pueblo Indians of the distant mesa cultures. But Moscoso had seen his fill of treasure hunting and most of the army agreed with him. He could quote the reports which Cabeza de Vaca had brought back from his wanderings along the Texas coast; they had all been unfavorable and painted a stark picture of primitive desert tribes who lived off grubs and prickly-pear shoots. The obvious course of action was to return to the Mississippi and try to get out of the country by sailing down the river to the sea. Along the Mississippi they would at least be sure to find catfish, wild grapes, and Indian corn to feed themselves. Accordingly, the army of Florida turned about and began retracing its steps.

In early December the Spanish arrived on the banks of the Mississippi for the third and last time. The return march had been straightforward and they were glad to see the river which by now was dominating the life of every man in the expedition. Originally the "Rio Grande" had been an obstacle in their path; now they hoped that it would prove to be the lifeline for survival. They had no inkling of the conditions they would encounter downstream; there might be thundering cataracts, whirlpools, or hostile Indians, but at least the river was a landmark in that dreary continent. It was the one tangible feature they could count on. They were no longer the army of Florida so much as the army of the Mississippi.

Moscoso handled his Mississippi operation with consummate skill. As soon as the Spaniards reached the river, he sent patrols to scout along the bank until they found a supply of food that would support the army for some time. At Aminoya, some distance upstream from the spot where De Soto had been buried, the patrols found what they were looking for—two small, prosperous riverside towns that were well stocked with provisions. Moscoso promptly moved his main force into one of the towns and sent a detachment to bring in all the food supplies from the other. Then the Spanish strengthened the fortifications of their new citadel and settled in for the winter, confident that they could withstand a siege and still have enough spare men to build boats for the river trip in the following spring.

Moscoso had chosen his site well; there were groves of tall, straight trees near Aminoya, and the Spanish troops had no difficulty in hauling back sufficient timber for the seven pinnaces which Moscoso calculated would carry his men to Mexico. It was essential to make these boats with much greater care than the old ferry barges because the pinnaces would have to face a long sea voyage along the Gulf coast. Luckily, one of the surviving Portuguese soldiers in the army had been a slave of the Moors in Fez, and there he had learned how to saw planks from raw lumber. Now he showed the Spaniards how to dig saw pits and cut the necessary planking. It was difficult work because there was an acute scarcity of metal for making nails and the planks had to be cut as thin as possible in order to keep the nails short. Oddly enough, the Spaniards do not seem to have considered using wooden pins in place of iron nails, and instead they stripped crossbows, slave chains, armor, and weapons for every last scrap of spare metal. They collected the stirrups that would no longer be needed and hammered them into simple anchors, twisted strands of horsehair and mulberry bark into ropes, and sewed crude sails from the skins of wild animals which the Indians brought in. The Portuguese ex-slave supervised the design and construction of the pinnaces with the help of four Basques from the Biscay coast. Two calkers, one from Genoa and the other from Sardinia, plugged the seams of the boats with a makeshift oakum concoction which they made by mixing together flax, mulberry bark, and threads of cotton plucked from native blankets. The ingenuity of the Spanish troops was remarkable and the work went well. Moscoso and his hidalgos knew that their lives depended on the skill of these humble artisans, and even the most aristocratic officers lent a hand at calking, hammering, and sewing.

The annual March rise of the Mississippi took them all by surprise and nearly ruined their painstaking efforts. The river suddenly overflowed its banks and spread across the surrounding countryside. The Spaniards were forced to take refuge in the high Indian grain lofts and tether their horses on rafts which floated up and down with the water. For two months the floods stopped work on the boats and by the time the Spanish had cleared away the ensuing debris, they learned that the Indians had plucked up enough courage to attack.

The Indian plan depended upon thirty spies who would enter the town unarmed and set it alight. This would signal a general onslaught by massed tribesmen concealed in the woods. The Spanish army would be trapped between the flames and their attackers, and with their ramparts collapsing they would be compelled to fight in the open against vastly superior numbers. It was a carefully developed plan, but the Indian war chiefs made one mistake—they tried to put Moscoso off guard by sending gifts of fish, shawls, and blankets to the Spanish army. This sudden generosity immediately aroused Moscoso's suspicions and, very quietly, he had one of the gift-bearers detained. The native was tortured until he revealed the exact details of the planned attack. Then Moscoso waited without giving the Indians any idea that they had been betrayed. When the thirty fire-raisers slipped into the town, they were promptly arrested and their hands were chopped off. Moscoso sent the maimed natives back to their leaders with the message that the Spanish would entertain every other treacherous visitor in identical fashion. It was a barbaric gesture, but Moscoso made his point; the Indians were frightened by his uncanny knowledge of their plans and they left the Spaniards alone until they departed for the sea.

In June the last phase of the withdrawal began. Hunters were sent out to kill as much game as they could find, the surviving pigs were slaughtered, and all but twenty-two of the cavalry mounts were butchered. The flesh was dried and salted for the voyage and foraging parties scavenged for edible roots, nuts, and corn. A cooper made water kegs, one for each vessel, and the pinnaces were launched. The boats leaked badly but they seemed serviceable enough, and Moscoso decided that the expedition should risk the trip. The men gathered their equipment and loaded it aboard with sacks and panniers of food. The horses were carried on rafts of canoes lashed together side by side. On July 2, 1543, the flotilla set out; it consisted of 322 Spaniards, 100 of the healthiest Indian slaves, 7 pinnaces, the horse rafts, and a cluster of dugouts. They left behind about five hundred other Indian prisoners, servants and porters acquired on their travels. Most of these unlucky natives were far from their tribal homes, and the majority undoubtedly perished.

Moscoso proceeded cautiously. The pinnaces were taking on a lot of water and they were difficult to row. Frequently it was necessary for two boats to lash alongside one another and help with bailing each other's bilges. The troops were not accustomed to rowing, and it took time for them to learn the most efficient way of steering and propelling their unwieldy vessels. The rafts of horses proved to be a great drag; they had to be towed behind a pinnace, and this slowed down the entire fleet as well as exhausting the oarsmen. Indeed, but for the four-mile-an-hour current, the expedition would have been stranded. As it was, Moscoso must have realized that the army had embarked on a one-way trip; they had no hope of retracing their path against the current and they were now committed to following the Mississippi to the sea, if they could escape the Indians and any natural hazards that might lie ahead. No one had the least notion what they would encounter nor how far they had to go before they reached the Gulf, if indeed the river emptied into the Gulf of Mexico.

On the first day's journey the Spaniards passed through the province of Guachoya, where the Indians came down to the bank to beckon them to land. But Moscoso was taking no chances; he ordered his men to stay in midstream and the army drifted slowly down the broad river, passing over De Soto's last resting place. That night they set up their bivouac at an isolated spot on the left bank, posted sentries, and slept undisturbed. However, the Indians were keeping a close watch on their progress, and when the Spaniards reached the next riverside town they found that it had already been evacuated. Moscoso sent a cavalry patrol ashore to investigate and the lancers came back with the welcome news that a few miles farther downstream there was a small settlement which contained stocks of corn. The army was desperately short of dried food, so Moscoso called a halt while the troops loaded the extra supplies. This delay almost cost them their lives, for a large fleet of Indian war canoes appeared while the bulk of the soldiers were on land. If the natives had attacked, they would have been able to destroy the Spanish boats, but instead the hostile fleet swept past and paddled downstream to the next town where land reinforcements awaited them.

Moscoso realized that he would have to strike before his enemies were organized, and the Spaniards scrambled back into their vessels and rowed at full speed downstream. The Indians had drawn up their forces on the bank, so Moscoso placed his best soldiers in the expedition's canoes and dispatched them in a frontal attack. This bold maneuver confused the natives, who received the impression that the white men were more eager to fight in boats than on land. The Indians had already been surprised by the invaders' armor and horses, and now they were not sure what secret weapon was in store for them. After some hesitation, they withdrew and watched the Spanish fleet from a safe distance. Moscoso landed his army on an open stretch of ground suitable for cavalry operations and hastily constructed a fortified camp.

The Indians did not attack that night, but next morning the Spaniards saw that the Indian fleet had been reinforced by a hundred more large canoes, each carrying sixty or seventy warriors. The native armada lay just out of bow shot, hovering in attendance upon the slow-moving Spanish boats. It was a tense situation and the white men knew that sooner or later the Indians would give battle. Moscoso could only press on and gain time with a show of strength. Before long the natives sent forward messengers in small, light canoes. These envoys pretended to bring an offer of peace but in reality they came to spy on the strength of the Spaniards. What they saw must have underscored the vulnerability of the ungainly Spanish boats, for when the scouts returned with Moscoso's rejection of their terms, the Indians swung their fleet into the path of the oncoming Spaniards. Once again Moscoso ordered forward his men-at-arms in their dugouts under the command of Captain Juan de Guzman. They were instructed to clear a path for the pinnaces, but this time the Indians accepted the challenge and Guzman's force was heavily engaged. In the skirmish the natives discovered that they were much more skillful boatmen than the Spaniards and managed to capsize the Spanish canoes. Weighed down by their armor, a dozen men-at-arms, Guzman included, were drowned before the remainder of the Spanish flotilla bore down and pulled the struggling men out of the river.

Now that the façade of Spanish invincibility had been shattered, the Indians boldly attacked the seven pinnaces. A vicious running battle took place as Moscoso urged his oarsmen to row forward and the crossbowmen tried to keep the natives at a distance. But the lumbering Spanish vessels had no chance of pulling clear and the nimble Indian war canoes darted in and out repeatedly, their crews shooting arrows and hurling spears at the white men. The engagement lasted all that day and continued through the night, for Moscoso did not dare call a halt but worked relays of oarsmen at the benches. Next morning the Indian canoes broke off the battle, which had carried them to the borders of their tribal territory. Content to have driven the unwelcome invaders from their domain, the natives turned around and paddled back upstream to their villages. But there was no respite for the weary Spaniards. Scarcely had the first Indian fleet vanished around a bend in the river than a second armada of fifty canoes put out from the bank and took up the chase. These Indians came from the next tribe downstream and, being fresh, pressed home their attack with great energy, coming so close inboard at one stage that they succeeded in taking off a native woman who was being held captive on one of the pinnaces.

For a second day and night the wretched Spaniards toiled downstream, taking it in turns to snatch a few hours sleep when not at the oars or fighting off the natives. Moscoso and every man in the expedition knew that they were running the gauntlet and that they had no choice but to continue until they reached the sea. The never-ending loops and meanders of the river were heartbreaking; the men slaved at the oars for hours, only to find that they had progressed less than a mile southward. The river's contortions made sailing difficult; doubling back and forth along the Mississippi a following wind became a headwind and then a following wind again and valuable time was lost putting the sails up and down. The canoe rafts carrying the horses moved so awkwardly they were an insupportable handicap to the other boats. Several times the Indians nearly succeeded in cutting off the slower rafts, and on each occasion the barges had to fall back to the rescue, endangering the entire flotilla. Reluctantly, Moscoso decided to sacrifice the horses for the safety of the other vessels. The Spanish put in to the bank and slaughtered most of the chargers, putting the horseflesh on one side for salting. Four or five of the horses were turned loose to run wild, but as they rowed on downstream, the soldiers looked back to see Indians appear from the bushes and kill the bewildered, abandoned animals.

At ten o'clock the next evening the native canoes finally gave up the pursuit and retired upstream. A small group of seven more canoes then came out from a backwater to harass the white men, but finding that they did little damage, the attackers went back home, leaving the Spaniards to float down the Mississippi in peace.

For seventeen more days Moscoso and his men traveled downriver. It was an eerie and uncomfortable journey. The banks of the river were clothed with dense, primeval forest which was made almost impenetrable by the interlacing tendrils of wild grape vines. Hawks wheeled over the silent forest and snow-white egrets stood motionless in the shadows under the bank. Occasionally great purple, russet, and yellow butterflies dipped and swooped around the boats, settling briefly on the gunwales before continuing their lumbering flight to the distant bank. The Mississippi was a broad expanse of dark brown water, at least a half mile across, and the boats moved sluggishly on the flood. The July sun caught them exposed without shade, and by ten o'clock in the morning the woodwork was uncomfortably hot to touch and the oarsmen had worked up a raging thirst. The water kegs were soon empty and had to be filled from the river, but it was several hours before the silt had settled enough for it to be drinkable. Even then the lukewarm liquid was gritty and foul to the taste. At night the army beached their vessels on a sand bar and the tired men slept while the sentries swatted the swarms of mosquitoes that settled on them. Dawn saw them once more on the river, tugging with blistered palms at the rough oar handles.

On July 16, after seven hundred miles of river travel, they

came within sight of the sea. They still had no idea where they were but at least the river section of their trip was behind and this was enough to raise their spirits. Moscoso ordered the army ashore and the soldiers repaired the boats for the sea voyage, filled the water kegs, and recouped their strength. Some of the officers suggested that the expedition would be better advised to turn eastward along the coast and head for Cuba, but Moscoso sensibly vetoed the idea on the grounds that the pinnaces were not sufficiently seaworthy to cross the Florida straits. He insisted that it was safer to follow the Gulf coast westward until they reached New Spain, though just how far they would have to sail was a mystery. One thing was certain: the army could not linger where it was, because the delta Indians had learned of its presence and were mounting an increasing number of sneak attacks, using spear throwers to hurl cane lances at isolated patrols.

On Wednesday, July 18, the expedition got under way for Mexico. For two days they rowed in fresh water which the Mississippi poured into the Gulf, and then the flotilla stood out to sea so that they could hoist their sails. The Spanish were lucky; the weather remained calm and the little boats, gunwales barely above the water, crept westward until they made landfall four days later on the barren Texas coast. Here the expedition stopped and Moscoso sent a party ashore to fill the water kegs before the flotilla coasted onward. It was a slow and painful crawl from headland to headland. The men suffered the torments of thirst and from swarms of mosquitoes that settled on their bare skin and sucked blood until the men's faces were so puffed up that they could not recognize one another. Once or twice they encountered severe storms that threatened to drive them onto the lee shore, and the oarsmen struggled all night at the oars in order to ease the strain on their flimsy anchors.

Finally, on September 10, fifty-two days after leaving the mouth of the Mississippi, they reached the Spanish settlement at the mouth of the Panuco River. Of the original 622 members of the Florida army, only half had returned, blistered and heavily bearded, their clothes in tatters, and their leader dead. Like living scarecrows the survivors limped ashore and sank to the ground to kiss the sand and give thanks to God for their unforeseen salvation. But the credit for their survival belonged to their own incredible resilience and to Moscoso. The easygoing man of pleasure had extricated his force almost without loss from the heart of the continent. Using excellent judgment, he had succeeded where the more dashing De Soto had failed. It was his reward that he was the only man to make a profit from the venture—he wooed and married a rich Mexican widow, taking her back to Spain, where presumably he lived the life of ease he had always craved.

Of the other survivors there is little record. A few stayed in the Americas to farm or joined other conquistador armies; some made their way back to Spain; and one or two took holy orders in thanks for their deliverance. Dona Isabella learned of her husband's death and died shortly afterward. Nothing was ever heard of the deserters who had chosen to "go native"; the North American continent swallowed them without trace; and in the years that followed Spanish colonial ambitions paid little attention to the "Rio Grande." There was nothing to stop a mounted expedition from tracing the river to its source in the interior, but De Soto's experiences had convinced the Spaniards that their efforts would be wasted. The Mississippi was not a highway to Golconda. A few trading posts were established near the delta but they did not prosper; the Spaniards turned increasingly to the problem of linking their older colonies rather than striking out into unknown territory, and it was not for another 150 years that white men sailed the Mississippi again. When they did, Spain was declining as a colonial power and the newcomers were Frenchmen arriving from the opposite end of the continent, the far northeast.

4

The Agent and
the Priest

IN THE SUMMER OF 1541, WHEN DE SOTO'S ARMY WAS
still pushing its way through the wilds of the lower Mississippi valley, a Frenchman, Jacques Cartier, arrived off the
mouth of the St. Lawrence river in Canada with a fleet of ten
ships. The newcomer was some two thousand miles to the
northeast of the toiling conquistadors and it was not his first
visit to the shores of North America. Cartier had made two
earlier voyages of exploration to the St. Lawrence Gulf and
this time he was returning there to plant a colony in "New
France."

Clearly this French venture in colonization infringed on
Spain's virtual monopoly of the New World, but Cartier had
the full support of his king, Francis I, and there was very
little that the Spaniards could do to crush the interlopers.
From the time of Columbus onward the Spanish authorities
had relied, rather hopefully, on a barrier of secrecy to protect
their American possessions from competitors; they refused to
publish maps of their colonies, forbade all pilots and navigators in Spanish employ to pass on information to foreign
powers, and threatened to seize any ships found trespassing in

Spanish colonial waters. Of course this policy was worth no more than Spain's willingness and ability to defend it against challengers, and in Central and South America the rewards had been so great that the Spanish authorities were prepared to back up their threats.

But in the north it was a different matter. In the first place, the Spanish geographers were not at all sure that the north of the continent was likely to contain native civilizations rich in gold and silver and it was therefore more sensible to concentrate their nation's exploring activities farther south where bullion had already been found. Second, Spain did not have the necessary strategic naval bases to protect the North Atlantic coast of America from incursions by the French, English, and Dutch, so that very soon these nations were scouting the fringes of the continent hoping to find the same fantastic treasure troves which the conquistadors had stumbled on in Mexico and Peru. Unfortunately for the Spaniards one of their galleons homeward bound from the New World was captured off Cape St. Vincent by a French privateer; on board the galleon was a cargo of Mexican booty that Cortés was sending back to Spain. Some of the plunder looted from the galleon found its way in due course to the French court, where it helped excite the cupidity of the French king and his advisers. Francis I was chronically short of money and he saw no reason why he should not profit as much in the opening up of the New World as his Spanish cousin. Accordingly, small expeditions were fitted out in Brittany and sent to probe the American coastline to the north of Spain's colonies. Naturally the Spanish emperor, Charles V, discovered that the French were poaching on his preserves and sharply pointed out that the Pope had awarded the western lands to Spain. If the French continued to flout Spanish claims in the New World, Charles threatened that his warships would be ordered to seize the intruding vessels and throw their crews overboard. Francis called Spain's bluff. In a caustic reply he maintained that America was open to all comers and that he "much desired to see Adam's will to learn how he had partitioned the world."

In any event, this bitterness between the two major European powers was all wasted effort and the Spanish need not have worried so much about French ambitions in Canada. Jacques Cartier's hopeful colonists soon found that life was too harsh for them in the strange new continent and they packed up and went home. For the next two generations New France was left mainly to the more enterprising fishermen of St. Malo and Brest who risked the Atlantic crossing each year in order to reach the teeming fishing grounds off northeast America. Going ashore to fill their water casks or to clean and salt their catch, these fishermen encountered tribes of coastal Indians and struck up a simple trade with them, exchanging trinkets and metal goods for the cast-off fur garments which the Indians had worn during the cold northern winter. Frequently the visiting fishermen found that they were making as much money from fur trading as from fishing and they began to turn their attention more and more to this profitable sideline. In this they were joined by groups of merchants from their home towns and these merchants provided enough capital to turn the rather haphazard system of native barter into a planned and regular trade. Permanent trading posts were established along the lower reaches of the St. Lawrence, and instead of waiting for the Indians to bring the furs to them, the merchants began sending their agents, young Frenchmen or half-breed Indians, into the interior to seek out tribes which had not yet heard of the white man and his demand for furs. These scouts, the coureurs de bois and voyageurs, were the vanguard of France's drive toward the Mississippi.

The character of this French exploration was something quite unlike De Soto's military tour de force. The Spanish conquistadors had given an impressive display of martial discipline as several hundred men, moving as a single unit, marched halfway across the continent. By contrast, the French explorers filtered across the countryside in tiny bands which seldom numbered more than half a dozen white men, making friends with the Indians rather than fighting with them, so that while the army of Florida blazed one solitary road through an unknown land, the French backwoodsmen succeeded in exploring a far larger swath of North America by hunting and trading with the aboriginal inhabitants. Nowhere is the difference between the efforts of these two European nations more clearly shown than on the early maps of what is now the United States and Canada. De Soto's extraordinary wanderings did so little to explain the geography of the southern part of the country that cartographers were obliged to leave the area blank except for stylized little drawings here and there of Indian villages which were scattered at random from Georgia to the Mississippi; yet in Canada the French travelers quickly collected enough information about the interior for their mapmakers to sketch in the complicated network of rivers, streams and portages which led from the St. Lawrence to the upper Great Lakes.

Naturally the success of the French fur traders and their agents reawakened the interest of the Paris authorities in developing Cartier's former colony. The new wave of settlers who since 1600 had emigrated to New France of their own accord were obviously prospering from their business in peltries and the home government did not have to be very farsighted to see that the dream of taking colonial profits from North America could at last be realized. France's first reward from her holdings in the New World would not be gold, silver, and slaves but a harvest of furs. This propect was enough to encourage the French government to allow increased colonization with the added hope that some time in the future the French-Canadians would also find rich mines or, best of all, a water route through New France to the Indies. Accordingly, during the early years of the seventeenth century France plunged into the scramble for North America. Shiploads of colonists were recruited in the mother country and went to farm the banks of the St. Lawrence. Newly arrived heads of families were given tracts of free land, and this acreage was increased with a special bounty if the colonists successfully sired a large family. Quebec was founded. Governors, intendants, customs officers, lawyers, tax collectors, and scribes came to New France. Priests also arrived; at first a small band of unassuming Recollets of the Order of St. Francis, and when they saw the size of the missionary task ahead of them, they invited the Jesuits to help in preaching to the Indians. Before long black-robed missionaries from the Society of Jesus were rivaling even the fur men in the exploration of the interior. While merchants sent their agents hundreds of miles inland to trade for furs among the untapped beaver streams of the Great Lakes basin, the priests also pushed westward with the same urgency to reach unknown heathen tribes and convert them to Christianity. Religion, trade, and exploration spread across Canada in unison and the effect was impressive. By 1650 the French had successfully explored a great triangular portion of the continent extending from the upper Hudson valley to the western shores of Lake Michigan and back to Quebec. As early as 1638 a French agent, Jean Nicolet, went by canoe from the St. Lawrence to Lake Michigan. Hoping that he would find the water route to China, Nicolet took along a ceremonial robe "of China damask, all strewn with flowers and birds of many colors," just in case he had an audience with the mandarins of Cathay. Reaching Green Bay, Wisconsin, Nicolet came within three days' journey of the Wisconsin River, a tributary of the Mississippi. But instead of Chinese mandarins, Nicolet found Winnebago chieftains assembled to greet him. Undeterred, the Frenchman dressed himself in his Chinese finery and, marching firmly up to the waiting Indian council, nearly scared off the entire welcoming committee by firing off two pistols under their noses.

For a moment it seemed that France was poised to discover the upper waters of the Mississippi within a century of De Soto's death. But Nicolet turned back in the land of the Winnebagos without ever crossing the watershed that divided the waters of the Mississippi from the Great Lakes. It was another thirty-five years before a Frenchman finally floated out on the Father of Waters, which coiled its way southward only 175 miles from the head of Green Bay. When Nicolet returned to the St. Lawrence, France's westward drive suddenly halted in midstride, and then fell back in full retreat. There were two main reasons for this sudden *volte-face*. First, Samuel Champlain died. He had been the genius of French-Canadian expansion for more than thirty years, its chief advocate, guiding light, and practical exponent. With his death much of the energy behind French exploration drained away. The second and much more important reason for the collapse of France's hopes in the Great Lakes region was the Iroquois trouble. The Iroquois were a confederation of five—later six—warlike Indian tribes living in a great arc along the flank of the French corridor leading to the Great Lakes. Well organized, treacherous and cruel, the Iroquois were the terror of the north woods. One Jesuit wrote: "They approach like foxes, fight like lions, and fly away like birds." The Iroquois were traditional enemies of the Hurons, an Indian tribe allied to the French and closely associated with the expanding influence of the white man. The Iroquois resented the interlopers and with a little encouragement from Dutch and English agents began, in 1643, almost twenty years of uninterrupted war to drive out the French, the Hurons, and their allies. The combined military power of the Iroquois was almost more than the French could handle, and the outnumbered Hurons did not stand a chance. Within a few years the network of trading posts and mission stations that stretched from the mouth of the St. Lawrence to Lake Michigan was in shreds. Iroquois war parties attacked settlement after settlement from Lake Ontario to Quebec, burning, scalping, and torturing. They virtually exterminated the Hurons in a relentless tribal war, burned Jesuit missionaries at the stake, and scattered the Christianized natives. Iroquois ambushes blocked the vital canoe routes, and fur traders went bankrupt as their cargoes were seized; even the distant tribes were too frightened of the Iroquois to bring their peltries to Montreal. For a while the continued existence of New France hung in the balance as Iroquois warriors chased French settlers out of their fields to shelter behind the wooden ramparts of Montreal and Quebec. Painted savages danced and howled in derision just out of cannon range and shocked the defenders by holding farcial celebrations of Mass to ridicule the Christians.

New France, so near to extinction, was saved by events which took place far away in the mother country. Young Louis XIV, the Sun King, demanded the reins of government from his ministers and determined that by his personal guidance he would restore the glory and greatness of France, not only in Europe but also in the distant forest wilderness of North America. The Sun King sought to build an empire and he was prepared to back his ambitions with men, money, and diplomatic intrigue. From North America he anticipated considerable rewards—the sea route to the Indies and riches as fabulous as those which Spain had won in the New World. The chief architect of his schemes was Minister Jean Baptiste Colbert, a former assistant to Cardinal Mazarin. Under his direction fresh troops and talented commanders were shipped out to the sickly colony on the banks of the St. Lawrence. In 1666 a well-equipped army of veterans under the gallant Marquis de Tracy marched into the Iroquois tribal lands of the Mohawk Valley and smashed their confederacy. More significantly, Colbert sent a new breed of administrators to Canada, self-made bureaucrats who were hard-working and efficient. The colony was still tiny and its future rested in the hands of a few leaders on the spot; these men were given sweeping powers. One of the ablest was the new intendant, Jean Talon, whose prime concern was to establish a healthy economy in New France.

Talon had a clear grasp of the need to develop agriculture as the solid base for the colony's future, but at the same time he was plagued by the French Crown for some repayment of the military expenses incurred in quelling the Iroquois. A stream of letters from Paris urged him to organize new explorations to discover and work any mines that might help swell the royal exchequer. The French authorities were still treating their northern possessions as if they were Mexico or

Peru, but Talon himself knew that Canada's real wealth lay in the value of her fur crop. He increased revenue by organizing the fur trade more tightly, and in response to the demands from Paris sent hand-picked Indian traders to explore westward. These scouts visited the shores of Lake Superior where the Indians reported copper deposits, and they investigated the waterways to see if it would be feasible to use sailing ships on the inland lakes. Their reports were disappointing; the copper deposits turned out to be isolated "erratics," mineraliferous boulders dropped by prehistoric glaciers, and numerous cataracts made the rivers impassable by anything but a light canoe. On the other hand the Great Lakes were navigable for large ships if the vessels could be built on the edges of the lakes themselves. Talon therefore looked farther afield—to the extreme western limits of French influence, where, according to the Indians, there was a great waterway leading to a sea on which floated tall ships manned by white men. If the Indians were to be believed, these white sailors used beads when they prayed. Talon decided to send an agent to investigate these rumors, chart the course of the inland waterway, search out any valuable deposits of ore, and report back on the presence of white men or the prospects for a new fur trade.

Talon had to tread carefully in planning this expedition. The outer fringe of French influence in Canada was controlled by Jesuit priests who had revived the remnants of their mission network around the Great Lakes as soon as the Iroquois were crushed. The "black robes" regarded the upper lakes as a private preserve for Jesuit activity and disliked the idea of secular interference in their domain. Talon could not proceed with his exploration program without the help of the priests, who had excellent contacts among the Indian tribes; yet the intendant, as a Crown officer, was also planning to curb the power of the Jesuits before they became too dominant in the backwoods. It was a delicate problem which called for considerable tact and Talon found a typically adept solution: he gave the leadership of the projected western expedition to a man who was regarded as a friend of the Jesuits, but who was, first and foremost, a loyal supporter of the intendant and his policies. The explorer Talon selected for this task was Louis Joliet.

Despite his importance in the opening up of North America and particularly in the exploration of the Mississippi, Louis Joliet remains something of a mystery. He is an important but shadowy figure whose background and character are seen in a series of brief glimpses.

Louis Joliet was born in New France in 1645 and is therefore the first white explorer of the Mississippi native to North America. He was the third son of a Quebec wagonmaker and wheelwright, though his father died when Louis was six years old. His mother, Marie, found another husband shortly afterward, as was the custom in a colony chronically short of women. The stepfather, Godefroid Guillot, must have provided the boy with some sort of education, for when he was seventeen Louis Joliet entered the Society of Jesus. A less likely candidate for an explorer can hardly be imagined; Joliet was a bookish youth, bourgeois and solemn. Even the Jesuits did not see missionary fiber in their novitiate, who was mainly interested in theological disputations and church music— gentle pastimes more suited to the seminary than the mission hut. But while he was with the Jesuits, Joliet acquired the formal education that later made him a reliable and accurate agent for the Crown. For some reason Joliet left the Jesuits after he had been with them for three years. Obviously he did not leave in disgrace, because that same year the bishop lent him 587 livres in Canadian money to pay for a trip to France. Joliet did not stay long in the mother country and there is not the least clue why he went on such a short and expensive jaunt. At any rate, he was back in Canada in the October of 1668, where once again he borrowed money from the bishop to purchase, among other things, "two guns; two pistols; six packages of wampum; twenty-four hatchets; a gross of small bells; twelve ells of coarse cloth; ten ells of canvas; forty pounds of tobacco. Cost: 354 livres 6 sols." His purchases were obviously trade goods for the Indian market and it is clear that Louis Joliet had finally decided to become a fur trader.

All this time, while Louis was training for the priesthood and visiting France, his elder brother Lucien had been establishing his own reputation as a bold and successful "voyageur." Lucien spoke several Indian dialects, and because he was a comparatively well-educated frontiersman, Talon had picked him as one of the scouts who were sent to look for the Lake Superior copper deposits. Lucien set out on this mission shortly after his younger brother returned from France, and it was the last time the brothers saw one another. Lucien succeeded in reaching Lake Superior where he hunted unsuccessfully for the elusive copper mines and his reports filtered back to Talon, though the voyageur himself never returned. Somewhere on the homeward leg of his journey through Iroquois territory Lucien Joliet vanished without a trace. It was left for Louis Joliet to step into his brother's shoes and continue the search for mines, furs, and the great river. If Lucien had lived, Talon probably would have chosen him to lead the Mississippi trip, and when the scout failed to reappear, it was natural to select his younger brother as a trustworthy substitute.

By now Talon was sifting through a mass of reports concerning this mysterious river of great size which the Indians called the "Messipi." Several fur traders reported hearing of a large forked river that lay south and west of Lake Superior, and from the Jesuits there were long, detailed memoranda about this Messipi. Fathers Dablon and Allouez of the Society of Jesus had heard about it at their mission of St. Francis Xavier near the head of Green Bay. The two priests had even ventured up the Fox River which emptied into Green Bay from the west and had visited the Mascouten, or Fire Indians, who lived near the watershed between the Fox and the so-called Father of Waters. Their report made interesting reading and had to be reconciled with the current theories on the geography of the unknown interior of North America. Ever since the survivors of De Soto's expedition had returned to civilization, there had been a great deal of speculation about the course of their "Rio Grande." The most popular theory held that there were several north-south rivers draining into the Gulf of Mexico, one of which was De Soto's river, and that all of them rose in a central range of mountains which divided the country in a great latitudinal arc. If this was true, the Messipi, which the French had heard about in the north, must empty into Hudson's Bay, the Atlantic Ocean, or the "Vermilion Sea," as the Gulf of California was called, and Talon's explorations would uncover a commercial water route penetrating deep into the heart of the country. It was a tempting prospect and a few optimistic geographers went so far as to postulate a continuous system of "Rio Grandes" and lakes along which ocean-going ships would be able to sail from the Atlantic to the Pacific. While many cartographers were confidently marking these "Straits of Anian" across the continent or shading in the central mountain range, there were level-headed theorists in Europe as well as in Canada who had guessed correctly that De Soto's "Rio Grande" and the French "Messipi" a thousand miles to the north were one and the same river.

Whichever theory was correct, it was in the best interests of France's imperial policy to be the first nation to learn the truth. If there were any commercial advantage to be gained from the unexplored waterway, she would be first in the field and her North American colonists could seize the initiative and forestall their rivals, particularly the English. Consequently Talon suggested to Louis Joliet that he lead a small private expedition to this Messipi, travel along the river, and find out where it flowed. Talon's offer had many of the features that characterized Charles V's royal license to De Soto. In both cases the Crown risked nothing. Talon had no funds available for sponsoring exploration, so Joliet was required to provide his own canoes, equipment, and provisions. In return the Crown graciously consented to allow their agent to recoup his expenditure by trading with the Indians he encountered on his trip. As a business proposition, this royal license was ludicrous; unless Joliet was lucky enough to find gems or bullion among the river tribes, he could not hope to cover his expenditure with meager profit from a single canoe-load of furs hauled back to civilization over the huge distances stipulated. The journey would take almost two years and during that time Joliet would be sacrificing the income from his normal fur-trading activities. Of course Talon probably enhanced his offer with hints that the Crown would provide extra rewards if Joliet's mission was successful. Sometime in the future, the adventurer could hope for a lucrative monopoly or a rich land grant, but first he had to go exploring on a shoestring budget, return home safely, and convince the authorities of the value of his discoveries.

It is difficult to understand exactly why Louis Joliet accepted the intendant's offer, when it ran counter to his own financial interests. It is possible that he wished to continue Lucien Joliet's work or he may even have hoped to trace his missing brother. Perhaps too Louis Joliet really did believe that there was money to be made in the Messipi venture, though this is unlikely. The most plausible reason for his acceptance is that Louis Joliet was genuinely curious about the far west and Talon's offer was an opportunity to gratify this interest. It was an unexpected chance to launch out in unknown places and it appealed to the same spirit which induced him to leave the seminary, sail to France, and then try his hand at the risky fur trade.

Talon's instructions to his new recruit were straightforward. After Joliet had arranged his business affairs in Montreal, he was to hire a squad of canoemen and proceed to the Jesuit mission post of St. Ignace at Mackinac, the "strategic triangle" lying between Lakes Huron, Superior, and Michigan. There he was to deliver a letter to Father Jacques Marquette of the Society of Jesus from his superior, Father Dablon. In the letter Father Dablon ordered Marquette to accompany Joliet on his voyage of exploration. It was understood that the two men would spend the winter at St. Ignace getting to know each other better, exchanging information, and preparing their equipment for an attempt on the Messipi the following spring. Clearly Talon had arranged for Father Marquette's participation in the venture as a further sop to the Jesuits.

As soon as he received Talon's commission, Joliet set about organizing his expedition. The first essential was to find experienced and reliable voyageurs who were willing to make the trip with him, but good men were hard to come by and it was not until October 1 with winter closing in that Joliet finally signed a formal partnership. He had persuaded eight voyageurs to share the risks and profits of the Mississippi trip; some of them would go with him down the river and the others would stay in the Great Lakes area to gather furs. By the terms of the contract Joliet agreed to pay the bulk of the expenses in return for half the profits when the company finally disbanded. On December 8, 1672, Louis Joliet, his younger brother Zacharie, who had signed the agreement, and the other voyageurs reached St. Ignace in their canoes and settled in for the winter.

The next five months proved to be a busy time for Joliet's party. The Canadians trapped or hunted beaver, fox, muskrat, and mink for their prime winter pelts and visited the Mackinac tribes to buy up their stores of furs. With hard work and judicious trading the voyageurs expected to take early advantage of the trading privileges Talon had granted them, and they hoped to accumulate a large cache of good furs before the expedition disrupted their business. Joliet himself could spare little time for making money; he stayed close to the mission house where he talked with Father Marquette. The two men discussed their plans for the summer trip, interviewed the Indians about the "Great Water," and managed to draw a rough sketch map of the Mississippi based on all the information available. It was not much, but at least they had a faint idea of where to find the river—when the ice cleared from the lake, their best route lay westward to Green Bay and then over the Fox river portage along the route which Fathers

Dablon and Allouez had pioneered. Their sketch map, a compass, a table of declinations, and an astrolabe was all the technical equipment at their disposal; for the most part they intended to rely on the traditional mainstays of voyageur travel, a lightweight birch-bark canoe, muskets, and common sense.

Father Marquette was not in the least worried about the dangers of the venture; indeed, he was more enthusiastic than the laymen. He was one of those old-style missionaries who had cheerfully faced martyrdom at the hands of the Iroquois twenty years earlier. It is difficult to get a clear idea of Marquette's real character from contemporary reports and the priest's own letters. At first glance there is something too good to be true about this missionary; he seems to be too devoted and a little too selfless. Yet as time goes on and Marquette moves down the Father of Waters, it becomes apparent that he was in every detail a saintly man. He was certainly very devout and perhaps somewhat naïve; and although he has been accused of being too ambitious in his pursuit of missionary success, Marquette was utterly dedicated to the idea of spreading Christianity to the North American aborigines. He pursued this ambition all the time he was with the Jesuits, and in the end he gave his life for the cause without fanfare or heroics. He remains a worthy zealot who was involved, almost by accident, in an important phase of American exploration.

Jacques Marquette was born in France, a son of a well-known and prosperous family of Laon in the Department of Aisne. The Marquettes were aristocratic and highly respected in the town; for centuries the family had provided judges, counselors, barristers, and government officials. The future explorer and missionary was born on June 1, 1637, the youngest of six children, and like many younger sons of good family he was destined for the Church. Apparently the ideal of service and religious duty ran strongly among his immediate kin, because the elder of his two sisters, Frances, founded a religious community of women known as the Marquette Sisters, devoted to teaching needy girls. Jacques Marquette joined the ranks of the Jesuits when he was seventeen years old and it was soon evident that the youth was suited to the austere and demanding life of the Society. After two years on probation he began a long, dreary round of teaching and studying at various Jesuit colleges throughout France. This kept him occupied for almost nine years and nearly extinguished the missionary ardor which his family background had instilled in him. Fortunately, his superiors recorded his progress in their three-year reports and their comments shed an interesting light on his development away from scholastics and toward practical field work. Marquette's "report card" read as follows:

Ingenium [General Ability]	*Judicium* [Judgment]
1655 Bonum	Sat Bonum
1658 Mediocre	Mediocre
1661 Mediocre	Bonum

Prudentia [Prudence]	*Complexio naturalis* [Temperament]
1655 Mediocris	Melancolica, Sanguines
1658 Mediocris	Biliosa, Melancolica
1661 Bona	Melancolica

During this time when his academic work was slipping, Jacques Marquette harped more and more on the idea that he should be sent as a missionary *in partibus infidelium*. He first volunteered for missionary work when he had been a priest for only two years, and the superior general of the Jesuits firmly rejected the application—he was to continue his studies until he was fit for overseas duty. At that stage Marquette was pleading to be sent to China or India, but when his requests were turned down and he began reading the exciting annual *Relations* of the missions in Canada, he widened his terms of reference. Year after year he agitated to be sent on missionary duties to the Orient or to Canada until finally his pestering had the desired effect. In 1665 the Jesuits in New France wrote to the Society that they were short-handed, and the superior-general decided to send the importunate Father Marquette to swell their ranks.

Even after he landed in New France, Marquette was restless. He was irked by the need to learn Indian dialects and he chafed to rush off into the field. At last, after two more years of studying Indian languages, he was considered to be ready for his duties and was ordered to assist the missionaries working on the shores of Lake Superior. It proved to be an uphill task, as thankless and unrewarding as he could have wished. The Great Lakes Indians were a shabby lot, dirty, quarrelsome, and fickle. Their tribal pride had been knocked to pieces by the better-organized and braver Iroquois, and as defeated refugees the Lakes Indians wandered aimlessly from one fishing ground to the next, or drifted in search of hunting grounds that were safe from Iroquois war parties. In winter they came to beg from the missionaries and in summer Marquette found himself trekking along in the wake of his migrating flock, his portable altar strapped to his back. This discomfort was usually repaid with heartbreak. The Indians rarely grasped the meaning of Christianity and they normally came to see the missionary out of curiosity or hoping for gifts. Marquette found that only the children, the maimed, and the very old wanted to be baptized; the others scoffed at his sermons and reverted to their tribal manitous, the animal spirits of their medicine men. Nevertheless Marquette tried to help the Indians given to his care. In his simple way he struggled to better their living conditions by teaching them to grow crops instead of hunting, and to hoard food, when it was plentiful, against a time of famine. He was usually unsuccessful; the Indians preferred to celebrate a good day's hunting with a nauseating orgy which left men, women, and children groaning and retching, sprawled on the ground with distended bellies.

During these years Marquette had only one complaint—he was working in an area where other missionaries had labored before him. Like many of his Jesuit colleagues, Marquette's highest ambition was to spread the message of Christianity to tribes no missionary had ever visited. He was not content to carry on where other Jesuits had left off, and he craved the opportunity to start his own mission post. He wanted to find a tribe that had never seen a "black robe" and convert the heathen by his own unaided effort. He questioned wandering Indians about their homes and the tribes they came from. He wrote letters to his superiors in Montreal beseeching them to send him to work among the farthest tribes, and he prayed to the Blessed Virgin that his wish would be granted.

Marquette's prayers were answered the day Joliet brought him Dablon's letter with its details of the forthcoming Mississippi journey. Marquette was ordered to accompany the expedition as its official padre, and on behalf of the Church he was to observe and record all that happened. Whenever possible he could assist Joliet as an interpreter and help with the drawing of maps. Furthermore he was granted permission to spread the Word of God to any tribes he met on the journey and on his return he was expected to recommend if missions should be set up in the newly discovered lands. It was all that Marquette had ever wanted, and it is typical of the man that he noted with pious thanks in his diary that Joliet brought him the good news on the feast day of his patroness, the Virgin Mary.

On Monday, May 15, 1673, the expedition set out. It consisted of Joliet, Marquette, and five voyageurs; the other men who had come up from Montreal stayed behind at Mackinac to run a small trading post and to look after the furs collected during the winter. The seven explorers traveled in two small canoes, light enough to be handled by one man in the bow and another in the stern; this meant that the priest would not have to paddle and that there would always be one man in each craft who could rest while his companions kept the canoe moving. For stores they took along dried maize and pemmican. Otherwise their equipment was minimal—trade goods, spare gunflints, powder and ball, a few cooking pots, axes, and some blankets. Marquette of course had his vestments, a traveling altar and holy vessels, while Joliet looked after the compass, astrolabe, and declination tables. In addition both men had a supply of writing and drawing materials for maps and journals.

After coasting around the shore of Lake Michigan for about a week, they reached Stinking Bay, as Green Bay was called, and visited the local natives, the Menominee or Wild Rice Indians. These were a peaceable tribe who derived their nickname from the main staple of their diet—the water rice that grows profusely in the marshes and shallow lakes of upper Wisconsin. In the fall the Indians would paddle through the masses of ripe grain and flail the heads of rice over the gunwales of their canoes, filling the boats like floating grain baskets. Then the rice was put into sacks and trampled until the chaff was separated, and the grain itself could be pounded into meal. The result, Marquette noted, was that "prepared in this way one finds wild rice almost as good as rice where no seasoning is added." The Menominee welcomed Joliet and his men but were horrified that the French planned to voyage down the "Big Water." They warned their visitors that the upper river was swarming with hostile war parties from the western tribes and that farther down there were terrible monsters which swallowed canoes at a single gulp. If this were not enough, the foolhardy white men would be burned to death by the fierce sun at the mouth of the river. Later it became obvious from these forebodings that even the isolated Wild Rice Indians had some inkling of the true course of the great river, but at the time the Frenchmen were puzzled and not a little amused by their dismal prophecies.

At the head of Green Bay the expedition stayed briefly with Father Allouez of the St. Francis Xavier mission station where they picked up fresh supplies before pushing up the Fox River. They advanced through beautiful countryside, and Marquette, who tended to take a rosy view of any frontier land, waxed enthusiastic about the gently flowing river which "abounds in bustards, ducks, teal, and other birds which are attracted by the wild rice of which they are very fond." Farther upstream the Fox crossed bands of hard rock that produced a series of rapids, but this was not a major obstacle for experienced canoe men and the party made excel-

lent progress. Above the rapids the river was interrupted by
the swamplike expanse of Lake Winnebago. The lake was a
maze of channels and half-submerged islands covered with tall
reeds, which blocked the view from the canoes. Joliet and his
party groped their way across, relying on the telltale weeds
that swayed like underwater weathervanes, pointing the direction of the main current through the lake. Eventually they
reached the mouth of the upper Fox and continued upstream
until on June 7 they arrived at the reed wigwams of the
Mascouten, or Fire Indians. This was the key point, the limit
of previous French exploration and the place where the expedition would be launching into the unknown. The Jesuit
missionaries had reached the village, and to mark their visit
they had set up a large wooden cross in the center of the
settlement. Marquette was overjoyed to see that the cross still
stood and that the Indians were leaving offerings in front of
it. He decided that among the local tribes the Miami Indians
"are the more courteous, the more open-hearted, and the
more handsome. They wear two long whiskers over the ears,
giving them a graceful appearance," whereas the "Mascoutens
and Kickapoos are boorish and look like peasants."

Joliet asked for, and was given, two guides to lead his
expedition over the watershed to the Messipi. On June 10
they left the Mascouten village and the same day reached the
portage which led to a small tributary of the Wisconsin
River. Here they unloaded the canoes and carried them two
and a half miles to the shallow waters of the westward-flow-
ing Wisconsin. The supplies were repacked under their tar-
paulins in the center of the boats, the guides turned back to
their village, and after Marquette had held a short service to
bless the project, the Frenchmen pushed off and started
downriver.

The upper reaches of the Wisconsin's feeder stream were
marshy and narrow, winding between many small islands, so
the canoes had to move cautiously through the shallows. Fortunately the river bed was sandy and the fragile birchbark
hulls were not damaged by the shoals; the boats drew so little

water that they could pick a slender channel between the worst obstacles. As the river deepened and grew broader, the countryside also improved; willow thickets gave way to a parklike savannah dotted with groves of walnut, basswood, and oak. The explorers noticed wild grapes, deer, and herds of buffalo more than four hundred strong. To Marquette's disappointment, and probably to Joliet's relief, they did not encounter any Indians, though doubtless the red men were watching the strangers from the shelter of the trees, wondering where the black robe and his companions were going. After a week's steady paddling the Wisconsin had grown into a sizable river running between heavily wooded hills, and on June 17 the explorers came to its junction with the parent stream. Before them lay the sought-after Big Water, a large river almost a mile wide flowing due south. In the middle distance they could see the line where the waters of the two rivers mingled, and on the far bank of the Mississippi rose a great wall of rocky bluffs, covered in thick forest except where the occasional white patch of limestone showed through the green. This was obviously the river the Indians called the Father of Waters; perhaps it was also the "inland sea" which might lead to the Pacific. At all events, the first part of their mission had been accomplished—they had found the river. Now their task was to follow it to its mouth.

Turning downstream the expedition floated along the Mississippi. On the right bank the high bluffs continued mile after mile, and on their left the countryside was a gently rolling panorama of dense woodland stretching to the horizon. The Mississippi wound southward in broad loops below the gray-blue line of the Iowa plateau. In places there were low tree-covered islands which constricted the channel, splitting the main stream into a network of small passages, scarcely two hundred yards broad. The current in the big river was much more sluggish that that of the Wisconsin and the paddlers had to apply themselves to their work. There was little to do or to notice. The Mississippi flowed onward gently and powerfully, the banks slipped by as though they would never change. Marquette looked hopefully for Indians but the river was deserted; Joliet took observations with his astrolabe and compiled a rough map of their course. Once they were startled by a wildcat that swam nonchalantly across their bows in full view of the paddlers, and Marquette mistakenly jotted down in his diary that they had discovered some new species of aquatic animal. Otherwise the explorers traveled peacefully and were lulled by their daily routine: the gentle gurgle of the canoes slicing through the water; the splash of the paddles at each downstroke; the patter of droplets flickering down from the upraised blades on the forward swing; an occasional clatter of paddle handle on gunwale during a careless stroke, or the creak of a thwart as one of the voyageurs shifted his position. The constant paddling hardened their shoulder and biceps muscles, and gradually their legs became accustomed to the cramped, half-kneeling paddling position. Their hands grew callused and their faces tanned in the reflection of the sun off the surface of the river.

At night the explorers nosed their canoes into the bank and clambered ashore to light a cooking fire. They roasted a few ears of Indian corn, picked wild fruit from the bushes, or cut off chunks of pemmican. Then, before darkness obscured the nearby thickets and turned them into potential ambushes, Marquette would recite a few prayers for their safety and success. It was dangerous to stay on the bank after dark, so the expedition always returned to their canoes, pushed out onto the darkening river, and Joliet would select a safe anchorage for the night. In the lee of an island or behind a sand bar where the current was slack, they dropped anchor and lay down to sleep in the bottom of the canoes. One man in each boat kept guard and the others stretched out among the bales of supplies.

By day Joliet kept his course along the west bank hoping to locate a tribe of Indians, the Illinois, whom he expected to find living on that side of the river. During the past few years an occasional Illinois tribesman had wandered into the Jesuit mission posts on the Great Lakes and talked, through interpreters, of his tribal home on the banks of the Father of Waters. The Jesuits of course were eager listeners because they were always seeking heathen tribes ripe for conversion, but the Illinois were equally important for Joliet. He wanted to contact them as potential allies; they were obviously friendly and it was possible that they had traveled all the way down the Mississippi and knew what lay at its mouth.

Eventually, some two hundred miles downstream from the mouth of the Wisconsin, the explorers caught sight of an Indian trail leading up from the water's edge. Recent footprints in the soft earth showed that the trail was in use, so, leaving the five voyageurs in the canoes, Joliet and Marquette went ashore and made their way inland along the narrow path, looking for aborigines. After his careful precautions each night against Indian attack, Joliet's bold excursion away from his canoes seems unaccountably foolhardy. Yet he had good reasons for running the risk, though perhaps he should not have taken Marquette with him, thereby exposing both senior men in the party to danger. At this stage of the journey it was essential for Joliet to make contact with some local Indians. The Frenchmen had been traveling down the river for a week without seeing a soul, and apart from the river's course and appearance they had learned nothing. Intendant Talon wanted to know about the river tribes, whether they were friendly or not, whether they were vassals of the Spanish, if they knew of a passage to China, whether they had precious gems, metals, or furs for sale. There were a thousand and one details which Joliet had to find out if his expedition was to be successful, and the natives were his only possible source of information. Besides, Joliet was a fair judge of Indian character and he realized that two white men stood an excellent chance of survival in a meeting with the Indians, provided the visitors were fearless and the savages had not seen white men before. He hoped that Marquette's presence would also be a help, not only as an interpreter, but because the "black robes" had acquired a general reputation for friendship which extended well beyond their line of mission stations. With luck the Indians would see the priest's garb before they let fly with their weapons.

After following the trail for four and a half miles Joliet and his companion came to "a village on the bank of a river and two others on a hillock about a mile away." The two Frenchmen had approached the encampments so quietly that no one had noticed them. Stepping out into the open, Joliet gave a loud halloo, at which some Indians working in a nearby field dropped their hoes and bolted into their village to report the arrival of two strangers. In a little while Joliet was relieved to see a ragged procession emerge from the village and head in his direction. Leading the column came four chieftains bearing aloft a calumet, the ritual peace pipe. Behind the elders hovered a motley throng of curious tribesmen, squaws, and children, who ventured forward to inspect the pale-skinned Frenchmen, a breed which the aborigines had certainly heard about but had never seen for themselves. After a brief ceremony with the peace pipe, the chiefs welcomed the white men and invited them to enter the village. There Joliet and Marquette had to undergo the full ceremony of Indian protocol, more puffing of the calumet, long speeches of welcome, and dancing displays. It turned out that the Indians were the Illinois the French had been looking for, so Marquette was able to translate their orations and reply with Joliet's prepared text on the benefits of allegiance with the "Great Captain of the French" in Quebec who was the dread enemy of the Iroquois. The latter point was well received by the Illinois, as they were yet another refugee group tormented by the Iroquois Confederacy.

After the preliminary round of speech-making, the French were entertained to a formal banquet, a gruesome four-course meal which the two visitors could not avoid for fear of offending their hosts. It began with "a large wooden platter of sagamité, as it was called, a generous supply of Indian corn boiled in water and seasoned with fat." As a token of esteem this soggy mess was spooned into the mouths of the explorers by the master of ceremonies. The second course was boiled fish; the master of ceremonies broke it into pieces, removed the bones with his grubby fingers, blew on the morsel to cool it, and then popped the tidbit into an open French mouth. Course number three, boiled dog, was politely declined, and the entrée, a buffalo hump, was ruined by the efforts of their host who insisted on hand-feeding his guests with the greasiest and most slimy portions. After the meal the Frenchmen were taken on a tour of the village and the Illinois showered them with pathetic gifts of "belts, garters, and other objects made of the hair of bears and wild oxen [buffalo]." It was a pitiful scene as the unsophisticated and wretched Indians tried hard to please their important visitors. The Illinois were a weak and peace-loving tribe who saw the French as potential protectors and wanted desperately to impress the white men. There was little that Joliet or Marquette could do to reassure them. Their own mission was to explore the river and they had little time to arrange treaties with needy tribes. However hard the Illinois tried to please, they were too timid to have ventured down the Father of Waters and they knew nothing about the lower river. After spending one night in the village, Joliet decided to return to his canoes and push ahead. The entire village escorted them back to the bank and presented them with two farewell gifts—a slave boy and a three-foot calumet decorated with feathers. Joliet accepted these presents graciously and promised to return in the fall; the other baubles he threw overboard as soon as the Illinois were out of sight.

Continuing down the river for another two hundred and thirty miles, the expedition encountered the "monsters" which the Wild Rice Indians had dreaded. These demons proved to be no more than weird rock pictures daubed in red, green, and black paint on a vertical cliff overlooking the river from the east bank. According to Marquette the figures in these petroglyphs were "as large as a calf. They have horns on the head like deer, a terrifying look, red eyes, a tiger's beard, a face somewhat like that of a man, the body covered with scales, a tail so long that it goes all around the body, passes over the head and turns back between the legs, ending in the tail of a fish." Evidently these rock manitous were powerful magic, because they had successfully discouraged the northern tribes from descending the river past their baleful glare. The French were more interested by the ability of the native artist "because skillful artists in France would find it difficult to paint them so well, aside from the fact that they were so high on the cliff as to make it hard to get to that spot conveniently and paint them."

Shortly after passing the rock monsters, the expedition came to the demon who was supposed to swallow their canoes. This evil spirit was nothing less than the mouth of the Missouri River which poured forth "a riot of entire trees, branches, and floating reefs which gushed from the river so violently that one could not pass through without great danger." Fortunately the tumbling roar of this huge tributary could be heard for many miles upstream and Joliet's voyageurs approached the junction cautiously so that they were able to pick a channel in the less turbulent Mississippi water which was pushed over to the left bank. Bouncing and gyrating in their light canoes through the maelstrom, the Frenchmen emerged unscathed and then shot the notorious "Chain of Rocks" rapids that exposed their jagged teeth a league downstream.

These rapids and the mouth of the Ohio several days' journey lower down were the last physical hazards which the party encountered. Neither was of much concern to experienced voyageurs who were trained on the turbulent waters of the Canadian backwoods. In fact, by the time the expedition passed the mouth of the Ohio they were much more troubled by the mosquitoes and hot sun of the warmer latitudes. But these were minor discomforts, and Joliet led his team efficiently and calmly as far south as the place where De Soto's corpse had been committed to the river depths 131 years earlier. At this point Talon's agent was faced with a difficult decision. By now it had become plain that the Mississippi drained south, not east nor west. This was the answer to

Talon's main question, and in addition Joliet had discovered
that the river was not commercially viable—there were no
mines, gems, or fur-trading Indians. Having learned this
much, Joliet had to decide whether it was worth continuing
the trip. His chief worry was that his expedition might fall
into the hands of the Spanish. None of the Frenchmen knew
whether the Spaniards had established garrisons or Indian
alliances on the lower Mississippi. If they had, the intruders
from the north would be arrested and clapped in jail; Talon
would never know the results of their exploration and the
French westward drive would be plunged into uncertainty. Furthermore the Missouri or Pekitanoui—the "Muddy
Water," as the Indians called it, looked a promising route
westward to the Pacific; it might be more profitable for future
expeditions to follow that river rather than the Mississippi.

While he was considering these conflicting interests,
Joliet's dilemma was taken out of his hands. Near the mouth
of the St. Francis river in present-day Arkansas, the Frenchmen came upon a village of Quapaw Indians on the west
bank. Joliet ordered his two canoes to steer toward the settlement, whereupon the inhabitants gave every indication that
they were preparing to attack the white men. A flotilla of
large dugout canoes appeared and circled behind the Frenchmen to cut off their retreat. At the same time a crowd of
yelling braves swarmed down to the bank and pranced about,
brandishing "bows, arrows, tomahawks, clubs and shields."
Desperately Joliet stood up in the bow of his canoe and repeatedly raised and lowered the Illinois calumet, while Marquette called out in Indian that the white men came in peace.
But the Quapaw could not understand Marquette's northern
dialect and they failed to recognize the pipe of peace. It was
an ugly moment, and luckily Joliet did not lose his nerve. He
ordered his voyageurs to keep paddling straight toward the
enemy and remained standing in the canoe waving the
calumet. Several of the younger warriors on the bank leapt
into the river and began swimming toward the French boats,
eager to capsize the light canoes and massacre the white men
as they floundered in the water. A hand reached up to grasp a

gunwale and war clubs went hurtling over the heads of the voyageurs. Then at the last second someone on the bank recognized the pipe of peace, and so great was the prestige of the feathered emblem that several of the older warriors jumped into the river to restrain the hotheads. The howling crowd faltered and their excitement died away in an embarrassed silence. Two of the senior braves swam up to the leading canoe and apologetically threw their bows and arrows into it. Then they clambered on board and gesticulated to the Frenchmen that they paddle to the village landing place.

All that day Joliet and Marquette worked hard at persuading the Quapaw that they were friendly. With much sign language and waving of the peace pipe the newcomers tried to make their point, and after an anxious night were escorted to the tribal capital farther downstream. There the calumet once again made the rounds and after a lengthy council meeting the chiefs decided not to kill the white men. To seal the agreement and convince their visitors, the Quapaw went through the full ritual of the calumet or peace dance and threw another of the sagamité, fish, and dogmeat banquets. By a stroke of good fortune one of the Quapaw chiefs knew a smattering of the Illinois language and through him the Frenchmen were able to learn about the lower river. Apparently the expedition was within ten days' journey of the sea where they would find the white men who "had rosaries and pictures." As further evidence the Indians produced guns, tomahawks, hoes, knives, beads, and an assortment of powder flasks of double glass. Joliet had no difficulty in recognizing Spanish trade goods, and because he did not understand the enormous distances over which the Indian trade took place, he presumed that his party was on the brink of entering Spanish domain. Furthermore the Quapaw warned him that the lower river was the haunt of piratical war fleets that preyed on unprotected travelers. After his recent narrow escape Joliet took this warning seriously and decided that there were enough reasons for turning back. Accordingly, on July 17, the French expedition started upstream for home.

It was a long, difficult, colorless journey against the Mississippi current and neither Joliet nor Marquette had much to say about it. Near the mouth of the Ohio they again met up with the Illinois Indians, who advised the explorers to follow the Illinois River up to Lake Michigan rather than use the longer route via the Wisconsin. Joliet sensibly took their advice and was delighted to find that the Illinois provided an invaluable short cut between the Mississippi and the Great Lakes. At the end of September the voyageurs carried their canoes over a portage near the future site of Chicago and launched them once more upon Lake Michigan. Then they paddled along the coast for three hundred miles until they regained the Jesuit mission at Green Bay. The approach of winter stopped the expedition from continuing on to Mackinac that year, so the party wintered with the missionaries. Joliet and Marquette spent their time putting together their notes of the trip, polishing up a fair copy of their reports, and drawing up a map of their explorations. The exacting conditions of his earlier missionary career had undermined Marquette's health, and during those cold winter months spent waiting at Green Bay he fell sick. The nature of his illness is not known, but by the time the spring thaw broke up the ice on the lake, Marquette felt that his weakened body would not withstand the hardships of the voyage back to Montreal, so he wrote to his superiors asking their permission for him to spend the next winter among the Illinois he had discovered. They granted his request, and with two voyageurs the ailing priest set out for the Chicago portage. It was a painful journey for the semi-invalid and the next winter caught his little group halfway across the Chicago portage. They would have starved to death but for the local tribes who brought food to the helpless white men, extorting gifts in return. The following spring Marquette struggled on in search of the Illinois and found them in time to preach for a few weeks. But the missionary knew he was near death and tried to limp back to his colleagues at St. Ignace. On the way he died, broken but happy, on the shores of Lake Michigan. Here his canoemen buried him and two years later the Christianized Indians exhumed his bones and took them with great affection to his old mission at Mackinac.

Joliet left Green Bay in the early spring of 1674, headed for Montreal. He took with him his journal, the new map of the Mississippi, and the slave boy whom the Illinois had presented him the previous year. It was a long but routine voyage and they moved quickly. By the end of June they had entered the home stretch and were on their way down the St. Lawrence to Montreal; only the rapids of Lachine lay between them and the city. It was late in the evening and the travelers were eager to return home. Joliet did not want to spend another night in the open, and so instead of portaging around Lachine he decided to shoot the rapids and arrive the same day. It was a disastrous decision. Their canoe went out of control and smashed into a rock, spilling its contents into the water. In a split second the fragile birchbark hull was shattered like an eggshell; the Indian boy was killed, and the trunk containing the map and report went to the bottom of the river. Joliet regained consciousness to find that he had been pulled to safety by two fishermen who had seen the accident. It was a cruel ending to his voyage of exploration.

Of course Joliet produced another map and report from memory but many of the details were missing. Marquette's version failed to fill in the gaps, for the worthy priest was a dull writer and a poor cartographer. His report was heavily biased in favor of missionary prospects and the only result of his effort was that for some time the Mississippi was called the "Rivière de la Conception." It was several years before either man received the recognition he deserved and by then they were already overshadowed by their illustrious successor, the Sieur de la Salle. Joliet continued to be dogged by bad luck. Intendant Talon had returned to France while the expedition was away, and his replacement was unhelpful. Joliet was refused a license to trade with the Indians he had discovered and he was even accused of misusing his commission for his own profit. Not until 1679, after he had led another trip, this time to Hudson's Bay to check on the British activities in that area, did he receive his reward from the French Crown. He was given the island of Anticosti in the Gulf of St. Lawrence and for a while he made a properous living from the rich fishing grounds of his fief. Then his grant was contested in the law courts, and as a final blow an English fleet, which arrived to attack Quebec, turned tail without doing anything more destructive than laying waste Joliet's estate on Anticosti.

The story of Joliet's last years is uncertain. He spent some time as a royal hydrographer mapping the sea approaches to the St. Lawrence and was a professor of hydrography in Quebec. By 1700, the year of his death, he had slipped from the scene. It was his fate that not only was he unlucky, but in some respects he was too good an explorer. If his Mississippi expedition had been packed with thrilling adventures, he would have caught the public's imagination. But, as it was, he conducted a businesslike trip which lacked glamor and hair-raising excitement. The results of his trip were disappointing, not only for the public that wanted tales of derring-do, but also for the authorities in New France who had hoped for a more profitable Mississippi civilization. Much of Joliet's reputation sank with the strongbox he lost at Lachine; Marquette's journal became the standard authority on the trip and soon afterward the exploits of La Salle eclipsed the earlier expedition.

5

The Visionary

WHILE FRENCH AGENTS LIKE THE JOLIET BROTHERS were boldly thrusting inland from their bases on the St. Lawrence, the English colonists farther south had also been probing westward from their settlements on the Atlantic seaboard. In fact, when Intendant Talon selected Louis Joliet for the task of investigating the rumored "Messipi" on behalf of France, the intendant was only just in time, because a handful of the more adventurous English settlers were poised to break through the barrier of the Appalachian Mountains and enter the Mississippi Valley. When Joliet cut short his trip down the river for fear of falling into the hands of the Spanish he was missing the point—the real threat to French expansion into America's heartland was not from the Spaniards who were bottled up behind their deserts in the southwest, but from the English colonists who were now surmounting the physical obstacle that had separated them from the Mississippi basin.

However, the Appalachian barrier was by no means the only disadvantage the English had to contend with vis-a-vis the French effort from the St. Lawrence. At first glance it would seem that it was a fairly straightforward matter for the English to find a route through the mountains just as the *coureurs de bois* had successfully found canoe routes around the flank of the hostile Iroquois Confederacy. Furthermore the English colonists were much closer to the Mississippi-Ohio drainage system than the French, and while a Montreal trader was normally obliged to allow at least fifteen months for a journey out to the Mississippi and back home again, an experienced Indian trader working out of Virginia could do the round trip in perhaps half that time. Yet despite this great handicap the French beat the English to the Mississippi because they were first in the field and because their rivals had no really strong incentives for successful exploration of the interior.

During the first half of the seventeenth century when French explorers were racing toward the Great Lakes, the English colonists remained firmly tied down to the coast. Each year more and more immigrants were arriving from England but they came to farm rather than to trade for furs and consequently the fringe of settlement spread only slowly outward from the harbors where they landed. Most of this population overspill took place along the line of the coast, and by 1670 there were English-speaking colonies from Carolina to Massachusetts, though inland the settled areas soon petered out into untouched wilderness. The colonists themselves were prone to spending more of their energy in squabbling among themselves than in countering the efforts of the French, and when it came to tackling the problem of moving up to the higher flanks of the mountains there were few pioneers interested in taking the risks involved. In the northern English settlements the only feasible road to the interior was the Hudson Valley and this led straight into an area already controlled by the French. It was in the middle and southern tier of colonies that the English faced into the unknown, and it so happened that in these colonies the settlers were doing so well with their lucrative plantation crops that they saw little point in challenging the Indians and the forbidding mountain ranges which they regarded as a reasonable and natural western boundary. Of course there were always a few bolder spirits, the occasional adventurer or a former Indian trader from the Dutch settlements, who preferred to make a living by gathering buckskin and furs of indifferent quality among the tribes of woodland Indians, but these frontiersmen, unlike the French fur traders, were of little significance in the colonial economy and their activities were usually frowned upon by the authorities. Such men could not compare with the dedicated priests manning the isolated Canadian mission stations or administrators like Talon who encouraged expansion because they knew that without new resources their colony would collapse. The English-Americans had no such presiding geniuses and by 1660 they could only console themselves with the comforting thought that in Virginia alone there were as many colonists as in the whole of New France.

The accession of Louis XIV made matters even worse for the English. The Sun King's grandiose schemes for an American empire found few imitators in England; Cromwell's Protectorate did more harm than good by creating dissensions among the colonists, and Charles II was happy to appease his powerful neighbor by curbing any activities of his American subjects which might be interpreted as running counter to French interest. Yet despite these discouragements there were men of influence in the English colonies who understood the need to beat the French in the contest for control of the interior. Chief of these expansionists was Governor William Berkeley of Virginia. In 1669 and 1670 he sent one John Lederer, a German doctor, to find a way west through the Appalachians. Lederer failed to find the pass he was looking for but a year later a semi-official exploring party of Virginians struggled across the divide and at last succeeded in reaching a tiny tributary of the Mississippi system, for on the opposite flank of the mountains they found a rivulet that flowed north and west. The Englishmen tried to follow this stream but were forced to turn back when their food supply ran out. Before Governor Berkeley could follow up their discovery there was news of the success of the Joliet-Marquette expedition and even the dullest geographer could point out that if the French established control of the Mississippi they would be able to hem in the English colonies. Even at this late stage the English held a potential trump card, for the foundation of Carolina meant that the line of their settlements now extended to the south of the Appalachian barrier. It was no more than a question of time before an Indian trader would find out that he could travel almost due west from Charleston to the confluence of the Arkansas River and the Mississippi and not encounter any terrain more formidable than virgin piedmont. Yet by the time this was known the race was well and truly lost; England was forestalled by the actions of a remarkable Frenchman who very nearly changed the entire course of American history.

René-Robert Cavelier, Sieur de la Salle, is the most tragic figure in the history of Mississippi exploration. Of all the Mississippi explorers he had the greatest vision, the most meteoric career, and the worst luck. In France he received royal patronage and financial assistance, but in Canada he struggled against hatred, greed, and envy. If La Salle had achieved his ambitions, a gigantic wedge of North America from Quebec to New Orleans to the Rocky Mountains would have become a French colony, firmly held for Louis the Magnificent by a chain of forts that started on the Atlantic and finished on the Gulf of Mexico. This was the empire that La Salle dreamed of, an empire whose key was absolute control of the vital spinal column, the Mississippi, reaching with its tributaries thousands of miles into the interior. If he had lived, perhaps La Salle would have finally built this colossus, but as it was, he died in an obscure Texas thicket, shot through the head by one of his own men. In some ways it was the inevitable conclusion to a turbulent and contradictory character.

La Salle was baptized René-Robert Cavelier on November 22, 1643. He was second son of a well-to-do wholesale merchant in the Normandy city of Rouen, and, as was the custom with the large, rich burgher families of France, René-Robert was given the distinguishing name 'de la Salle' from an estate owned by the Cavelier family. La Salle's intellectual talents were recognized at an early age and his father encouraged him to enter the Society of Jesus, because the Jesuits provided the best education available in France at that time. La Salle was an able student even by the high standards of the Jesuits and his teachers praised his academic excellence, particularly in mathematics, and his high moral character. Ironically, the hard-working priests were carefully training a young man who would develop into a great foe of their order and would strive to destroy the Jesuit plan to dominate Canada.

It did not take long for La Salle to become disenchanted with the highly regimented rule of the Jesuits and he left the Society to go out into the world and run his own life. It was the first manifestation of a restless spirit that would not suffer any authority but its own, and that drove La Salle to ignore both his health and his fortune in pursuit of a career. Under French law La Salle had already forfeited his share in the family estates by entering the Society of Jesus, so when he emerged from the seminary he was penniless. To tide him over, his family arranged to pay him a small annual income, some three to four hundred livres a year, and with this cash in his pocket La Salle sailed for New France in 1666 to make his life in the colony.

It was not entirely a step in the dark. La Salle's elder brother Jean was already at Montreal, where he was a priest with the Sulpician Order. Jean Cavelier was unlike his younger brother, more content to follow the ways of the priesthood, and he was already a rising star among the Sulpicians, who were on the point of launching a great campaign to oust the Jesuits from power in the Canadian backwoods. The Sulpicians needed allies and agents in this crusade and La Salle could scarcely have timed his arrival more profitably. Almost at once, through Jean's help, the shrewd, twenty-three-year-old Norman was given an estate at Lachine, the same place where Joliet later disastrously capsized his canoe. The Lachine estate was in the fief of the Sulpicians and they gave it away for an absurdly cheap price—La Salle had to improve the estate and pay a silver medal weighing one mark every time the property changed hands. Of course the land was still in a primeval condition, dense forest and foaming river, but it was a key site controlling the portage which the fur traders' canoes used on the way down to Montreal. La Salle was off to a flying start and he made every effort to follow up his advantage. He built a fort, cleared the land, brought in settlers, set up a trading post, and parleyed with the Indians. The Sulpicians were well pleased with their energetic tenant as they watched him tackle the job of making Lachine the first Sulpician steppingstone westward into the interior. Like the Jesuits before them, they failed to realize that La Salle was working toward his own ambitions and not in the interests of his overlords. For the moment their interests coincided, but when these ambitions diverged, La Salle was prepared to break with his sponsors.

Logically, once he had built his palisades and storehouses, the young Norman had only to sit back and watch the furs roll in, his peasants raise crops, and his fortune snowball. But La Salle was not a merchant; in fact, throughout his career he was a poor businessman and lost money on most of his deals. La Salle had come to New France not to make money, but to make his mark on the colony's history and follow a destiny in the unknown west. Running a combination trading post and estate was not to his taste, however much money he made. Far superior in talent, education, and imagination to the run-of-the-mill colonists in Canada, La Salle was a lone wolf. He could well have become a *coureur de bois*, wandering among the Indians, trading, hunting, trapping, having children by Indian squaws, growing half-savage in the backlands, and finally leaving no more trace of his existence than a wild animal. But La Salle was too disciplined and too gifted to waste himself that way; he dreamed of the Far West, and determined in his quiet, uncompromising way to search out new lands and tame the wilderness. In the vast unknown heart of North America he planned a great empire built by his own efforts as a tribute to France.

Accordingly, when Lachine was firmly established, La Salle took a trip to Montreal to see the Sulpicians. His request to the bishop was shattering; he proposed that his benefactors should buy back the estate they had given him. This suggestion was not so unreasonable as it first might seem, for La Salle had transformed the original grant, sunk considerable capital and labor into the estate, and greatly improved the value of Lachine. Naturally the Sulpicians were irritated to learn that their exemplary tenant wanted to move, and tried to keep him anchored by repurchasing only part of the Lachine property. La Salle promptly sold off the remainder to a rich blacksmith, and having washed his hands of landed property, turned inland toward the wilderness and his ambition.

The Sulpicians decided that something could still be saved from their association with the talented La Salle and proposed that if he was going off exploring in the backwoods, he might do well to join forces with a group of Sulpician missionaries. These were embarking on a westward voyage to track down unconverted Indians whose tribes had not yet been found by the Jesuits. Partly to repay his obligations to the Sulpicians and partly to conceal the extent of his own plans, La Salle agreed to combine his four canoes with the three canoes of the Sulpician expedition led by Dollier de Casson, a giant of a man who had once been a renowned and dashing cavalry captain before he had turned priest. The imposing De Casson and the taciturn La Salle worked well together, for they were both dedicated men; so long as their paths lay together there was no friction, but when their aims differed, they broke up without regret.

The La Salle-Sulpician expedition set out on July 6, 1669. The explorers were well provisioned and confident—La Salle had accepted payment for Lachine in stores and trade goods.

As matters turned out, they were too confident; they had overlooked their lack of experience in backwoods life. This was La Salle's first real trip into the wilderness, and the Sulpicians were complete novices in exploration. This was their maiden venture to challenge the supremacy of the Jesuit missionaries. To make matters worse, their Dutch interpreter spoke excellent Iroquois but atrocious French, so communication between him and his employers was a hit-and-miss affair.

To avoid the Jesuit-held territories to the north and west, the expedition set a southerly course to Lake Ontario. This route took the sweating paddlers straight into the domain of the hostile Iroquois Confederacy. The French were soon in trouble as man after man was laid low by the unaccustomed physical strain, the poor food, and the constant discomfort. One of the priests, obviously on his first long-distance canoe journey, wrote home in mingled wonder and complaint:

"Your lodge is as extraordinary as your vessels; for after paddling or carrying the canoes all day, you find mother earth ready to receive your weary body. If the weather is fine, you kindle a fire and lie down to sleep without further trouble; but if it rains you must peel bark from the trees, and make a lean-to by laying it on a frame of sticks. As for food, it is enough to make you burn all the cookery books ever written; for in the woods of Canada one can live well without bread, wine, salt, pepper or spice. The ordinary food is Indian corn, or Turkey wheat as it is called in France, which is crushed between two stones and boiled, seasoning it with meat or fish, when you can get them. This sort of life seemed so strange to us that we all felt the effects of it; and before we were a hundred leagues from Montreal, not one of us was free from some malady or other. At last after our misery, on the second of August, we came to Lake Ontario, like a great sea with no land beyond it."

Paddling out onto the broad waters of Lake Ontario, the expedition followed the line of the south shore until they beached their canoes at Irondequoit Bay, an inlet of Lake Ontario, east of the site of Rochester. Here they were intercepted by Seneca Indians of the Iroquois Confederacy and escorted to the nearest village. The French gladly went along with the Indians, for in their naïvete the Sulpicians were looking for converts and La Salle was hoping to gather information about the interior. They were sharply introduced to the cruel realities of Indian life. From the outset the Senecas were antagonistic toward the newcomers, as the Confederacy had just received word that renegade French soldiers at Montreal had murdered an Iroquois chief. Although the culprits were publicly executed by a firing squad against the town ramparts, the damage had been done and the fragile French-Iroquois truce was in ruins. The Senecas regarded La Salle and the Sulpicians as spies and refused to extend anything more than the barest minimum of Indian courtesy. To make their attitude clear, the Senecas produced a young Shawnee prisoner, who they knew would have been an ideal guide for the Frenchmen on their trek into the unknown lands of the West. When the French offered to buy the Shawnee, the Seneca warriors responded sadistically; they lashed their prisoner to a stake, burned the youth terribly with red-hot musket barrels that were stroked and stabbed all over his body, flayed him alive, scalped him, and then ate the pitiful remains of their victim. This gruesome spectacle lasted for six hours in the presence of a gloating crowd of Iroquois and before it was half over the Frenchmen were sick to the stomach and begged to be excused from the entertainment. Even the most starry-eyed of the missionaries realized that their own lives were now in danger if the Seneca became bold or drunk enough to seize them. Returning to their canoes, the French made good their withdrawal from the savage company of the Iroquois and paddled on down Lake Ontario, nauseated by their experience and much less optimistic about the chances of success for their venture. At the extreme western tip of Lake Ontario the expedition met Louis Joliet's brother Lucien, the voyageur, who was on his way back to see Intendant Talon with his report on the copper deposits of Lake Superior. Lucien Joliet was a strong supporter of the Jesuits and he now saw a chance to help the Black Robes by heading off the bewildered Sulpicians. He strongly recommended that the aspiring missionaries turn northwest where they would find plenty of Indians to convert. Strictly speaking, this was true, but Lucien Joliet failed to mention that the Jesuits had got there before the Sulpicians and the newcomers would be garnering in a field that had already been reaped. The best that can be said for Lucien Joliet is that he lured the Sulpicians away from the deadly Iroquois and diverted them into an area which Talon wanted to see developed.

La Salle tried to veto the change of direction, for he was still interested in the West and in particular he wanted to investigate the Iroquois rumors of the "Ohio" or "Beautiful Water" that evidently lay somewhere south of their position. However, Dollier de Casson and the other Sulpicians had made up their minds; they preferred to listen to the voice of the experienced voyageur and were once again afire to hasten among the benighted heathen. La Salle bowed to the inevitable and, wishing them all success, informed them that he would take his canoes back to civilization. The Sulpicians were sarcastic about his cowardice and prepared to push ahead with their own plans. On the last day of September the priests lashed together a crude altar made of paddles balanced on forked sticks, blessed La Salle and his voyageurs, and then left on a fruitless journey which eventually led them back to Montreal, having converted not a single Indian, though they did bring back the first map ever drawn of the Great Lakes area.

As soon as the priests had paddled safely on their way, La Salle informed his men that they were not going to Montreal but were heading south toward the Beautiful Water. La Salle had no intention of abandoning his half-formed plans for an inland empire and he was clever enough to realize that if he could find the Ohio River it might give him mastery over the heart of the continent. The withdrawal of the Sulpicians was a blessing in disguise; without their constant quest for native congregations La Salle could travel much faster, as he was interested in exploration, not in souls. It was never a part of La Salle's character to share his plans and dreams with others; he preferred to keep his ideas to himself and he was glad to be rid of the priests with their unending discussions and reports. Throughout his life, La Salle's nature was to work on his own without publicity or interference, and in these early days of his Canadian career he had much to do. It was a time for scouting, probing, and exploring; a time to test the possibility of his theories, to see how the land lay, and to plot the details of his grand design. Fame could come later; for the moment La Salle intended to lay the groundwork and get a head start on his rivals.

Unfortunately for historians, when La Salle decided to turn south and drop out of sight, he did a very thorough job. It is known that he persuaded his voyageurs to accompany him into the lion's mouth, deep into Iroquois territory; and that the following winter his men lost their nerve and deserted their leader, preferring to steal his possessions and cut eastward to sanctuary with the Dutch and English colonists on the Atlantic seaboard. Betrayed and left destitute in snow-bound forests either uninhabited or known only to the Indians, La Salle should have died, but he did not. There was something in his burning ambition, his untiring self-discipline and iron will that made him unquenchable. His life's work was scarcely begun and he refused to let it be snuffed out. La Salle was not an exceptionally robust man and his contemporaries were never impressed by his size or physique; he was, in fact, a thoroughly ordinary-looking person, rather prone to fever. Yet he drove himself to meet physical demands which would have broken stronger men. When he found himself alone and inexperienced, without guides or canoemen in the heart of the wilderness, instead of turning back, La Salle pushed ahead toward the Ohio. He was the first Frenchman known to have reached the river, though he maintained his usual silence about his discovery and it is not certain when or where he first saw the Beautiful Water. There is only the evidence of the early maps which mark the river and add the words, "the river discovered by the Sieur de la Salle." He was never inclined to boast of his deeds and during those days in the wilderness his silence is even deeper than usual. For months he roamed the dense forests that blanketed the northeast corner of the continent, marking the trails, making friends with the tribes, including the Iroquois, and gathering data about the geography of the land. No search parties left Montreal to find him for there was no one sufficiently concerned about his safety. Even Jean Cavelier, his brother, believed with the other Sulpicians that La Salle was unreliable, impractical, and perhaps a little mad. From time to time reports trickled into Montreal about La Salle: he had been seen by *coureurs de bois;* the Indians talked about a white man wandering among them; the famous voyageur Nicholas Perrot reported that he met La Salle in the summer of 1670, hunting on the Ottawa River with a party of Iroquois braves. All this time La Salle was steadily enlarging his knowledge of the interior. He acquired woodcraft; explored the streams, portages, and lakes; and learned how to deal with the Indians. He had suffered the uselessness of interpreters so now he studied eight different Indian dialects.

When La Salle finally emerged from the wilderness, he had formulated his great plan, the blueprint for his life's course. He envisaged a vast heartland empire, stretching south from the waterways of Canada, through the Great Lakes, and down the Mississippi to the waters of the Gulf of Mexico. Even before Joliet and Marquette paddled down the Mississippi, La Salle was convinced from his talks with the Indians that the great river emptied into the Gulf. The sweep of this empire would encompass the entire basin of the Mississippi, the Ohio, and the Missouri, bounded on the south by the sea, on the east and west by the Appalachians and the Rockies, and reaching into the barren pinelands of the northland. Knitting together this far-flung domain would be the waterways of the Great Lakes–Mississippi system. Here sailing vessels, pirogues, barges, and canoes would carry furs, timber, ores, settlers, farm produce, and manufactures. France would bestride North America like a colossus; one foot at Quebec, the other at the mouth of the Mississippi. The English and Dutch would be hemmed in behind the eastern mountains and the Spanish-American empire would pale into insignificance by comparison with its French neighbor. It was a dream far greater than De Soto's hopes for a petty kingdom; far more imaginative than Joliet's industrious mapping of the course of the central river. La Salle was a visionary who saw North America oriented north-south, not east-west as matters turned out. He was gifted with the foresight to prophesy the immense wealth which later made the heartland the richest region on earth. It was his tragedy that he was ahead of his time, commanding too few men and not enough resources. Yet there was hope; if the waterways could be secured, then from them in course of time would radiate trade, government and power. First there had to be French explorers and cartographers, next French soldiers, then traders, until finally there would be men and equipment enough to colonize the fertile land with an industrious catalyst of farmers, shopkeepers, and craftsmen.

This grand design formulated by a young man—La Salle was not yet thirty—was awe-inspiring. There is evidence that he came to his conclusions long before Joliet mapped the upper courses of the Mississippi, and that La Salle wrought out the entire intricate project single-handed without consulting any colleague or borrowing a single idea from other men. These plans transcended all earlier schemes, and in their scope and detail they surpassed anything that had yet been envisaged for the New World. The "Great Plan" still stands as a monument to La Salle's grasp of imperialism, though in his own time most Canadians believed that the rash young man suffered from delusions of grandeur and that he had been driven mad by his solitary life deep in the forests. There was a grain of truth in their doubts, for La Salle embellished his central theme with some scatterbrain fantasies. For example, he had a plot to lead an army of French regulars and war-painted Indian braves across the deserts of Texas, overthrow the Spanish in New Mexico, and seize the gold and silver mines there. But even La Salle's more down-to-earth plans were far beyond the provincial minds of the French settlers in Quebec or Montreal. They wanted to live peacefully, placate the Iroquois, barter for furs, make money, and go home rich. They wanted no part in these seemingly madcap plots to overrun half a continent; it was better to leave the interior well alone and not disturb the Indians.

La Salle's visions, however, found powerful sympathizers. Most influential of these supporters and the most important figure in Canada was the recently appointed governor of New France, Louis de Buade, Count of Palluau and Frontenac. It is impossible to appreciate how closely La Salle came to achieving his far-reaching dreams, without first considering the support, power, and encouragement which Count Frontenac gave him.

Frontenac was a man after La Salle's own heart. When the count came to Canada he was fifty-two years old and had nothing to lose; his private fortune had been dissipated and his wife was deeply involved in the tortuous intrigues of court life. Frontenac, a stern but ambitious soldier, was hopelessly out of place in the subtleties of palace politics. Although he was as unscrupulous as the rest and did not refrain from subterfuge and deceit, the undercurrent of innuendo and artifice was not his style; Frontenac preferred threat and power play. Actually, his wife considered him to be a stumbling block in the path of her career, so when the governorship of Canada became vacant, it was no surprise to the elegant courtiers of Louis XIV that the boorish Count Frontenac should be shipped off to Quebec.

Frontenac arrived in Canada late in the summer of 1672 and immediately made it clear that in the future the governor would take active and personal control of the colony. Flamboyant and ruthless, Frontenac made his mark. Almost immediately he clashed with the vested interests in Canada—priests, merchants, and civil servants—most of whom would have preferred to be left to their own devices. But at the start of his governorship, Frontenac's impact was so strong that he swept aside all obstacles the Canadians put in his way. Later, opposition to Frontenac stiffened until Louis had to recall his imperious governor, but not until Frontenac had achieved more than any of his predecessors.

The link between Frontenac and La Salle is understandable. On the one hand was the governor, eager to enhance the prestige of his administration and quietly make a fortune in doing so. On the other hand stood La Salle, experienced, traveled, well-educated, and burning with colossal schemes for empire in the wilderness. More important, La Salle was uncommitted to any of the existing factions in Canada—Sulpician, Jesuit, merchant or otherwise. Frontenac intended to build a cortege of his own and in that group La Salle became a leading figure in all matters relating to the Far West.

The first step was to deal with the Iroquois who were reasserting their former power. Until the Confederacy was tamed, neither La Salle nor Frontenac could make any headway inland. La Salle went out among the tribes of the Five Nations, who already knew him from his woodsman days, and persuaded the Iroquois chiefs to meet Frontenac for a grand council at Cataraqui on the shores of Lake Ontario. Frontenac handled his end of the affair brilliantly. To calm the stay-at-home merchants of Montreal and Quebec, he stated that his only intention was an "armed tour" of the upper parts of the colony. As soon as the colonists murmured their half-hearted support of the project, Frontenac struck: he requisitioned all the men, canoes, and stores he needed for the trip and, spurning all complaints, took his fleet of 120 canoes up the St. Lawrence. With him went four hundred men: conscripts in homespun, painted and feathered Huron warriors, French regular troops of the Carignan-Salières regiment in their white breeches and cross-belts, and two flatboats mounted with cannon and covered in gaudy red and blue patterns to impress the Iroquois.

It was the biggest convoy that the French had ever floated

on Lake Ontario and it was a complete success. Frontenac drove his men mercilessly; canoes and flatboats were manhandled over or around the rapids, hunting parties fanned out to obtain fresh meat, and everywhere the aristocratic governor was seen urging on his men, sharing their food, heaving on the tow ropes and hacking paths through the underbrush. It is said that Frontenac lay awake all one night worrying that the biscuit ration would get wet and ruin the expedition. All this trouble and effort paid off, for when the French army finally arrived at Cataraqui, they paddled toward the shore in perfect battle formation, flatboats wallowing in the center of the line, the canoes sweeping out in crescent horns, drums beating, and the royal standard flying. It was a grand spectacle. The Iroquois were vastly impressed. Frontenac proceeded to drive home his point. He organized color guards, pickets, escorts, and dress parades with the regular troops decked out in their best uniforms. Orderly lines of tents were erected with all the pomp and panoply that the French could muster. Frontenac himself strutted about in his full-dress uniform complete with ruffles, sword, gold braid, and medals. Gifts were showered on the delighted Iroquois. With superb aplomb Frontenac treated the Iroquois like children; he spoke down to them, promising them trade, gifts, and protection if they behaved. In the future, he said, they were to be guided by no one but "men of character like the Sieur de la Salle." Count Frontenac, the high-born novice to the backwoods, overawed the ambassadors of the Iroquois Confederacy by sheer force of character, and a formal peace was negotiated. Among the terms of the treaty was an important clause allowing the French to maintain a fort on Lake Ontario. It was the first step westward in the grand design that Frontenac and La Salle shared together, and the new fort, named Fort Frontenac, became the most important base inland from Montreal.

Frontenac returned to Montreal without losing a single man, and soon La Salle was on his way to France to see Colbert, the Minister of Marine, who was responsible to King

Louis for Canadian affairs. La Salle carried fulsome letters of recommendation from Frontenac, and at Versailles he showed an unexpected ability to use them to good advantage. La Salle proved himself to be a far better courtier than Frontenac. In the all-powerful Colbert, La Salle, the self-made burgher's son, dealt with another self-made member of the bourgeoisie. Minister and explorer understood one another perfectly, and La Salle left Paris well satisfied with the results of his meetings with Louis' chief adviser. By royal order La Salle had been raised to the rank of an untitled noble and had been given the new Lake Ontario fort for his own uses. In return he had promised to refund the Crown for the royal expenses in building the fort, to maintain the garrison at his own expense, and to bring in settlers. It was a tremendous step forward: La Salle had progressed from Lachine to Fort Frontenac, a move that took him 180 miles farther inland toward the empire he sought. Frontenac, too, was delighted; through La Salle he now held a major interest in the strategic center of the fur trade, and before long the beaver pelts would be contributing to the restoration of the Frontenac fortunes. It was an ideal arrangement for both partners, and La Salle hurried back to Canada to take command at Fort Frontenac.

La Salle did well as the proprietor of the new fort. With the same energy that he had shown in developing Lachine, he quickly fulfilled his obligations to the Crown. He built barracks, a mill, a bakery, a guardhouse, and a forge. Nine small cannon were mounted on the ramparts, and four vessels, ranging from twenty-five to forty tons, were built for lake traffic. All was well at Fort Frontenac, but in Montreal and Quebec trouble was brewing. The merchants were plainly jealous of La Salle's commercial advantage on the lake, the Jesuits resented the Recollet Friars he imported to staff the chapel at the fort, and many of the established colonists were openly jealous of his runaway success. These hostile factions began a campaign to destroy the upstart, a campaign that did not cease until his death. Letters were sent to Paris complaining of his conduct and accusing him of everything from smuggling with the Dutch to inciting rebellion among the Indians. In Canada La Salle's enemies delayed his supplies, neglected his fur shipments, and tampered with his men. All this would not have affected La Salle but for the bitter opposition of two parties: the financiers, who had loaned him money to pay for the improvements at Fort Frontenac and now wanted to oust the pioneer so as to take all the profits; and Intendant Duchesneau who was responsible for financial and civil administration in the colony. Duchesneau was a powerful man, powerful enough to challenge even Governor Frontenac, and his enmity was a grave threat to La Salle's hopes.

La Salle chose to ignore the gathering storm clouds and in the fall of 1677 set out once more for France to report on his stewardship of Fort Frontenac. He had firmly established the second phase of his Great Plan, now he proposed to unfold a really big step—the financial and administrative development of a southerly route from Fort Frontenac to the Mississippi. Luckily La Salle had influential friends in Paris who had already helped him on his previous visit, and in his absence they had been preparing the way for his second round of talks with Minister Colbert. In one memorial to the minister, the new lands of the interior were described as "all so beautiful and fertile; so free of forests, and so full of meadows, brooks and rivers; so abounding in fish, game and venison, that one can find there in plenty, and with little trouble, all that is needful to the support of flourishing colonies. The soil will produce everything that is raised in France. Flocks and herds can be left out at pasture all winter; and there are even native wild cattle [buffalo], which, instead of hair, have a fine wool that may answer for making cloth and hats.[1] Their hides are better than those of France, as appears by the sample which the Sieur de la Salle has brought with him."

However, La Salle's second request to the Crown was not so unqualified a success as his first negotiations. He asked for

[1] Hatmakers were the chief buyers of beaver pelts, Canada's main export at that time.

permission to control all western lands he might explore and develop over the next twenty years. At the same time he promised to relinquish his share in the trade carried on between the upper Lakes and the people of Canada. It was a shrewd move designed to placate the disgruntled merchants of Montreal, but Colbert was not so easily duped and, furthermore, was beginning to suspect that the young Norman was growing too powerful in the colony. In answer to La Salle's petition, the Crown proposed a watered-down version of his ideas. La Salle could explore as much as he liked, especially for the will-o'-the-wisp water route to Cathay, but he was allowed only five years in which to make good and develop his discoveries. Further, he was expressly forbidden to interfere with the Montreal fur trade and instead was allowed the monopoly in buffalo hides. This was a hollow gift, for the buffalo-hide business was profitless due to the high transportation costs on the bulky, low-value skins. Of course, the entire cost of his "great leap westward" was to be paid by La Salle; De Soto would have recognized the "Crown wins all" conditions of royal favor.

La Salle's acceptance of this royal patent shows that he was not interested in money. Already he had a virtual gold mine in his control of Fort Frontenac; by collecting furs at the fort, even the most idle commandant would have become a millionaire within a few years. Instead, La Salle wanted to take a second plunge into the wilderness without even waiting long enough to repay the money he had borrowed for the expansion of Fort Frontenac. If La Salle had been content to wait five years and repay his debts with the profits from the fur trade, he might have succeeded in his dreams; as it was, the visionary refused to delay. He was a man of quick action who listened to no one. Quiet, shy and reserved, he pushed ahead with his plans for exploration and the debts he left behind became the lever which his enemies in Canada used to topple his half-built empire.

Colbert and the king had their own reasons for curbing La Salle's ambition. The policymakers in Paris were becoming increasingly concerned with the problem of colonial expansion versus colonial concentration. Colbert was worried that if La Salle or anyone else drew off too many colonists on wild western adventures, the root stock in New France would be weakened and dissipated. It was dangerous to let the colony spread inland too fast and too far: it could easily become overextended and vulnerable to attacks from the Dutch and English. In addition, a sprawling colony would be difficult to control and Colbert had no intention of easing his grip on New France. These problems were identical, on a larger scale, to those which La Salle was failing to face as he rushed ahead with his master plan. If La Salle had waited to test and strengthen each step of his westward push, he might have built his empire. But the steps proved to be weak or rotten so that their collapse was inevitable and, in the end, robbed France of half a continent. King, Minister, and La Salle were all to blame, but the real culprits were the petty-minded colonists of Canada who deliberately sabotaged the plans of a man whom they neither understood nor liked.

With the king's patent in his possession, La Salle managed to borrow enough money in Paris to launch his plans for a network of forts and trading posts to reach from Fort Frontenac to the Mississippi. Then he sailed for Canada, taking with him as second-in-command an Italian, Henry de Tonti, who proved in later years to be his most loyal and fearless supporter and who also was to become one of the outstanding explorers of the Mississippi. Also on board went thirty carefully selected artisans—"pilots, carpenters, smiths and other useful Artists"—and enough anchors, cordage, and sails to rig out two small sailing barks which La Salle planned to build on the Great Lakes and the Mississippi; the boats were to be the vital links in a chain extending from Montreal to the Gulf of Mexico.

Unlike De Soto, who had been forced by his ignorance of North American conditions to equip his army of Florida with everything from foodstuffs to flintlocks, La Salle knew exactly what supplies were needed to carry out his plans. The

Frenchman had learned from his hunting and exploring trips with the Indians that hardy pioneers could live off the land in summer, provided they were skilled backwoodsmen and had a well-stocked base where they could pass the winters. The only supplies which La Salle had to import from the mother country were specialized articles of manufacture (and the men to use them) which were still unobtainable in New France. On the other hand La Salle's real need was for money —capital to invest in the construction of fur-trading posts, cash to pay his artisans and canoemen, and credit from the powerful merchants of Quebec and Montreal until the fur crop of the interior began to flow back along the communications network which La Salle was hoping to build along the waterways of the continent.

While La Salle was taking care of financial and supply problems along the lower St. Lawrence, his assistants began to expand operations out of Fort Frontenac. Their preliminary move was to build a blockhouse on the Niagara River, the door to Lake Erie and the Great Lakes beyond. It was harsh work; the ground was frozen solid and the men were forced to pour boiling water on the earth to soften it before they could dig the foundations. The local Indians—Senecas of the Iroquois Confederacy—were restless; they resented the intrusion of the white men and knew perfectly well that once the portage around Niagara Falls was secure, the newcomers would control the four great lakes above. Before long La Salle arrived on the scene and with his magic touch the Indians were temporarily placated. But scarcely had this danger been averted when a disaster occurred. The vessel carrying the precious ship supplies from France went aground due to the insubordination of the pilot, who flatly disobeyed La Salle's instructions. Only the anchors and cables were saved from the wreck. It was a major blow to La Salle's fragile plans, hounded as he was by the five-year deadline in his royal patent. According to one of his men: "It would have made anyone but him [La Salle] give up the enterprise."

But La Salle refused to abandon his project. He stubbornly insisted that the work at Niagara be pushed forward even though every piece of improvised equipment had to be dragged up a steep twelve-mile portage around the thundering cataract. It was cruel work in the subzero weather of a Canadian winter and the men needed to be fortified with frequent draughts of brandy. The hired workers were restless and disheartened by the shipwreck as well as by malicious rumors of La Salle's impending financial collapse. La Salle cheered them on, though it was obvious that he would have to return to Fort Frontenac to scotch the rumors and procure fresh supplies. Accordingly, in February he set out on the grueling 250-mile trek to his base with two of his strongest men and a sledge. For food they carried only a bag of parched corn. With this meager equipment they proposed to walk through the snowbound northern forests, across ice-covered lakes and streams until they reached civilization. If they lost their way, there was no hope of rescue, for even the Indians shunned the wilderness when the snow lay banked as high as the lowest branches and the trees crackled like musketry in the intense cold. La Salle was not in the best of health when he set out; for some time he had been suffering from an inflammation of the eyes, probably snowblindness. Yet he drove himself forward, when each step of the journey must have been torture. Two days before his party reached Fort Frontenac the last of the corn gave out, and they finished the last lap with only melted snow to fill their stomachs. The three men staggered into the fort more dead than alive. In the depths of winter they had covered a trail that few dared to travel in the easier days of summer. Only a desperate man would have been so foolhardy and probably only a fanatic would have got through.

Despite these brave deeds, La Salle, like the hero of a Greek tragedy, was gradually losing control of the situation around him. Surly Indians, mutinous *coureurs de bois*, natural hazards—these were threats which La Salle could overcome by superhuman exertion and leadership. What he did not understand and entirely failed to crush were the attacks of his

[124]

enemies in Montreal. With the support of Intendant Ducheseau, they were foreclosing on their loans to La Salle, seizing his goods, demanding repayment in the courts, impounding his shipments of furs, and discrediting him as a madman or a fool. It was a deliberate and effective campaign against the explorer; the sale of Fort Frontenac alone would have easily paid off all the money La Salle owed, but in his absence Fort Frontenac was no longer his to sell. The deed and title to the fort were now under violent litigation. Only Governor Frontenac could have prevented La Salle from being robbed while his back was turned, but Frontenac himself was embroiled in a host of other squabbles. La Salle could only beg his creditors for more time, leave the matter in the hands of his lawyers, and disappear back into the friendlier desolation of the forests.

Above the great falls at Niagara the master carpenters brought from France had at last finished the sailing vessel that was to navigate the upper Lakes. Under Tonti's command and with the blessing of the Flemish missionary Father Louis Hennepin, the 45-ton bark slid down from the stocks and onto the waters of the Niagara River. It was a moment of triumph for all those who had labored through the hard winter. The little bark was no more than a crude fishing smack, but she rode on waters where no sailing vessel had ever floated. She boasted five small cannon, and on her prow was carved the likeness of a griffin—part lion, part eagle—a tribute to Count Frontenac whose coat of arms included the mythical beast. The *Griffin*, as she was christened, was La Salle's great hope. She gave him absolute mastery of the Great Lakes. He had often promised that he would make the griffin fly above the crows, meaning that Frontenac would triumph over the black-robed Jesuits. Now it seemed that his words would come true.

At first all went smoothly. Under swelling canvas the little *Griffin* sailed along Lake Erie, through Lake St. Clair and on to the broad expanse of Lake Huron, until at last she reached Michilimackinac at the junction of the three great upper

Lakes. The uncouth settlement of Michilimackinac, which Marquette had called Mackinac, was the focus for the Lakes trade. In the center of the village stood the house and chapel of the Jesuits behind a ring of palisades; to the right, a Huron village of shabby cabins made from bark laid on wooden frames; to the left, the chunky daub-and-beam houses of the French merchants, smoke rising from the slender chimneys which poked through their shingle roofs; and, close by, a haphazard huddle of squalid wigwams belonging to an unwashed conglomeration of Ottawa Indians and other refugee tribes. Traders, *coureurs de bois*, Indians, priests, half-breeds, trappers, voyageurs, squaws, and soldiers rubbed shoulders in this rendezvous of the North. Michilimackinac was a brawling, boisterous and semi-savage place. Indians came to poke and stare at the white man's marvels or to beg for cheap "trade brandy"—a poisonous concoction made of untreated wood alcohol, tobacco juice, molasses, ginger, and even a little real brandy, which was virtually guaranteed to drive the drinker out of his senses. The merchants preferred to have their own imported wine and watch the visitors sell, barter, or steal. White men came to trade guns, furs, beads, liquor, knives, kettles, mirrors, tobacco, and scarlet cloth. Day-to-day life was a hectic, vicious affair. Every man looked after his own interests, formed or broke partnerships at will. The French-Canadian frontier, like its American counterpart, had a temporary existence, and now this existence was threatened by a small, clumsy sailing vessel that dropped anchor in the bay and fired off a ragged salute from its cannon.

It is uncanny how La Salle failed to gauge the hatred he was stirring up. The withdrawn Norman had built a defensive wall around his feelings until he completely isolated himself and failed to notice the reactions of his competitors. Perhaps he chose to ignore his enemies because he was confident that he would overcome them. But at Michilimackinac La Salle was hated. The traders knew that if La Salle succeeded in his projects, they would be driven out of business; the priests feared the decline of their influence among the natives; and even the Indians were hostile, for they were an easy prey to the highest bidder and La Salle's enemies had been among the tribes spreading evil gossip against the interloper. La Salle was facing tremendous odds, yet he never grasped the need for positive action against his enemies and did nothing at Michilimackinac to strengthen his position. Already most of the men had defected from an advance party sent by La Salle from Niagara with trade goods to prepare the way amongst the Great Lakes Indians. La Salle found his scouts bribed, debauched, and insubordinate. There was no choice but to press on. The *Griffin* sailed west to Green Bay, where La Salle loaded the ship with furs and sent her back to Niagara. It was a sad error of judgment. Bedeviled by his creditors, La Salle wanted to stave off their demands with the furs aboard the *Griffin*, but while La Salle and most of his men remained at Green Bay, the invaluable and essential *Griffin* was committed to the hands of an untrustworthy pilot who had already wrecked one boat at Niagara. She was never seen again.

The *Griffin* sailed for Niagara on September 18, 1679, and shortly afterward La Salle put out from Green Bay with fourteen men in four heavily laden canoes. The plan was to coast south along the shores of Lake Michigan to the Chicago portage. There they would meet up with more men under Tonti who was coming direct from Michilimackinac, and build a stockade to secure the portage leading to the Mississippi. La Salle's journey down the lake shore was a nightmare. September is late in the year to begin a major canoe trip and the flotilla was unwieldy and slow. But with the five-year deadline driving him forward, there could be no delay. The weather was miserable and several times bad storms forced the paddlers to beach their canoes through the pounding surf. On these occasions the travelers were lucky to escape with their lives and the half-drowned stragglers had to be pulled from the icy water. One man who should never have made the trip was Father Gabriel, a sixty-five-year-old missionary. He began to suffer from periodic blackouts brought on by hunger and exposure and no one expected him to survive. But somehow he clung on and even revived sufficiently to cheer up his companions with his unflagging sense of humor. Wet, cold, and disheartened, the little band limped forward. Food ran out and even the skill of Nika, a Shawnee brave who had attached himself to La Salle with doglike devotion, failed to bring in any game. On the verge of starvation, the travelers were forced to land and eat carrion left by turkey buzzards. This kept them alive until conditions improved and, after almost six weeks of toil, they finally reached their destination on the Chicago portage and settled down to await the arrival of Tonti with fresh men and supplies.

Spending the winter on the barren shores of Lake Michigan was a grim prospect. La Salle's men demanded to push on southward to the Illinois Indians who had befriended Joliet and Marquette, but La Salle refused to abandon Tonti. Even if his men deserted him, La Salle told them that he would stay behind to wait for his lieutenant; in the meantime they could keep themselves busy building a stockade.

Tonti arrived with the first snowflakes. He had spent an equally uncomfortable journey reaching the meeting place and brought the bad news that the *Griffin* had failed to touch at Michilimackinac on her homeward voyage. La Salle was plunged into gloom about the fate of his precious boat, but there was no time to check on her fate. Without delay the united parties headed southward across the portage and down the St. Joseph River to the supposed location of the Illinois encampment. The foolishness of the late start was becoming increasingly clear. Food was scarce and Nika the Shawnee went off on longer and longer hunts to find game. The Frenchmen paddled on uncertainly. Hands froze on paddles, the men's bearded faces were powdered with frost, and their lungs rasped in the chill air. At night the travelers slept with their moccasins tucked under their warm bodies so that the leather did not freeze iron hard by morning.

One day, while Nika was out hunting, the canoemen overshot the portage that led to the Illinois River. Snow had covered the trail and without Nika's trained eye to help him, La Salle missed the landing place. A little farther on, La Salle went ashore to look for the path, but lost his bearings and found himself adrift in the snowbound forest. When his leader failed to return, Tonti ordered a halt. The men landed from the canoes to light signal fires and scour the woods for their commander. It was useless; La Salle was swallowed up by the dense forest. All that night the expedition waited for La Salle to return, while the snow swirled down in the flickering light of the campfire. La Salle, floundering through the snow and the underbrush, was too experienced a woodsman to panic. Casting in a wide circle, he succeeded in groping his way back to the river bank and turned along it. At about two o'clock in the morning he caught sight of fire gleaming in the thickets, and, thinking that he had discovered his party, he went up to it. To his surprise there was no one to be seen, and a single couch of dried grass near the fire told him that he had disturbed a solitary Indian, probably out hunting in the snow. By now La Salle was too exhausted to go any farther, so with admirable coolness he called out to the unseen savage lurking in the darkness that he intended to borrow the bivouac. He then arranged a barricade of bushes around the site and calmly lay down to sleep until daybreak. Next morning tracks in the snow told him that the dispossessed hunter had spent the night prowling in circles around the bold intruder who had stolen his bed for the night.

With daylight to help him, La Salle had no difficulty in rejoining his companions, and when Nika returned from hunting, the expedition found the portage. Shouldering the canoes, they set out on the five-mile trek across a low, swampy plain toward the Illinois River. On this march, one of the voyageurs, by the name of Duplessis, tried to kill La Salle. Duplessis may have been bribed to assassinate La Salle or he may have borne his leader some personal grudge. Whatever the reason for his action, Duplessis had raised his gun to shoot La Salle in the back, when the man next in file saw the danger and struck up the weapon so that the murder attempt failed. Coolly La Salle chose to overlook the incident and the column marched on to the launching place at the source of the Kankakee River, a tributary of the Illinois.

Obtaining enough food for the hungry travelers was a constant problem. Despite Nika's skill, the Shawnee was having great difficulty in keeping the expedition supplied with game. The deer were winter lean and the hunter was reduced to shooting scrawny wild geese and swans. This did not satisfy the half-starving men and discontent was rumbling among the half-breed voyageurs, when the expedition came across a large buffalo bull mired down in a mud wallow. The huge beast was shot and twelve men heaving on ropes and hawsers succeeded in dragging the carcass free. Here was meat in plenty and the party feasted on buffalo steak before moving on. They reached the first Illinois village near a lookout cliff called Starved Rock, but the settlement was empty. The 450 or so tribal huts were in good repair, and the tribe itself was elsewhere. Puzzled by this, La Salle took some corn from a village store bin, leaving trade goods in exchange, and moved on down the river until, at the junction of the Des Plaines and Kankakee, he at last caught up with the main band of the Illinois tribe. After their friendly reception of Joliet and Marquette, La Salle was confident that he could build his Mississippi outpost among these hospitable natives.

He was disappointed. At first the Illinois received the newcomers warmly, rubbing their feet with bear's grease as a token of esteem. But a few days later a chieftain of the Miami Indians turned up with some advice for his Illinois cousins. The Miami had been sent by La Salle's enemies and his mission was to destroy La Salle before he won over the Illinois to his schemes. The Miami told a horrified Illinois council that La Salle was a spy from the dreaded Iroquois, and that La Salle had many friends among the Iroquois, having lived among them. Soon the "tigers of the forest" would follow their scout and attack the peaceful Illinois. Furthermore, La Salle wanted to descend the Mississippi in order to raise the lower river tribes against the Illinois, who would then be trapped between the two armies and exterminated. It was a clever story with just enough truth in it to make the tale plausible—it so happened that the Iroquois were preparing a spring invasion of the Illinois lands. The visitor distributed presents and vanished, leaving the Illinois to deal with La Salle.

This bloodthirsty plot dreamed up by La Salle's rivals might have succeeded if the organizers had not overlooked his genius in handling the Indians. Luckily for La Salle, a friendly council member warned him of his danger. La Salle sensed that something had gone very badly wrong; and he knew that unless he showed prompt firmness, his entire party would be massacred out of hand. With characteristic determination, he went at once to parley with the council of Illinois war chiefs. He protested his friendship with the tribe and pointed out that the Miami envoy had not waited to face La Salle himself. It was a flowery, effective speech by a brave man and the Illinois respected La Salle's courage. They hesitated, and then agreed to wait and see how matters turned out with their white visitors. It was a valuable breathing space, but it was dearly bought. That night six of La Salle's men, including two irreplaceable carpenters, took fright at the Indian hostility, lost their nerve, and deserted. Disheartened by this never-ending treachery, La Salle moved the expedition's camp a little way downstream of the Illinois settlement. There, on a prominent bluff overlooking the river, he ordered a protective stockade to be built. The new fort he named Fort Crèvecoeur —"Fort Heartbreak."

La Salle was increasingly turning in on himself; he withdrew into a shell to brood upon the misfortunes which were mounting up around him and his grand design. It was the same change which had overtaken De Soto generations before in the wilderness of the continent. Both men felt the terrible burden of isolation. Neither was accustomed to sharing the load of leadership. Now, as La Salle faced one calamity after another, he became increasingly bitter. There was still plenty of fight left in him, but as time went on, he lapsed deeper into loneliness, a solitary and tragid hero figure.

When the defenses of Fort Crèvecoeur had been erected, La Salle proposed building a sister ship to the *Griffin*. The new vessel would operate on the Mississippi, and, because his carpenters had deserted, La Salle designed the boat himself. She was to be a 40-ton bark, armed with cannon and surrounded by high bulwarks to protect her crew from Indian arrows. With excellent supplies of good straight timber close at hand, the work went well. La Salle improvised a saw pit and found out how planks could be cut from the tree trunks. But time was still a vital factor and La Salle knew that he could not spend long at Fort Crèvecoeur. His fragile chain of forts now stretched from Fort Frontenac to the Illinois and each link in the chain was feeble; it was time for him to hurry back and strengthen the entire system. Accordingly, after six weeks of hard work in which the boat was half-completed, he decided to re-allocate his men. A skeleton crew would stay on at Crèvecoeur to complete the vessel while a second party explored the upper waters of the Mississippi for future navigation; he himself would return to Frontenac for supplies. The upriver party was to be led by one of the best and most reliable voyageurs, Michel Accau, who spoke several Indian dialects. With him would go another experienced man, Picard du Gay, and the priest, Father Hennepin, whose account of his adventures on this side excursion would in due course make him one of the most notorious Mississippi travelers.

When Hennepin and his two companions had set off by canoe on their northward voyage of exploration, La Salle selected four of the toughest voyageurs and prepared to head back to Lake Ontario. Tonti was to take command at Crèvecoeur, complete the boat, hold the stockade, and wait for La Salle to return with reinforcements. In the meantime La Salle intended to check on the whereabouts of the *Griffin*, still unaccountably missing, and gather together the anchors, ropes, sails, and other equipment needed for the Mississippi vessel. La Salle was spreading his hopes thinner and thinner.

The truth of the matter was that he had spread his meager resources beyond their breakingpoint. With one party exploring the upper Mississippi; another group at Crèvecoeur; men at Michilimackinac, Green Bay, Niagara, Fort Frontenac; and his own band heading overland to Lake Ontario, La Salle's organization was perilously overextended. Somewhere, something would snap and then the whole structure would fall apart. But La Salle had no choice. He was spanning thousands of miles in his developing network; with volatile Indians in the West, hostile rivals on the Great Lakes, and jealous civil servants in Montreal, he had to be everywhere at once, soothing, counterattacking, and organizing. This frantic dash back to Fort Frontenac during the spring thaw led him straight into the path of an Iroquois army on its way to attack the Illinois, and broke every law of backwoods travel. It almost killed La Salle, and in the end failed to save his dreams.

Early spring is an unpleasant time to travel by foot and canoe from the Illinois to Lake Ontario. The route lies through difficult country—forest, marsh, and rocky hills. The spring weather is notoriously fickle; at night the temperature drops low enough to kill a man who is caught unprepared, and by day the skies pour down a depressing mixture of sleet, snow, and torrents of rain. While the rain and rising temperature melt some of the snow cover, the soil underneath remains frozen and impermeable so that the melt water cannot drain away and the ground becomes a cold, soggy morass of bogs, ponds, and rivulets. In shaded corners the snowbanks lie untouched beneath crusts of ice and river travel is made difficult by squadrons of jagged ice floes. La Salle and his four men, together with the essential Nika, had to make their way through this bleak scene, over unknown trails and portages, and past tribes that were unfriendly to strangers. La Salle had no illusions about the difficulties of the trip; he wrote: "Though the thaws of approaching spring greatly increased the difficulty of the way, interrupted as it was everywhere by marshes and rivers, to say nothing of the length of the journey, which is about 500 leagues in a direct line, and the danger of meeting Indians of four or five different nations through whose country we were to pass, as well as an Iroquois army which we knew was coming that way; though we must suffer all the time from hunger; sleep on open ground and often without food; watch by night and march by day, loaded with baggage, such as blanket, clothing, kettle, hatchet, gun, powder, lead and skins to make moccasins; sometimes pushing through thickets, sometimes climbing rocks covered with ice and snow, sometimes wading whole days through marshes where the water was waist-deep or more, at a season when the snow was not entirely melted— though I knew all this, it did not prevent me from resolving to go on foot to Fort Frontenac, to learn for myself what had become of my vessel [the *Griffin*] and bring back the things we needed."

The journey was every bit as bad as La Salle described; the ice in the streams made it necessary to pole the canoes through a channel battered out with clubs and axes, or drag them overland like sledges. On the portages the men squelched knee-deep in swamp. Before they had gone very far, the waterways became blocked with ice and driftwood, so they had to hide the canoes and proceed on foot, crossing the streams on makeshift rafts of branches and rushes. Brambles and thorns cut their faces and slashed their clothes to ribbons. Their moccasins wore out on bleeding feet and they had to stop while new moccasins were made from the spare leather they carried. Sometimes they were forced to spend the night curled up like cats on tree stumps, the only dry places above the spongelike ground. To confuse hostile Indians and discourage them from tracking his party, La Salle started brush fires to erase every trace of his trail. He also stripped the bark from trees and scrawled Iroquois hieroglyphics in charcoal on the bare white trunks—an established custom of Iroquois raiding parties and, for La Salle, a ruse designed to scare off all but the most confident pursuit. On some mornings the men woke up to find their clothes "frozen stiff as sticks," and valuable hours were wasted thawing the garments before a fire. One by one the men fell sick under the ordeal, until even Nika was spitting blood. Only La Salle seemed inexhaustible. He nursed the invalids, and urged them forward. Two of the voyageurs were so ill that he sent them direct to Michilimackinac, while he and the others built a fresh canoe. There was no birchbark available for the hull, so they used elm instead, stripping the tight spring bark from the trunk after they had loosened it with boiling water. On Easter Monday, 1680, after one of the most incredible feats of endurance in the history of French Canada, the Sieur de la Salle and three followers reached the blockhouse at Niagara. From the Illinois to Niagara, they had covered over one thousand miles of the most desolate countryside imaginable in the record time of sixty-five days.

The news at Niagara was very bad indeed. The *Griffin* had failed to show up. No one on the lakes had seen the little vessel since she left Green Bay and she had undoubtedly foundered. The ship, so essential to his plans and built with such labor, was a total loss. With her went down a thousand crowns' worth of cargo. At Quebec Intendant Duchesneau had succeeded in stopping another shipload of artisans bound for Fort Frontenac. Further, a storeship carrying more than 22,000 livres worth of La Salle's goods had been totally wrecked in the difficult channel at the mouth of the St. Lawrence. From Green Bay to Fort Frontenac, La Salle's farflung line of outposts was starved of supplies, manned by disgruntled hirelings, and tottering toward collapse.

With disaster looming over him, La Salle, exhausted and sick from his journey, took three fresh men from Niagara, and started out for Fort Frontenac and Montreal. The wornout companions of the Illinois journey he left at Niagara, but La Salle could not spare himself. Only his intervention could save his organization from ruin. At Montreal he heard more bad news: several of his fur-carrying canoes had been wrecked in the rapids, and during his absence on the Illinois his enemies had sequestered most of his property in Montreal.

La Salle worked like a madman to stave off total defeat. Within a week he had borrowed enough money to quiet his creditors, and had collected enough supplies to relieve Fort Crèvecoeur, many hundreds of miles away in the heart of the continent. Without pausing, La Salle turned back toward the wilderness, determined to bring help to Tonti and his isolated little band on the Illinois before the Iroquois invasion swamped them. At Fort Frontenac on his return trip came the cruelest blow. La Salle learned from two wandering trappers that most of the men he had left with Tonti had mutinied. It was reported that the mutineers had murdered Tonti, burned the half-built ship, thrown all the remaining trade goods, guns, and ammunition into the river, and fled from the scene of their crimes. The mutineers had then paddled up to Michilimackinac and spread the revolt, seizing the furs left there by La Salle's agents. Next they had descended on Niagara and plundered the blockhouse. Now twelve of the rebels were on their way by canoe down the west shore of the lake to Fort Frontenac with plans to kill La Salle, the chief witness against them.

La Salle's course of action was clear. The rebellion had to be stamped out quickly and thoroughly. Selecting nine of his most trusted men from Fort Frontenac, La Salle set off with them by canoe to surprise the mutineers. Coasting a little way along the shore of Lake Ontario, La Salle picked a site where a small headland jutted out into the lake. Here, in the lee of the headland, La Salle set up an ambush. Some of his men took up their positions on the shore while La Salle and the best paddlers waited in a canoe under the bushes of the high bank. Before long their prey approached in two canoes. As the leading canoe came past the ambush, La Salle's boat shot out from its hiding place and the startled mutineers found themselves looking straight into the muzzles of rifles held by La Salle and his grim-faced men. Surprise was complete. Both canoeloads of mutineers fell into the trap and surrendered without a fight. But this did not account for all the enemy; there was one more canoe to be dealt with, which had lagged behind. Sending his prisoners under guard to Fort Frontenac, La Salle and his men set off up the lake to find the last batch of mutineers before they escaped. At about six in the evening they sighted their quarry and gave chase. The mutineers saw that their plans had failed and decided to make a run for it. Turning their canoe toward the land, they paddled frantically for the shelter of the pine-clad beach. La Salle and his men chased them as fast as possible, but the rebels landed before the pursuit got within range. Realizing that it would be difficult to dislodge the enemy after they had taken up defensive positions among the rocks and trees, La Salle dispatched four of his men to circle behind the mutineers and cut off their retreat. As the evening ebbed away, the mutineers decided to break out of their stronghold and escape. Launching their canoe, they paddled off furiously into the gloom. Immediately La Salle was after them. He called out, demanding that the rebels surrender, but was answered with renewed paddling and hoots of derision. Without hesitation La Salle's men fired a volley which killed two of the mutineers outright and abruptly ended the drama. Taking the renegades back to Fort Frontenac, La Salle placed them all under guard to await the arrival of Governor Frontenac.

It was now well into the spring of 1680 and time was running short for La Salle. He had held the king's patent for two years and had accomplished very little toward his goal. There was still one slim hope: that Tonti and a handful of loyal followers had survived the mutiny at Fort Crèvecoeur, saved the half-built boat, and retained the axes, adzes, hammers, chisels, and other equipment necessary to complete the vessel. Although there was no definite news from the Illinois, La Salle must have interrogated the captured mutineers and learned that the first reports of their rebellion had been exaggerated in one respect: Tonti had been absent from the camp on a scouting mission when the mutiny took place, and the Italian might yet be alive, just as La Salle had once managed to survive after his voyageurs had deserted him near the Ohio. At any event La Salle decided to find out for himself what had happened at the nascent fort on the Illinois. A small relief force was fitted out and, with La Salle leading it, started off on the long, hard trail back to the Illinois. Time and again La Salle had proved his personal courage; now he showed his iron determination and unbending will once again. He proposed to retrace his path in order to pick up the fragments of an enterprise that most men would long since have abandoned. His ships were lost, his forts wrecked, his storehouses plundered, and his creditors were clamoring for their pound of flesh; yet in the face of all these pressures La Salle set out to retrieve his dreams. At first, the return to the Illinois was an easy trip. There was good hunting and the party traveled quickly. But as they reached the outskirts of Illinois tribal territory, the Frenchmen began to see sights that made them retch. The Iroquois invasion had finally struck; La Salle's party was traveling in the wake of an Iroquois army. On every side there was evidence of Indian ferocity. The little hamlets of the Illinois Indians had been ravaged—huts torn down or burned, fields destroyed, caches and storehouses ransacked. Graves were broken open and the bones of the dead scattered on the torn earth. Whatever the Iroquois could not carry away, they smashed or burned. Wolves and carrion birds picked over the land; broken and disfigured corpses lay scattered about. Here and there a lone corpse strapped upright to a stake marked the spot where the Iroquois had spent a few sadistic hours, torturing a writhing victim. Along the banks of the river, La Salle could trace the march of death. Each day the terrified Illinois had struggled a little farther downstream—the peaceable men, women, and children seeking to escape their horrible scourge. Each day, the Iroquois army had kept pace, setting up camp on the opposite bank within sight of their frenzied victims. In a gruesome game of cat-and-mouse, the Iroquois had tormented their prey; cutting off a hunting party; launching a sneak raid; torturing a captive to death within earshot of his comrades. In places there were macabre little charnel circles where the Iroquois had burned or half-eaten an isolated group of Illinois women and children whose menfolk had abandoned them to their fate. Through this sickening scene La Salle and his men paddled toward Crèvecoeur. With sinking hearts they examined each torture stake to find some indication whether the victim had been a white man. But there was no sign of Tonti or his men. The palisade at Crèvecoeur had been thrown down and the camp stripped of every item. The Iroquois had gone so far as to extract every nail and ounce of metal from the half-built sailing vessel, for all metal was precious to the savages. The boat itself still lay on the stocks, and scrawled on one plank were the sinister words of an unknown mutineer:*"Nous sommes tous sauvages."* La Salle hunted for Tonti all the way down to the junction of the Illinois with the Mississippi, but there was no sign of his Italian lieutenant. Despondently La Salle turned back. He left behind a message for Tonti, in case he had survived. The letter was tied to a conspicuous tree near the water's edge, and to discourage the Indians from meddling with it, La Salle hung up a board showing himself and his men in a canoe holding up a pipe of peace. In the letter La Salle said that he was returning to Lake Michigan and hoped to rendezvous there with his missing lieutenant.

6

The Fatal River

L A SALLE SPENT THE WINTER OF 1680 AND THE
following summer at his shabby Fort Miami on the
Chicago portage. If his enemies thought they had defeated
him, they were wrong. La Salle had been abandoned and
betrayed by his Canadian colleagues, and the Indians,
seduced by his foes, had turned against him. But he was not
yet crushed. The time had come for La Salle to launch a
counteroffensive and he did so with brilliance. He resolved
to turn the tables on his enemies. The crux of his counter-
attack was a scheme to win over the Indians living between
the Mississippi and the Great Lakes. If he could persuade
these tribes to support him, he would kill several birds
with one stone. He would block the Iroquois who menaced
his flanks; deny his enemies their accustomed spies, furs,
and agents; secure the pivotal point of the Mississippi–Great
Lakes route; and put together a loyal group of redmen to
defend his interests and execute his projects. The idea was
a monumental dream. A prudent merchant would never
have conjured up such impractical visions. The settlers of
New France regarded the Indians as untrustworthy, vicious
nuisances, and, at best, tolerated them. La Salle now pro-

posed to bind these wild heathens into a coherent, useful force. The idea was impossible, dangerous, and stupid. La Salle, the visionary, almost made it work.

Starting out with a base at Fort Miami, a handful of soldiers, the green memory of the Iroquois massacres, and a supply of trade goods, La Salle set to work. He was trying to weld together an odd assortment of tribes who spoke different languages, shifted vaguely from one hunting ground to the next, were dispirited by repeated defeats at the hands of the Iroquois, and were traditional enemies among themselves. Nearly all that year, 1681, La Salle toiled to put his idea into effect. He talked with the various wandering bands of the Illinois of the river—Miamis from the lake shore, Shawnees from the Ohio Valley, Outagamies and Potawatamies from the west, Abenaki and Mohican exiles from east of the mountains. To all of them La Salle explained the benefits of a great federation of the tribes based on his camp on the Illinois. There the allies would find fair trade, help in hard times, and a rallying point against the Iroquois. To band after band of Indians La Salle preached his message. He walked or canoed for hundreds of miles; sat through uncomfortable hours of dull tribal councils; smoked innumerable pipes of peace; went through formal adoption ceremonies into different clans; gave presents, harangued, pleaded and boasted in the accepted Indian style. During the spring he suffered again from snowblindness and by summer he had exhausted himself with work. La Salle was more than a theoretical planner of Indian federations; he was one of the few men with the qualities to bring such an alliance into existence, and, little by little, he began to unite the tribes in a loose-knit community based on the Illinois country. Best of all, he at last heard that Tonti had turned up, alive and well, and was waiting for him at Michilimackinac. With that good news, La Salle told his Indian friends to wait for his return and paddled off to join forces with his lieutenant. The two men then traveled to Montreal to see Governor Frontenac and lay before him the third phase of La Salle's grand enterprise.

What La Salle suggested to Count Frontenac was no less than a joint Indian-French thrust from the Great Lakes down to the Gulf of Mexico. In some ways it was a bizarre notion. Instead of employing French voyageurs who had nearly always let him down, La Salle intended to rely heavily on his Indian allies. The expedition would have a hard core of trustworthy Frenchmen, but the bulk of the hunting, paddling, and scouting would be done by Indians from La Salle's Illinois community. La Salle saw nothing strange in the idea of Abenaki Indians, whose cousins had terrorized the Puritans in New England, paddling down the length of the Mississippi to explore and claim the river for Louis the Magnificent.

Once again Frontenac grasped the genius of the plan and threw his weight behind La Salle's schemes, knowing it was high time to profit from the results of Joliet's trip, some eight years before. To raise money for the new venture, La Salle sold part of his monopolies and borrowed from his family; then he and Tonti set off for the Illinois with the colorful crew that made up the expedition. The party consisted of twenty-three Frenchmen and eighteen Abenaki and Mohican Indians in their feathers and breechclouts. As was their custom, the Indians refused to travel without their families, so the party included ten squaws and three children. This large group may have seemed too unwieldy, but La Salle knew better. His Indians were armed and well-trained in the use of their weapons; they were less likely to desert than the French voyageurs, because, as De Soto had noted, the Indians preferred to stick together once outside their own tribal territory, for they distrusted "foreign" tribes and had no idea how to get home. As for the women folk and children, La Salle knew that the squaws would be expected to cook, gather food, do more than their fair share of the portaging and paddling, live on scraps, and do all the camp chores, thus leaving their men free for hunting and scouting.

On December 21 the expedition passed through Fort Miami. In a straggling file, tribesmen, voyageurs, soldiers, and Membré, the expedition priest, walked southward over the frozen river courses. The canoes were placed on sledges and piled high with tents, spare powder and shot, axes, guns, cooking pots, blankets, tobacco, trade goods, and all the paraphernalia of a long-distance voyage. After some 120 miles on foot, the break-up of the ice on the Illinois river allowed the expedition to launch its canoes and paddle down to the junction with the Mississippi. The Father of Waters was still sending down dangerous chunks of drift ice, so La Salle ordered a halt while his entire company prepared themselves for the great trip downriver, past the point where Joliet had turned back, and on to the sea—if the Spanish did not stop them. When conditions were safer, the expedition paddled out onto the main river and hurried southward.

For many miles it was an uneventful trip. The Indians, accustomed to their northern forests, were intrigued by the open prairies and rolling bluffs as the countryside opened out. Father Membré looked hopefully for river Indians to convert, but there were none in sight; the local Indians probably kept well out of the way when they saw the outlandish birchbark cockleshells with their decorative patterns of blue, black, and red. The canoes moved steadily through the water and the weather gradually improved. To feed the expedition, fish were caught from the river, and the Indian hunters, trained in the bleak northern woods, had no difficulty in bringing down enough game in the fertile prairies and river bottomlands. At night when the vessels were beached, La Salle posted sentries and the campfire was lit. Indians and French worked well together and, for once, La Salle found himself in charge of a smoothly running operation. The travelers passed the mouth of the Missouri and the junction with the Ohio. Without fuss or bother La Salle descended past the farthest point that Joliet and Marquette had reached, the place where they had turned back for fear of the Spanish, and from now on the voyage became more exciting, more mysterious, and the travelers tensed for the unexpected. Near the third Chickasaw bluffs the expedition landed, as was their custom, to allow the Indians to replenish the stocks of food. While the hunters were away, a voyageur, Pierre Prudhomme, wandered off to explore on his own. When his Indians returned and Prudhomme failed to appear, La Salle worried that the missing man had been ambushed by the local natives. The hunters were sent out again to look for the missing man and came back to report that they had found fresh Indian tracks. It was ominous news and La Salle hastily ordered a palisade to be constructed as a defense against the unseen natives. For five days the expedition stood to arms, waiting for an attack that never came. Then La Salle's scouts surprised two Chickasaw Indians in the woods, and through them managed to make contact with the local tribesmen, who proved to be friendly but had no idea of Prudhomme's whereabouts. On the sixth day the missing man limped into the stockade; he was woebegone and apologetic. Like La Salle some time before, he had lost his bearings in the dense undergrowth and spent a miserable time blundering through a confusing welter of brush, swamp, and forest. Partly in relief and partly to cheer the bedraggled figure, La Salle named the tiny outpost Fort Prudhomme, and, leaving Pierre Prudhomme and a handful of men in charge of the stockade, set off again down the river.

By now it was March, and the advancing season as well as the more southerly latitude, was changing the landscape. The Frenchmen and Indians from the stern wilds of Canada found themselves in a gentle, warm land they had never experienced before. There were sultry days with the early morning mist curling off the river; red and orange sunsets against a theatrical backdrop of cloud and sky; tree moss hanging in wraiths from the contorted cypresses; swamp and canebrake; strange birds, beasts, and flowers; the undergrowth alive with the constant whirring of strange frogs and insects.

On March 13, as the canoes were groping their way through a thick fog, the paddlers heard the chilling rhythm of a war drum and the yelps of an Indian war dance. Hurriedly La Salle put in for the opposite bank and his men leapt ashore. They cleared away the undergrowth with their hatchets, felled trees and dragged them into position to form a breastwork; ammunition, powder, and supplies were rushed into the stockade, and, as the fog dispersed, the travelers took their places behind the fragile defenses to meet whatever was coming. The French, nervously fingering their weapons, need not have worried. The Indians were Quapaws, the same warrior clan which had harassed De Soto and Moscoso so sorely and had scared Joliet, but this time they had no thought of attacking the intruders. Even if the natives had wanted blood, the little stronghold and the guns of its defenders would have deterred them. Instead the Quapaws dispatched a single dugout canoe to investigate, and when La Salle held up a peace pipe, all tension melted away.

The expedition crossed over to the other bank, where they were welcomed as if they came from another planet. The Quapaws were immensely pleased with their strange visitors, parading them around the local villages, feting them, and putting on the usual dances and ceremonies of friendship. They might not have been so pleased if they had understood what La Salle was doing. While Father Membré preached a totally incomprehensible sermon to the assembled tribesmen, La Salle and Tonti marched off to the village square. There they set up a large wooden cross embellished with the French coat of arms, and with cries of *"Vive le Roi!"* and fusillades of guns, claimed the land for France and its peoples as subjects of Louis XIV.

From now on, as La Salle moved swiftly downriver, the land-grabbing routine became standard procedure. Village after village was claimed for France in the presence of ignorant and applauding natives, who were intrigued by the bearded white men with their graceful canoes and noisy weapons. Some three hundred miles below the mouth of the Arkansas River, the expedition came across the sun-worshiping Taensa Indians and Tonti took the opportunity, with Father Membré, of visiting the tribal capital. The Frenchmen saw orderly dwellings of sunbaked mud with their dome-shaped roofs, the Temple of the Sun with its sacrificial bones and perpetual fire tended by two ancient sages, and the king's wives honoring their lord and master every time he spoke by howling like wolves in deference to his great wisdom. Father Membré noted with astonishment that the large alligators, several of which the French killed and ate, were born of eggs, "like chickens."

The expedition hurried on, passing tribes of the lower river—the Natchez, Koroa, Ouna, and the Tangipohoa. Only once were the canoeists greeted with arrows, and on that occasion La Salle prudently passed by on the other side of the river. Elsewhere the explorers were unmolested, until at last they reached the point where the broad stream divided itself into three great distributaries before flowing through the delta to the sea. La Salle took the western arm, Tonti the middle passage, and a reliable voyageur followed the eastern branch. As La Salle moved slowly down the current, the river flowed thickly between dreary shores of reed and marsh. The water was salty and sluggish, and the horizon was bounded on all sides by a whispering wall of yellow-gray weeds. The canoes moved clear of the marshes and there before them lay the Gulf of Mexico, blue, tranquil, and without a sail or Spaniard in sight. For the first time a white man had journeyed from the St. Lawrence to the Gulf through the heart of the continent, with only a few short miles by land over insignificant portages. From the beginning of his career La Salle had postulated a central river highway; now he had proved that it existed. He knew for certain that his great waterway was a reality, that there were no whirlpools, monsters, or unconquerable Indians to bar the passage. Above all, he had not seen a single Spaniard to challenge the Frenchmen from the north. It was a moment of personal triumph.

When his party had reassembled on the shore, La Salle held a ceremony to claim the lands for France. A column was set up, bearing the inscription: "*Louis le Grand, Roy de France et de Navarre, Regne; Le Neuvieme Avril, 1682.*" and beside the column they put a large cross, beneath which was buried a leaden plate scratched with the words: "Ludovicus Magnus Regnat." Father Membré blessed the enterprise and gave thanks to God. Then, La Salle proclaimed the legal formula—giving Louis and his successors the "possession of this country of Louisiana, the seas, harbors, ports, bays, adjacent straits, and all the nations, peoples, provinces, cities, towns, villages, mines, minerals, fisheries, streams, and rivers, within the extent of the said Louisiana, from the mouth of *the great river* . . . and the rivers which discharge themselves thereinto, from its source beyond the country of the Nadouessioux [the Sioux Indians] . . . and as far as its mouth at the sea, or the Gulf of Mexico . . ."

With one stroke La Salle was presenting his sovereign with the heart of a continent, an area many times larger than the whole of France and named in honor of the new overlord. It was a magnificent gesture, and all, as the historian Francis Parkman pointed out, "by virtue of a feeble human voice, inaudible at half a mile."

The irony of La Salle's situation was that even as he stood at the pinnacle of success on the shores of the Gulf of Mexico, the tide of events in far-off Quebec was overwhelming him. Frontenac had made so many enemies during his governorship that his position was seriously threatened. When La Salle and his expedition began to retrace their path toward Canada, Frontenac was falling from power. By a cruel stroke of fate La Salle was delayed by serious illness as he passed back through Fort Prudhomme and by the time he reached the Illinois country, his supporters in Montreal and Quebec were in full retreat before the enemies of the "'Great Plan." La Salle, believing that the realization of his Mississippi empire still lay within his grasp, worked feverishly to consolidate his base on the Illinois. But he could make no headway without supplies of trade goods, gifts for the Indians, weapons, and other equipment from Canada. His flow of matériel was being choked off to a mere trickle. He learned that Count Frontenac had been recalled to France, and the new governor, a retired naval officer by the name of Le Febvre de la Barre, was a weak-willed old man, firmly under the control of the anti-La Salle faction, which was determined to throttle

La Salle's growing success and maliciously isolated him in his wilderness outpost. La Barre was persuaded to send troops to seize Fort Frontenac, the storehouses at Niagara and Michilimackinac, and the installations on the Illinois. Faced with complete disaster, La Salle had only one hope—to go over La Barre's head, direct to the king in Paris. In 1683 La Salle sailed once more for France.

For seventeen years now La Salle had devoted his life to building a French empire in the backlands of North America. He had consistently based his plan on an approach that moved inland from the established French colony on the St. Lawrence. Now the policymakers in Paris decided to switch La Salle's activities to the mouth of the Mississippi, which the explorer had shown lay uncolonized by any European power. La Salle was becoming involved in international politics. Seignelay, the new French minister, devised a two-pronged plan. If he could establish the ambitious La Salle on the Mississippi delta, not only would France control the vast river basin, but a French settlement on the Gulf of Mexico would threaten the Spanish-American empire. Relations between France and Spain had deteriorated into open bickering and La Salle would now be a weapon in the hands of the French. In Paris, La Salle was offered royal patronage in colonizing the Mississippi delta.

La Salle was enthusiastic about Seignelay's plan. He even resurrected his old idea of leading a combined French-Indian expeditionary force across Texas to attack the Spanish in their New Biscay colony. It was a harebrained plot, but Louis XIV was accustomed to success and La Salle's Mississippi navigation had proved that combined French-Indian operations were feasible. The invasion was therefore included on La Salle's agenda even though no one had the least concept of the harshness of the Texas deserts or the enormous distances involved. Seignelay's machinations were bedeviled by his basic ignorance of the geography of America and this proved to be La Salle's ruin.

On this note La Salle's fourth and last adventure began. At

[148]

1.

1. De Soto, from *A History of the Mississippi Valley* (1903).
[By courtesy of the Harvard College Library.]

2.

2. *The Battle of Mobila*, from *Life of De Soto* (1858).

[By courtesy of the Harvard College Library.]

3. *Discovery of the Mississippi*, by William H. Powell.

[United States Capitol Historical Society.]

4. De Soto's army. building their barges, from *Life of De Soto* (1858).

[By courtesy of the Harvard College Library.]

3.

5.

5. *Midnight Mass on the Mississippi over the body of Ferdinand
De Soto, 1542,* by Edward Moran.

[By courtesy of the United States Naval Academy Museum.]

6.

6. La Salle, from *A History of the Mississippi Valley* (1903).

[By courtesy of the Harvard College Library.]

7. Presentation of the peace pipe, from *Histoire de la Louisiane* (1758).

[Copyright British Museum.]

7.

Marche du
Calumet de Paix.

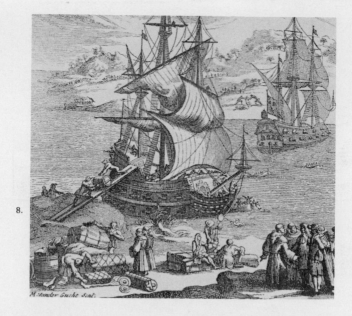

8.

8. Landing at Matagorda Bay, from Hennepin's *New Discovery* (1698).

[By courtesy of the Curator, James Ford Bell Collection.]

9.

10.

10. Beaver and Indian buffalo ("beeve") hunt, from Lahontan's *Voyages to North America* (1703).

[Copyright British Museum.]

9. La Salle's death, from Hennepin's *New Discovery* (1698).

[By courtesy of the Curator, James Ford Bell Collection.]

11.

11. *The Cruelty of the Savage Iroquois*, from Hennepin's *New Discovery* (1698).

[By courtesy of the Curator, James Ford Bell Collection.]

12.

13.

13. A buffalo, from Hennepin's *New Discovery* (1698).

[By courtesy of the Curator, James Ford Bell Collection.]

12. The Falls of Niagara, from Hennepin's *New Discovery* (1698).

[By courtesy of the Curator, James Ford Bell Collection.]

14.

14. Captain Jonathan Carver, from his *Travels* (1781).

[By courtesy of the Curator, James Ford Bell Collection.]

15. The Falls of St. Anthony, from Carver's *Travels* (1781).

[Copyright British Museum.]

15.

16.

16. Sioux Indians, from Carver's *Travels* (1781).

17. Zebulon Pike, from his *Expeditions* (1895).

17.

18. Fort Snelling in 1848, from *Das Illustrirte Mississippithal*.

18.

19.

19. Glazier's lake, from 1891 account of his trip.
[By courtesy of the Harvard College Library.]

20. Frontispiece of Beltrami's *Pilgrimage* (1828).
[By courtesy of the Curator, James Ford Bell Collection.]

20.

21.

21. *Members of the Expedition*, from Glazier's *Down the Great River* (1889).

[By courtesy of the Harvard College Library.]

first all went well: the delta scheme had full government support, and Louis reprimanded La Barre and ordered him to restore to Tonti, as La Salle's agent, all the forts, goods, and installations in Canada that the governor had seized. For his delta colony La Salle was empowered by royal license to select material as good as that which De Soto had put together for his ill-fated Florida venture. There were to be four vessels in the fleet which would carry the colonists to the Gulf coast: a ketch, a storeship, a tiny six-gun frigate, and the *Joly*, a 36-gun ship of the line in the royal navy. Crown agents went to Rochelle and Rochefort to gather recruits. For a hard core La Salle took along a few experienced Canadian voyageurs and, like De Soto, several members of his own family, among them his nephew Moranget and his brother Cavelier. A hundred soldiers were enrolled besides artisans, laborers, gentlemen of fortune, and shopkeepers. Several families, women and children included, signed up for the colonization project, as well as a batch of young women, attracted by the prospect of almost certain marriage. Unhappily the quality of these hopeful colonists was not all that could have been desired; there were rascals, thieves, and vagabonds in the company. The worst feature of the preparations was the organization of a split command; La Salle was to head the colony once it was put ashore, but Beaujeu, the ranking naval officer, was to be responsible for the convoy and navigation to the place of disembarkation. The two leaders disliked one another from the start—La Salle because he detested sharing authority with any man, and Beaujeu because he considered La Salle an inexperienced and undisciplined upstart. Even before the ships set sail, both men were firing off letters of complaint to Paris. Beaujeu found La Salle totally ignorant of naval matters, whimsical and suspicious; La Salle accused his colleague of loose talk and overstepping his responsibilities. They squabbled endlessly over precedence, command of the soldiers, loading of the ships, and even the food that would be served during the voyage.

The four ships eventually set sail from Rochelle on July

24, 1684, on a wretched trip. Almost at once the *Joly* snapped
a bowsprit and the flotilla had to put back to port until a new
spar was fitted. Then, on the transatlantic voyage Beaujeu and
La Salle continued to quarrel violently about everything from
the filling of the water casks to the best destination in the
French West Indies where the ships were supposed to stop
over for supplies. La Salle was terribly strained by the endless
arguments and, already weakened by the succession of fevers
he had suffered in Canada, had a nervous breakdown. By
the time Beaujeu brought the convoy to Santo Domingo, La
Salle was in such poor shape that he had to be landed to
convalesce. While their leader tossed and turned, babbling
with fever, his carefully planned expedition fell apart. The
ketch was captured by Spanish pirates and all its stores were
lost; besides which, the Spanish authorities got to know of
France's intentions to poach in the Gulf of Mexico, hitherto
considered a Spanish preserve. Soldiers and sailors from the
expeditionary force roamed about on shore, carousing and
debauching themselves in the heady atmosphere of the lush
island, until there was hardly a man fit for duty. The troops
contracted the local fevers and diseases which they took with
them to the intended colony, a curse none of the planners had
foreseen.

Slowly La Salle recovered his health and when he was
strong enough to do so, resumed command. He realized that
unless the expedition left the debilitating atmosphere of Santo
Domingo immediately, his project would disintegrate entirely. Already the men were deserting in droves, disheartened by the gloomy prophecies of French buccaneers who
had sailed the Gulf coast. Toward the end of November, four
months after leaving France, the remaining three ships
weighed anchor and set their course for the Mississippi. They
were steering into unknown waters, for the Spanish had long
forbidden the Gulf of Mexico to foreign ships on pain of
death, and only pirate vessels had slipped in and out on their
secret raids. Not a single pilot aboard La Salle's vessels knew
the coastline accurately, and while it was Beaujeu's responsi-

bility to make landfall, La Salle had to pick out the mouth of the Mississippi where the colony was to be planted.

The flotilla came within sight of the coast on December 28 and promptly turned *westward* to follow the sweep of the land until the Mississippi delta was found. Beaujeu, La Salle, and the pilots were already well astray. They were all convinced that they had been sailing against a strong easterly current which had delayed their penetration into the Gulf. This misunderstanding, coupled with a cartographical misplacing of the Mississippi delta toward Mexico, led La Salle to believe that his expedition was still east of the delta. In fact, they had already overshot the mouth of the river and every mile took them farther and farther from their goal. It was a mistake for which the navigators were not entirely to blame. They did not have an accurate method of determining longitude, and, because the coastline ran roughly east-west, locating any position on it was largely a matter of guesswork. On his canoe journey from Canada to the mouth of the Mississippi, La Salle had tried to determine the longitude of the delta, but his readings were subject to the wide margin of error usual to the times. His main hope was to recognize the delta by sight, but it was almost impossible to correlate his observations from a canoe with the view from a ship's deck a mile or so offshore. To make matters worse, Beaujeu refused to jeopardize his ships by hugging the land too closely. He stood well out to sea while the lookouts hopefully scanned the low silhouette of the coast for the Mississippi distributaries. It was a difficult task. The flat, dreary coastline offered no landmarks; surf, sand bars, lagoons, and beaches were bleak and featureless. One section of the coast looked very much like the next and the expedition wallowed steadily away from the delta.

At last, nearly four hundred miles past the river's mouth, La Salle realized that he was hopelessly lost. But because of his quarrel with Beaujeu, there was no question of the two commanders getting together and making the best of their situation. The weather was becoming increasingly stormy and the ships were frequently losing sight of each other. Tempers were frayed and the colonists, bottled up in the overcrowded ships, were becoming more and more despondent. No one wanted to extend the stuffy, uncomfortable voyage a day longer than necessary. Under these conditions La Salle made a terrible mistake. Eager to rid himself of Beaujeu and moved by a mystic faith in his own destiny, he decided to land his colony—settlers, supplies, and livestock—on the barren Texas coast. Once ashore, they would find the great river and launch the Lousiana colony. It was the most stupid decision La Salle ever made. He had no idea where he was, the country was utterly bleak, and by disembarking from the ships his unwieldy expedition was losing its mobility. La Salle overlooked the fact that he was no longer leading a tough, experienced band of voyageurs accustomed to hard traveling; now he commanded a disorganized and weak conglomeration of men, women, and children, nearly all of whom were sick. These unreliable townfolk were complete novices to the customs, conditions, and demands of a pioneer life. Nevertheless La Salle gave the order and the landing began at the mouth of Matagorda Bay, nearly three weeks' travel on foot from the Mississippi.

The disembarkation was a shambles. In pounding surf the small boats were tossed about or capsized; worried colonists clutched their belongings and staggered ashore, drenched and dispirited. On the beach there was chaos: confused soldiers scuttled back and forth, not knowing what to do; supplies were muddled in a vast jumble; tents and baggage dumped haphazard on the sand. On the ships it was discovered that some of the stores had been stowed in the ballast and could not be put ashore for fear of endangering the lading of the vessels. A party of men went wandering off inland and almost at once got involved with a band of the local natives, a mangy lot who scraped a pitiful existence in the barrens by living off grubs and prickly pear in times of famine. La Salle, already at full stretch trying to sort out the bedlam, had to tramp off with a squad of soldiers to rescue the wanderers before they came to blows with the Indians. In his absence, matters got even further out of control and the captain of the storeship, the *Aimable*, tried to sail closer in shore under a full press of canvas. The ship ran firmly aground on a sand bar, and, by the time La Salle got back to the beach, the unhappy *Aimable* was careened helplessly over on her side. La Salle desperately rounded up all the available light craft, and with dinghys and dugouts the more responsible men began to unload the stranded ship. Several boatloads of gunpowder and flour were safely landed before the wind began to freshen from the sea. Soon the gathering storm forced all unloading to stop and the rising waves began to pound the helpless *Aimable*. The heavily laden storeship broke apart; her seams gaped and the crashing waves gutted her from stem to stern. On the sands there was pandemonium as the luckless colonists saw their supplies swallowed up by the unfriendly sea. Many of the lighter goods from the *Aimable's* hold were washed ashore and La Salle sent the strongest swimmers into the plunging breakers to retrieve what flotsam they could. A troop of Indians who turned up and opportunely joined in for plunder had to be chased off with muskets. When the storm blew itself out, the *Aimable* was a broken hulk on the shoals, while the unhappy survivors huddled on the beach in makeshift tents and shelters contrived from the damaged casks, bales, and bundles of their equipment. With the *Aimable* they had lost nearly all their provisions, 60 barrels of wine, 4 cannon, 1620 cannonballs, 400 grenades, 4,000 pounds of iron, 5,000 pounds of lead, most of the tools, a forge, a mill, boxes of arms, and nearly all the medicines.

It must have been obvious to La Salle, as well as to Beaujeu, that the projected colony did not stand a chance of survival after this disastrous beginning. But La Salle was obsessed with his plans for a settlement. He still had the *Joly* and the six-gun frigate *Belle*. Now he proposed that Beaujeu take the *Joly* and coast eastward until he found the Mississippi. La Salle and the colonists would either set up a fort where they were, or if that proved impractical, march along the coast until they linked up once more with Beaujeu. To help them, the shallow-draught *Belle* would stay behind to explore the coastline and its inlets. A few days later, Beaujeu set his sails and the *Joly* vanished over the horizon. On board went several colonists, already disillusioned with the whole project. Beaujeu never came back to Matagorda Bay.

Looking over his sorry band of colonists, La Salle knew that his first task was to get them off the unprotected beach and safely ensconced in a more suitable spot. This had to be done quickly; already men were dying, five or six each day, from bad food, disease, and brackish water. There were no ovens for baking bread and the French were reduced to eating a soggy porridge of flour mixed with sea water. The coast Indians, although few in numbers and desperately poverty-stricken, were becoming bolder. They managed to creep into the camp to steal blankets and other badly needed supplies, and the soldiers La Salle sent out to punish the thieves were mauled during a night attack on their bivouac. The survivors came limping back with two dead and several wounded, including La Salle's hotheaded nephew Moranget, who had led the patrol. The Indians then lit a prairie fire upwind of the beachhead and for a moment it looked as if the advancing inferno might blow up the powder store. Just in time, La Salle and his Canadian veterans organized a counterfire to burn off a protective ring round the camp before the creeping line of the main fire engulfed the entire settlement.

After the fire, La Salle moved his forlorn group of settlers to a more suitable spot at the head of the bay. There the colonists feebly began to work on La Salle's Fort St. Louis of Texas. It was a shabby, pathetic affair. There was very little wood near at hand, so most of the dwellings were mere shanties of patched tarpaulin stretched over makeshift frames of driftwood laboriously hauled up from the beach on gun carriages. A ragged picket fence was put up to protect the supplies of gunpowder and brandy. Fields were laid out and half-heartedly tilled, but the young crops soon withered under the strange conditions. The livestock, so painstakingly shipped from France, fared little better: cattle, pigs, chickens, and goats sickened and died, until a bare handful were left alive, jealously guarded by the famished colonists. As work gradually progressed on more solid structures at Fort St. Louis, the number of invalids increased alarmingly. The crude sick bay was packed with men suffering from malnutrition, sunstroke, festering sores, and a host of diseases for which there were no medicines or known cures. The debauchery of Santo Domingo was now reaping a heavy toll; fever ran like wildfire through the camp and its scarecrow victims lurched about with hollow cheeks and sunken eyes. They went out into the prairie looking for strange herbs to cure their illnesses, and several men were bitten by rattlesnakes. They died screaming with pain.

La Salle gradually lost hope. He went out on a series of expeditions, near and far, to locate the vital Mississippi River or the Spanish settlements. Each time the explorers came back a little weaker and with nothing to show for their efforts. His men sensed the gathering despair in their leader and the dwindling colony sank into apathy. A terrible boredom settled over Fort St. Louis; the flat prairie was a monotonous, dull ocean, broken only by the black dots of buffalo grazing in the distance; the blue sky weighed heavily on the tiny fort and its antlike garrison; the men felt trapped and scourged in the hopeless struggle to make their mark on a hostile land. As day succeeded day, the death count remorselessly ticked away the list of the living, and life at Fort St. Louis ebbed.

La Salle was approaching the same state of mind that De Soto had shown in his last hours of despondency on the banks of the fatal river which had deluded both leaders. La Salle's dream was finally crumbling and, like De Soto, he withdrew more and more into himself, to suffer and brood in silence. On the last day of October he led out a desperate expedition to locate and attack the Spanish colonies to the west. Fifty of the strongest men went with him, some wearing home-made corselets of staves to protect them from Indian arrows. Few returned. The soldiers, half-trained sweepings from the gutters and jails of Rochelle and Paris, got lost, died of thirst, or deserted. La Salle built a stockade far inland and left a squad to garrison it; these men and the deserters were never heard from again. They died from thirst, starvation, exposure, or Indian attack. Worst of all, the little frigate *Belle*, which was exploring the coast, ran aground and was lost. La Salle's last link with France had snapped: the colony was marooned.

By now La Salle's pathetic colony was reduced to about forty souls, less than one quarter of the original number who had so foolishly landed on the bleak coast. All but seven of the women had died and half the surviving men were in such poor health that they could not travel. Undernourished and racked with illness, the living had long since given up hope of rescue from the sea; their only escape now lay inland to the Mississippi, if they could find it, and up the river to Canada. A last expedition was organized. The men gathered every scrap of equipment, ransacking the fort for boots and blankets, even cutting up the spare sails of the *Belle* to make clothing for the adventurers. With twenty of the fittest men, including his brother Cavelier and his nephew Moranget, La Salle intended to march northeast until he reached the Mississippi. There the expedition would turn upstream until they came to one of the outposts which Tonti was supposed to be building along the line of the great river, and arrange for a rescue party of Canadian voyageurs to relieve the ill-omened Fort St. Louis of Texas.

On January 7, 1687, La Salle set out. It was a gloomy leave-taking. All those who stayed behind at the fort realized that their fate rested with the pathetic expedition. Those who were leaving were subdued and careworn, knowing that they had only a slim chance of getting through to Canada. The harsh pessimism of their commander did not encourage them. For the last time La Salle was starting a bitter and cruel journey to save his ambitions. He had done all in his power to establish his southern colony; now there was nothing left but to pick up its shattered pieces.

The story of that last ill-fated trip is clouded in a mist of half-truths, doubt, and uncertainty. The French were a motley band thrown together by circumstances. Besides La Salle, his brother, and his nephew there was the pilot from the wrecked *Belle*, a priest by the name of Douay, the surgeon Liotot, Nika the Shawnee hunter, and a blackguard called Duhaut who had invested in the colonial project. It was a very ill-assorted group and as the days passed, their mutual likes and dislikes were sharpened by the constant strain of traveling together over an unending landscape of prairie, thicket, and densely overgrown valleys. Food was a constant problem and the subject of countless quarrels; they picked berries, shot buffalo, or traded with the Indians for supplies. At night the party huddled around the campfire, endlessly discussing the route and their chances of reaching Canada alive. They crossed several rivers on home-made rafts or "bull boats" made of buffalo hide stretched over wicker frames. From time to time foul weather halted all progress for days on end while the men moped beneath crude tents of buffalo skins. In the fight for survival there were more and more quarrels among the men. Tempers snapped. Petty hostilities grew into violent hatreds, factions developed, until, like snarling dogs, the expedition was ready for an internal explosion that would rip it apart. Only La Salle could have averted disaster, but he was a broken reed, too harsh, reserved, and uncompromising in his disappointment.

On March 15 food was running low, so La Salle dispatched a gang of men to retrieve a cache of supplies that had been set up during an earlier sortie from Fort St. Louis. Seven men went out, including the surgeon, Tiessier the Pilot, Nika, the disgruntled Duhaut, and an ex-buccaneer by the name of Hiens who was German by birth but had probably sailed aboard an English pirate ship for he was sometimes known as "English Jem." This group located the cache without difficulty but found that all its contents had rotted and were spoiled beyond saving. Their dismay was lessened when Nika with his usual skill managed to shoot two buffalo. While the dead animals were being butchered, one of the men returned to fetch help from La Salle's party to bring in the meat. La Salle sent his fiery-tempered nephew Moranget to take charge. He arrived at the hunters' camp in time to brew up a violent quarrel with Duhaut and the buccaneer. The reasons for the quarrel were as trivial as could be imagined: by frontier custom the successful hunters were entitled to keep the marrow bones and other choice portions of the beast, but Moranget demanded the entire carcass. A furious argument ensued which brought to the surface all the underlying hatreds in the group. It was an ugly scene and Moranget invoked the authority of his uncle La Salle, threatening the men with severe punishment if they did not obey orders. To Duhaut, Tiessier, and Hiens this was the last insult they would take from the arrogant Moranget. In a swirl of hatred and envy, they abandoned reason and turned their passions against their leader and those faithful to him. That night Duhaut and the others concocted a plot to murder Moranget, Nika, and a manservant called Saget. In the small hours of the morning Liotot the surgeon executed the bloody task. With an ax he hacked Saget and Nika to death as his victims lay asleep by the campfire. Moranget, mortally wounded and unable to utter a word, thrashed about in his death throes until the ringleaders compelled one of their more faint-hearted accomplices to finish off the wounded man. These atrocities sealed La Salle's fate. The murderers knew that only one man could bring justice to them in that desolate wilderness far from civilization. If the guilty were to escape punishment, La Salle had to die. There was no alternative. The conspirators settled back to await the appearance of their captain.

Meanwhile, some six miles away at the main camp, La Salle became anxious when Moranget failed to return. There had been an undercurrent of mutiny in the camp and La Salle had a sense of foreboding about the fate of his party. He talked the matter over with Joutel, his lieutenant, and on the morning of March 18 he decided to investigate matters for himself. Setting out with Douay the priest, he began walking toward the hunter's camp, its site already marked by the circling flight of two buzzards attracted to the corpses. As the two men approached the camp, La Salle fired off his gun to attract the attention of the hunters and announce his arrival. Duhaut and the other assassins slipped into the protection of the bush and took up their positions in a shallow gully which covered the approaches to the camp. As soon as La Salle came in sight, one of the mutineers showed himself and with studied insolence refused to answer La Salle's questions concerning the whereabouts of Moranget. Stung to anger by the man's rudeness, La Salle advanced on him while the decoy fell back in feigned nervousness toward the gully. When La Salle had moved into point-blank range, two shots rang out in quick succession. La Salle pitched forward, dead before he hit the Texas soil, a musket ball through his brain. The dead captain's body was stripped by his murderers and dragged aside to a thicket where it was left to the wolves and birds of carrion. The conspirators then advanced on the main camp, taking with them the terrified priest, and seized control of the expedition proposing the utterly impractical system that each man in turn should take command for a day.

The triumph of the mutineers was short-lived and they soon quarreled over the division of the loot from La Salle's belongings. Hiens, the buccaneer, shot down Duhaut, and the surgeon was also killed. With bloody anarchy on all sides, Joutel, Douay and the pro-La Salle faction managed to escape and with the help of the Indians were taken on a two-month trek which finally brought them, in a state of near-collapse, to a point near the junction of the Arkansas river and the Mississippi. Here the faithful Tonti had set up a tiny outpost as part of La Salle's scheme for a chain of forts from the St. Lawrence to the Gulf. Tonti himself was away fighting the Iroquois but he hurried back to see the survivors when they reached his headquarters on the Illinois and gave them all the help he could to see them safely back to France. For some reason, it was not until the survivors reached France that they revealed the full details of La Salle's assassination and the fate of the Texas colony. Perhaps they were afraid of being impli-

cated in his death. By then it was too late; the murderers had
escaped to live with the Indians, and Louis the Magnificent
did not consider it worth the expense to fit out an expedition
to rescue the remaining colonists at Fort St. Louis of Texas.
Only the Spanish, jealous of their western domain, showed an
interest. No less than four expeditions sailed from Vera Cruz
to find and destroy the feeble French settlement. They un-
covered the hulks of the *Aimable* and the *Belle* but of the fort
there was no trace. It was not until a French deserter turned
up in the Spanish province of New Leon that a land expedition marched across the Rio Grande and made its way to Fort
St. Louis. They found it garrisoned by corpses, dead from
smallpox and Indian attack. The palisades were in ruins and
the houses were empty shells. All that remained were rumors
of white children and women living among the Indian tribes,
captives from the last defense of the fort. For years the
rumors persisted and occasionally a white survivor escaped
from the Indians and turned up on the Mexican frontier. Of
La Salle's "Great Plan," only Tonti's forts survived, a poor
relic of so much ambition and toil.

During his lifetime La Salle held in his hands all the
threads essential to success—royal patronage, the support of
Frontenac, financial backing, friendship with the Indians, vision, personal talent for planning, hard work, endurance and
energy—yet all these trickled like water through his grasp.
Why did he fail? There can be no certain answer, but the
clue probably lies in his timing and his character. His dreams
were ahead of his century and premature in their execution.
Canada and the Mississippi were not ready for La Salle and
his schemes; his efforts were spread too thinly over too vast an
area. Yet La Salle might have succeeded if he had advanced
deliberately and had organized a network of faithful and efficient followers to carry out his plans. But he met with hatred,
treachery, and envy from the people he relied on in Canada
and in Texas. Even if his enemies did not understand La Salle
and considered him a threat to their existence, their fierce
opposition to his progress needs more explanation. Looking

back over his career, it seems that for some reason the burgher's son from Rouen was seen as a stormy petrel. All too often his shyness—and he was very shy indeed—was taken for disdain or arrogance. He stirred up ill-will wherever he went and he rarely commanded the affection of lesser men. The king, his ministers, and the governor of Canada understood him and threw their entire support behind the quiet Norman; yet the trappers, bushrangers, and fur traders, with whom he spent most of his days, all too often disliked La Salle and did everything in their power to bring him down. He lacked the common touch, and that failing proved to be his undoing. Yet even in death he was a noble and tragic figure. His most staunch follower and life-long admirer, the Italian Tonti, called La Salle "one of the greatest men of his age." It is an excellent epitaph. In due course the torch of the Mississippi dream passed to Tonti, as Moscoso had carried on when De Soto died. Like Moscoso, Henry de Tonti proved less idealistic, more practical, and in the end achieved more concrete results than La Salle the visionary.

7

Iron Hand

WHEN LA SALLE'S ASSASSINATION REMOVED THE leading character from the drama that was now rapidly unfolding along the Mississippi Valley, his place on the center of the stage was taken by his second-in-command, Henry de Tonti. For nine difficult years Tonti had worked in the shadows of the renowned Sieur de la Salle; now, quite unexpectedly, he found himself heir to La Salle's dreams and half-finished ambitions in a New World which was changing rapidly. At Montreal and Quebec, in the British coastal settlements, and among the Anglo-Dutch of the Hudson, the tempo of expansion was quickening. There was a surge in the scramble for America; the prizes were the profits of the fur trade, the allegiance of the Indians, and possession of the interior. The deciding factor was, of course, the direct struggle for supremacy in the northeast corner of the continent where the midget colonies of New France and Massachusetts struck at one another with raid, counterraid, and intrigue. But the intercolonial rivalry was also an important motive in the efforts of the explorers whether they were traders, government agents, or missionaries. France had stolen a march on England by making the basic discovery that the Mississippi flowed south to the Gulf of Mexico, and she had followed up this advantage by establishing a flamboyant claim to the entire area drained by the Ohio, Mississippi, and Missouri without even knowing the extent of this region. However, there was nothing to prevent England challenging the validity of this claim provided that English agents could cross the Appalachians and enter the great central valley. So a situation developed in which English explorers and traders moving westward from their coastal settlements encountered French agents working in the opposite direction from their headquarters on the Mississippi. Both groups were intent on persuading the Indians to trade with them alone and both sides were prepared to employ deceit and treachery in the struggle. It is no surprise, therefore, that England's most successful agents were a Dutchman, Arnout Viele, and a renegade French voyageur, Jean Couture, who defected to Carolina. In 1692 Viele, an enterprising *boschloper*, pioneered a route for the English from the Mohawk to the Ohio and not only persuaded the Shawnee living in that area to trade with Albany but also successfully tapped a large portion of the lower Great Lakes Indian market. Farther south Jean Couture, who had once worked under La Salle, showed the Carolinians that their traders could take trains of pack horses up the Savannah River, cross to the Tennessee, and so win through to the tribes of the Mississippi valley. His work complemented a trip in 1698 by one Thomas Welch, a Carolinian, who opened up the even easier route direct from Charleston to the mouth of the Arkansas. Significantly, this venture isolated even more thoroughly the Spanish colonists in Florida so that the real contest for the Mississippi was left to the French and the English. These two nations pushed their activities inland—one down the line of the Great Lakes, the other down the Ohio—their collision course was set for the Illinois settlement. There, at Fort St. Louis of the Illinois, was Henry de Tonti, left behind by La Salle to manage the affairs of the upper Mississippi valley.

Henry de Tonti was one of those people who seems to

have been born for a life of adventure. His father, Lorenzo de Tonti, was a young Italian banker living in Naples when the Neopolitan lazzaroni rose in revolt against the tyranny of their Spanish viceroy, the Duke of Arcos. The rebellion was headed by an Amalfi fisherman, a ruffian called Masaniello, who led the mob in storming the duke's palace. Lorenzo de Tonti threw himself so wholeheartedly into the popular cause that he and Salvatore Rosa, the famous painter, were made Masaniello's lieutenants. While Masaniello became drunk with power and strutted about Naples like a comic-opera dictator, Lorenzo captured and held for the rebels the important bastion of Gaeta, north of the city. However, the rule of the lazzaroni turned out to be an eight-day wonder; Masaniello so enraged the mob with his brutal antics that they assassinated him in the market place. The revolt collapsed and Lorenzo was forced to take his wife and flee into exile in France. During these tumultous days their first son was born— Henry de Tonti, who came to be known as La Salle's "faithful lieutenant."

Lorenzo arrived in Paris as a down-at-heel political refugee without friends or money; luckily for him France at that time was ruled by an Italian, Cardinal Mazarin, in the minority of the twelve-year-old Louis XIV. Mazarin's great problem as head of the state was to keep the French exchequer from bankruptcy and it was not long before Lorenzo de Tonti, the exiled banker, came forward with an ingenious method of filling the royal coffers. Tonti had concocted a primitive form of life insurance by which the Crown would receive a large amount of capital contributed in small shares by the bourgeoisie. The interest on this capital would accrue to the investors after most of the original contributors had died. The scheme was practical and clever—to this day it is known as a "tontine," after its inventor—and successive governments in France used the system to raise money. Unhappily, Tonti himself received little reward for his idea; the first attempt at putting the tontine into practice was a failure and Lorenzo was thrown into the Bastille where he stayed for eight years.

In 1677 he was released but never succeeded in returning to favor, so that for the rest of his life he had to be supported by his children.

One of the oddest features of early Mississippi exploration is the extent to which it was a family affair. We have seen how De Soto took several members of his family on the Florida adventure and how La Salle was surrounded in Canada and Texas by various cousins, a brother, and several nephews, including the young fool Moranget who triggered the final tragedy of assassination. Henry de Tonti was no exception to this "family rule." Two of his cousins by the name of Desliettes, the Frenchified form of Di Lietto, were officers in the regiments of New France. Two other cousins were well-known voyageurs: Sieur Greysolon de la Tourette and his brother Daniel Greysolon Duluth, after whom a major American city is named. Furthermore, Tonti's younger brother Alphonse was one of the first swindlers in the history of Canada. Alphonse applied to join up under La Salle but was refused; undeterred, he came to Canada on his own initiative and set himself up as a merchant. Before long Alphonse was doing so well that he was appointed commandant at Michilimackinac and then at Detroit. Alphonse, being a thorough cynic, did not hesitate to misuse his official position to line his own pocket. At that time it was extremely difficult to obtain a license to trade with the Indians and Alphonse busily searched for some way of avoiding the official regulations. In 1700 he mentioned in a letter that there was "no recourse for *honest* folk since the abolition of the permits to trade." It occurred to Alphonse that if the authorities would not allow him to trade, there was nothing to prevent him using his power as commandant of an isolated western fort to make some clandestine deals with the savages in his area. At Detroit he hit on the happy idea of swapping his fort's supply of gunpowder for furs brought in by the Indians. The scheme was a huge success and Alphonse did such a roaring trade with the savages that the settlers at Detroit began to worry that if the Indians ever decided to attack the fort, the garrison would not have enough powder to fire a single cannon. After numerous complaints by the settlers he was supposed to protect, Alphonse was removed from Detroit. Shortly afterward he wangled the post of commandant at Fort Frontenac and enjoyed two more years of inglorious peculation before he was dismissed in disgrace for extortion and illicit trading with the Indians. Alphonse then redeemed his reputation by fighting gallantly against the Iroquois until he was reappointed to his old command at Detroit. He was still at the fort in 1727 when he died. Needless to say, it was found after his death that he had returned to his old ways; the financial affairs at the fort were in a shambles.

Naturally Alphonse's bad reputation rebounded on his brother, Henry, and Henry de Tonti was frequently and quite unjustly tarred with the same brush. In fact, Henry was heavyweight caliber, while his brother was not. Men who knew Henry, and others who wrote about him after his death, consistently describe his unswerving devotion to La Salle and his staunch support of him when the future looked blackest and everyone else had abandoned La Salle as an idle dreamer. Again and again the same adjectives are used to describe Tonti: brave, faithful, loyal, energetic, courageous, devoted. This praise is accurate and well-deserved, but the historians and commentators usually miss the essence of Tonti's personality; he remains a half-figure, the second-string player on a team whose captain steals the glory and captures everyone's attention. Tonti was much more than the classic "faithful lieutenant"; he experienced more than his fair share of adventures and hairbreadth escapes in the wilds. For seventeen years after La Salle's death, Tonti carried on the dream of the "Great Plan" and came nearer to putting the idea into practice than did La Salle. Perhaps Tonti's story was forgotten because there was no place for an Italian in French-Canadian folk legend. Yet during twenty-five difficult years Henry de Tonti labored for the cause of France on or near the Mississippi. The river became the focus of his career and he was undisputed authority on all questions relating to its exploration, navigation, settlement, commerce, and Indian life.

Even a brief glance at Tonti's life before he emigrated to Canada reveals the strength and depth of his character. At the age of eighteen, when Joliet, Marquette, or La Salle would have been more at home in the quiet of seminary cloisters, Henry de Tonti was learning the rough-and-tumble life of a professional soldier in the armies of Louis the Magnificent. In 1668, Tonti makes his first appearance as a cadet in the French army and two years later he is serving as a *garde marine* in the Mediterranean fleet based on Toulon and Marseilles. By then his father had been locked away in the Bastille and there was no one at Court to help the young officer on his way up the promotion ladder. Fortunately for Tonti there was plenty of fighting to be done and battlefield promotions to be gained in the Wars of Devolution which Louis XIV was busily waging to expand his possessions at the cost of the Spanish monarch Charles II and concurrently to enhance the prestige of the Sun King. The Mediterranean was a cockpit of war and young Tonti saw action in several campaigns. Three times he served aboard ships of the line and four times he went to sea on war galleys. His campaigning took him to Sicily to fight under the fleur-de-lis of France, and at Messina he was promoted to the rank of captain-lieutenant of a brigade. Then, at Libisso, there was a disaster that would have put an end to the career of a lesser man. The Spanish forces attacked and during the battle Tonti's right hand was blown off by an exploding grenade. It is said that while waiting for the surgeon to attend to his wound, Tonti himself trimmed the bleeding fragments at the end of his shattered wrist. At Libisso he was also taken prisoner, but his commander must have already considered the young Italian too valuable to lose; in an exchange of prisoners Tonti was traded for the son of the Spanish governor of Metassa. Tough and resourceful, Tonti recovered from his injury and made his way to Paris where he petitioned the king for help. He was lucky; Louis gave the battle-scarred Italian an outright gift of three hundred livres for his services to the French Crown. Promptly Tonti volunteered to return to active duty aboard the galleys and despite the missing right hand he was soon back in Sicily fighting in another campaign.

Then, in 1678, the war ended. By the Treaty of Nimwegen Louis patched up his quarrel with Spain and started to cut back his large wartime armies. Droves of professional officers were discharged and with them went Tonti, a superfluous veteran. The future looked bleak for the young officer; his only trade was soldiering, and a foreigner with only one hand had no place in the new streamlined French army. Tonti's hopes lay with the patronage of the Prince of Conti and with Abbé Renaudot, both men of influence who knew his excellent record as a fighting man. By a happy coincidence, they were also leading advocates at Court of the Sieur de la Salle with his extraordinary schemes for an empire of the Mississippi. Thus when La Salle visited Paris in the year of the peace, looking for men, money, and royal support, his arrival was a windfall for Tonti. Abbé Renaudot suggested to La Salle that Tonti would be a good man to use in Canada, and La Salle, already bitter about the treachery and desertions among his Canadian employees, gladly agreed to try out the young Italian as a backwoods leader. Tonti jumped at the chance. On July 12, 1678, he traveled to La Rochelle where he found La Salle assembling the artisans and equipment for the Great Lakes sailing ships that would link together the pieces of the grand enterprise. The two men, the lonely suspicious Norman and the twenty-eight-year-old Italian soldier of fortune, took an instant liking to each other. It was a friendship that lasted until La Salle's death.

On July 14 their ship, the 200-ton *St. Honoré*, sailed for Canada where Tonti was to begin his long, hard apprenticeship in the half-savage ways of the voyageur, *coureur de bois*, and squaw man. It was a life to which the one-handed Italian seemed peculiarly ill-fitted, but as the days passed, it became clear that Tonti reveled in the crude conditions of the outback. Even La Salle, usually so reserved in his opinions, was amazed

by his new recruit's drive and determination in the strange
new world of the colonies. Shortly after reaching Quebec La
Salle wrote delightedly to the Prince of Conti:

> M. de Tonti has always shewed so honest a manner toward
> me, that I cannot overstate my joy in having him with me
> . . . he has surpassed my highest hopes . . . His honesty
> and intrinsic worth are well enough known to you, but per-
> haps you would not have believed him capable of doing things
> for which a strong constitution, a knowledge of the country,
> and the free use of two arms seem absolutely necessary. Never-
> theless, his energy and ability make him capable of anything.
> He leaves in a season when the ice discourages everyone else,
> to command a new fort two hundred leagues from here . . .

If there was such a person as a "natural" frontiersman,
Tonti was that man. By birth he had little to lose if he gambled everything on a career in the colonies; by training he
was tough and disciplined; by nature he was a man of few
words, observant, brave, and practical. He came to New
France with every intention of making his future there and
was prepared to put up with the discomfort, suffering, and
difficulties of a pioneer. Rather to his surprise Tonti's maimed
limb proved to be more of an asset than a hindrance. An
artificial hand had been fitted to the stump of his wrist and
this arrangement was weird enough in the eyes of the Indians
to raise Tonti immediately to the role of a powerful war
chief. Tonti always wore a glove to cover the artificial hand,
so it is not known whether it was made of copper, brass, or
iron, nor is there any record whether it was articulated or
not. But whatever the metal and mechanics of the artificial
limb, the Indians regarded it as the strongest of strong medicine and Tonti took care to spread their respect; he was quite
willing to use his ready-made club to knock an Indian dizzy
or break a few teeth. The savages were delighted by this
display of white man's magic, and among the tribes Tonti
soon became known as "Cut Arm" or "Iron Hand."

From the beginning of his days in the Canadian wilderness
Tonti made his position clear to the Indians, priests, and

voyageurs alike: he was La Salle's man and would not tolerate
interference, carping, or negligence in the affairs of his patron. Tonti had been trained in a hard school and he was
determined to bring the discipline of the battlefield to the
chaos of the backwoods. Inevitably he had to compromise, but
not until he had made his point. His first task was to supervise
the building of the *Griffin* at Niagara, and it has been told
how he pushed his men relentlessly in order to have the job
finished quickly despite the rigors of winter. It was characteristic of Tonti that he took his responsibilities seriously; when
Father Hennepin tried to meddle in the building of the
Griffin, Tonti bluntly told the priest to mind his own business and confine his opinions to spiritual affairs. Hennepin
retired in a huff but he never interfered again.

In 1680 Tonti went from Niagara to the Illinois country
where La Salle had decided to built Fort Crèvecoeur. When
La Salle set off on his remarkable spring trek across Canada to
Fort Frontenac to fetch supplies, Tonti was left in charge of
the construction of the outpost. It provided him with a bitter
lesson in the differences between commanding regular troops
and persuading unruly half-breeds to execute a chore that
required patience and sustained hard work. When the stockade was only half complete and the bare ribs of the Mississippi sailing vessel still lay on the stocks, a messenger arrived
with instructions from La Salle that he wanted a new and
better fort built on Starved Rock, a commanding bluff upstream from Crèvecoeur. Dutifully, Tonti went off to reconnoiter the site; while he was absent his voyageurs seized their
chance to desert. Before vanishing into the woods, they stole
as much plunder as they could carry off from the stores and
threw the remainder, including the precious weapons, gunpowder, and trade goods, into the river. Tonti returned to
find himself abandoned without supplies in the middle of Indian country and only the doubtful friendship of the Illinois
Indians for protection. With him were two loyal voyageurs
and two Recollet priests who had accompanied the expedition, one of them the intrepid old Father Gabriel de la

Ribourde. With so much dead weight in his command, Tonti would have been well advised to withdraw to the safety of Michilimackinac at once, but it seems that the soldierly Italian still lived by his military training. La Salle had ordered him to hold Fort Crèvecoeur and the Illinois country; obediently Tonti tried to do this with two noncombatants and two voyageurs who had nothing but their muskets and a few days supply of ammunition. It was out of the question to continue work on the boat or even to maintain Fort Crèvecoeur, so Tonti moved his party to the Illinois village and grimly settled in to wait for La Salle's return. It was a courageous decision but it nearly cost all of them their lives.

At first all went smoothly. The two priests contentedly found a place to live in the village and began taking lessons in the language of the Illinois so that they might be able to preach to the Indians. Tonti and his voyageurs did some desultory fur trading to pass the time away. In this rustic calm the months slipped gently away. The ice broke up on the river and floated southward in paper-thin sheets; spring melted the last snow and the trees of the surrounding forest burst into leaf. The Indians scratched up tiny plots of land with their hoes and planted a few kernels of corn. The summer months brought the ripening of the crops and plagues of swarming mosquitoes. As the days shortened into fall the hunting parties went out in force to bring in stocks of venison for the coming winter and the village lay empty except for the women going about their daily routine and the children fishing in the river. It was a deceptive, unruffled peace in a backwater of the continent; before long the Illinois would become the focus for white man's politics, trade wars, and conflicts.

Then, one day in mid-September, an Indian runner came panting into the Illinois settlement with the chilling news that an Iroquois raiding army of Senecas was on the warpath and had approached undetected within a day's journey of the village. Immediately there was pandemonium among the Illinois. Most of the tribe wanted to flee westward to escape the cruel

Iroquois; the younger hotheads spoke up for a battle with the invaders; and suddenly there was a wild rumor that La Salle was leading the Senecas. All the latent Indian mistrust of the white men burst into flame; yelling braves surrounded the Frenchmen demanding revenge on the treacherous guests who had lived among them. Tonti and his companions found themselves in real danger from the savages who wanted to make living torches of the foreigners. The Italian tried to calm the Illinois, but they were half-crazed by their traditional dread of the ferocity of the Iroquois and would not listen to reason. In desperation Tonti volunteered to prove his friendship by leading the Illinois in an attack on the invaders. His suggestion took the tribesmen by surprise and the hubbub ceased while the Illinois considered his offer of help. As long as they could remember, the Illinois had been attacked by the armies of the Iroquis Confederacy; on each occasion the Illinois had been beaten and badly mauled, until now they were so cowed by the reputation of an Iroquois war party that all their courage drained away, and, paralyzed by fear, the tribe waited for the annual onslaught of their traditional persecutor. Now, it occurred to their leaders, they might stand a chance of victory behind the guns of the prestigious white men.

On their side, the Iroquois had always regarded a raid on the Illinois as more of a sport than a war; it was a pleasant diversion for the warriors, taught the Illinois to respect the power of the Confederacy, and provided the young men with a chance to practice their martial skill. When it was all over, there was plunder, prestige, slaves, and gory spectacles of torture and ritual cannibalism. Therefore it was a shock for the Seneca army when the Illinois, after accepting Tonti's offer of leadership, sallied out from their village with every appearance of enough pluck to put up fierce resistance with the help of a few Frenchmen. The last thing the Iroquois wanted was a brush with the French. The Confederacy had learned its lesson from Frontenac's expedition and tried to steer clear of open, unplanned hostilities with the white men. Tonti's appearance at the head of the Illinois forces threw the Senecas into confusion and the Italian seized on his tactical advantage. He advanced to parley with the Iroquois in the hope that he could bluff them into a peace treaty.

Holding up a wampum belt, a traditional "white flag" similar to the peace pipe, Tonti and three of his companions started out across the gap that divided the two armies. If Tonti was still thinking in terms of European chivalry and the protection offered an envoy under an emblem of truce, he misjudged the arrogance of the Iroquois. The French had not advanced more than a few steps before the Senecas opened fire. Immediately Tonti sent his men back and coolly walked on by himself toward the waiting lines of half-naked savages, garish with streaks of war paint, their topknots bristling like the horsehair plumes of Roman legionnaires and their bodies stinking of stale urine. A young Seneca warrior, eager for glory, sprang forward and stabbed Tonti in the body. Luckily for the Italian it was a glancing thrust and the knife blade was deflected by a rib. As Tonti staggered under the blow, another Seneca grabbed the wampum belt and hurled it contemptuously on the ground; Tonti's hat was snatched from his head and gleefully hoisted aloft on a musket barrel to taunt the watching Illinois. Only the last-minute intervention of the more staid tribesmen saved the Italian's life; they cautioned the young men against killing a white man, though one scalp-hungry warrior continued to stand behind the white man and, as Tonti quaintly put it, lovingly "lifted up my hair every now and then." With this ghoul tickling his scalp, Tonti breezily bluffed the Iroquois war leaders, claiming that they were overmatched by the Illinois who held 1,200 warriors, allies, and sixty armed Frenchmen in reserve at their village.

After some consultation the Seneca chiefs replied that they were prepared to hold peace talks. It was a typical Iroquois trick; their army had not spent several weeks marching across difficult country to be turned aside by the word of one man. The wily councilors were playing for time to test the truth of Tonti's threats and to find some way of getting rid of the French. Tonti, who was by now spitting blood, went back to the Illinois lines to settle the details of the truce. The Illinois were stunned by the success of their bluster and gladly provided a hostage as part of the treaty agreement. Unfortunately the young man they selected to send back with Tonti was so eager to please the Iroquois that he promptly blurted out that his tribe was overjoyed to make peace with the invaders as most of the Illinois men were away on hunting trips, leaving their village unprotected. In Tonti's words: "I had much difficulty in getting out of this scrape. The Iroquois called me to them and loaded me with reproaches; they told me that I was a liar to have said the Illinois had 1,200 warriors besides the allies that had given them assistance. Where were the sixty Frenchmen who I had told them had been left at the village?"

The pretense was over, now that the Senecas knew the weakness of the opposition. The Illinois knew better than to trust the peace pledges of the Iroquois; they burned their village and withdrew to the temporary safety of an island in the middle of the river. Tonti and his companions remained behind in a cabin, surrounded by the bivouacs of the invaders, who, although professing peace, began building a fleet of canoes to attack the island refuge. Tonti sent word to the Illinois warning of the impending onslaught and advised the entire tribe to escape while there was still time. Eight days after their arrival, the Iroquois war leaders summoned Tonti to appear before them. After the usual formalities, the meeting got down to business. Six bales of beaver pelts were ceremonially carried in and placed before Tonti as he sat facing the solemn circle of chiefs. Then the Iroquois spokesman rose to address the waiting Italian. Using the oblique double-talk and symbolism of Indian diplomacy, the Seneca explained the meaning of each bale:

The first two bales were "to inform M. de Frontenac that they would not eat his children and he should not be angry at what they had done."

The third bale was a plaster for Tonti's wound.

The fourth was some oil to rub on his and his companions' limbs on account of the long journeys they had taken.

The fifth, that the sun was bright.

The sixth, that the Frenchmen should profit by the sunshine and leave next day for the French settlements.

The thinly veiled hint that the Frenchmen should accept a bribe and clear out enraged Tonti. Springing to his feet he sent the bales tumbling in all directions with a hearty kick and stalked out of the meeting. That night he and his men barricaded themselves in their cabin, waiting with loaded guns for an attack that would wipe them out. Next morning there was still no sign of the Iroquois' intentions and Tonti had cooled down enough to realize that his situation was untenable; the Illinois showed no signs of putting up a fight and the white men were living on borrowed time at the mercy of the Iroquois. Tonti decided to withdraw and seek shelter at the Jesuit mission of Green Bay.

The flight to Green Bay completed Tonti's frontier education. In every detail the journey was as unpleasant as La Salle's dash to Fort Frontenac. The Illinois had taken all the good canoes with them to the island and the Iroquois had commandeered almost everything else that would float for their projected invasion. The only canoe which Tonti could obtain was scarcely river-worthy. Paddling upstream in this leaky cockleshell, Tonti and his men had no idea whether the Iroquois would leave them alone or ambush and massacre them. Every few miles the travelers had to go ashore to repair the battered hull of their canoe, stitching the seams, calking with pine gum or sticking on patches of cloth and bark. On one of these halts, the seventy-year old Father Gabriel wandered off into the woods to pray, and while he was thus absorbed, the gentle old man was surprised by a gang of marauding Kickapoos. They clubbed in his skull, scalped him, and threw the corpse into a deep hole. Years later Tonti learned the fate of the indefatigable and cheerful missionary when his breviary turned up in the possession of a Wisconsin tribe.

Tonti waited for Father Gabriel as long as it was safe to

do so, but that evening the white man saw Indians skulking in the shadows of the thickets and the travelers were forced to move on if they were to save their own lives. Glumly they strained their aching muscles to paddle and portage their decrepit canoe to the waters of Lake Michigan, then coasted along its western shore. For weeks the refugees lived on roots, nuts, and wild garlic which they grubbed from under the snow blanket of early winter. In the bitter cold, the jagged ice slashed their moccasins to ribbons and they were forced to cut Father Gabriel's old beaver cloak into strips to bind their feet. A voyageur strayed from the party and survived in the woods for ten days by melting down a pewter plate to make bullets and using a live coal to replace his missing gunflint. Tonti fell dangerously ill and his legs puffed up alarmingly. One of his companions was so hungry that he tried boiling and eating pieces of leather cut from an Indian shield; next day he was suffering so badly from stomach cramps that Tonti had to call a halt. In the last stages of exhaustion their luck finally turned; a band of friendly Indians discovered them and brought the emaciated survivors to the mission station at Green Bay.

The following autumn Tonti rejoined La Salle, who had seen the ravages of the Iroquois invasion and given up all hope of ever seeing Tonti alive again. Then in the summer of 1682 they made the historic first navigation of the Mississippi to its mouth on the Gulf of Mexico. There Tonti added his name to the procès-verbal by which La Salle claimed the entire Mississippi valley for Louis the Magnificent.

The next year while La Salle returned to France to make arrangements for his ill-fated Louisiana colony, Tonti stayed behind in the Illinois country. His task was to establish and hold a French settlement that would secure this pivot area for the Mississippi empire. It was a considerable undertaking; Tonti had not only to win the Illinois to his side, but had to fend off determined attacks from his Canadian rivals and the officials in Montreal who did not like to see a semi-autonomous colony arising in the heartland. To make matters worse, the English were becoming a real threat. They were ruthlessly inciting the Iroquois Confederacy to attack all outlying French settlements and were backing their word with bribes of guns, ammunition, powder, and rum. The latter was particularly effective, as the Indians had acquired a craving for strong liquor of any kind and British rum undersold the more expensive (and better) French brandy.

For his stronghold on the Illinois Tonti went back to the natural fortress of Starved Rock overlooking the Illinois River. The place took its name from an earlier episode when a band of Illinois Indians had been trapped on top of the rock by a Potawatomi war party. Rather than surrender, the Illinois had preferred to starve to death. It was an excellent site. The rock rose up from the water's edge in a sheer cliff 150 feet high. On two other sides were dizzy precipices, and only from the landward approach was there any access to the flat crest where Tonti established his position, Fort St. Louis of the Illinois. Trenches were dug for the foundations, tree trunks trimmed and planted as a rampart, loopholes cut, and saplings interwoven between the uprights. A sturdy gateway was constructed, powder and shot brought in, a watch tower raised, and later, small cannon were added. Tonti even designed a wooden contrivance that would allow defenders to hoist water from the river in times of siege.

Then the Italian began to populate his domain. He invited the Illinois, the Miamis, the Chouanons, and all those who would pledge allegiance to Sieur de la Salle and the French Crown to come to Fort St. Louis and set up their cabins, shacks, tepees, and wigwams in the shelter of the fort. Using La Salle's authority, Tonti gave to French settlers grants of land complete with rights of hunting, fishing, dovecote, fortification, and low justice. The newcomers were also given permission to trade with the Indians on the condition that they did their business at the fort and nowhere else. Voyageurs were signed on; their mission was to seek out the fur-trapping tribes of the dim interior and barter for peltries. Tonti agreed to furnish canoe, merchandise,

[177]

and weapons; the voyageur brought back the furs and the profit was divided equally. Other *engagés* were hired to run the canoe link with Montreal, taking furs out and bringing supplies in. One bill of lading for a canoe arriving at the fort in 1688 included a writing desk—awkward cargo to carry across the portages and a menace to the delicately balanced birchbark hull. Indians journeyed to the Illinois from as far away as the borders of Spain's Mexican colonies. At Starved Rock the aborigines exchanged their furs and skins for trinkets, cloth, bright red blankets, muskets, powder and shot, beads, knives, paint, hatchets, tools, musket flints, needles and thread, bacon, bread, tobacco, brandy, and nests of "kettles," as the cooking pots were called. The savages even relied on the French to supply them with arrowheads. Not all the brandy reached the natives; some of it went down French throats, for, as one Canadian officer explained, "a drink of brandy after a meal seems necessary in order to cook the bilious meats and the crudities they leave in the stomach." The price of everything from brandy to writing quills was calculated in beaver skins: one large buffalo hide was valued at two beavers; a small buffalo hide at one beaver. Transactions between one Frenchman and another were also computed in terms of beaver pelts; when Oliver Morel de la Durantaye, an officer in the Carignan regiment, had his gun repaired by Tonti's armorer, his bill came to "eleven beavers," and a blanket he purchased at the commissary cost him "six beavers."

Life at Fort St. Louis was never dull. No one knew what would happen from day to day—fistfight, childbirth, or theft. Indians from outlandish tribes emerged cautiously from the forests and strangely painted canoes grated on the shingle of the landing beach. In March of 1684 a strong Iroquois war party attacked the fort, and despite their natural defenses, the garrison was hard pressed. Three times the savages stormed against the palisades and three times Tonti and his men beat off the attack. There were casualties on both sides and for a few days the Iroquois threw a blockade around

Starved Rock before withdrawing to their forest cantons. But even with Iroquois war parties hovering in the background, the Frenchmen, half-breeds, and friendly Indians at the Rock shrugged off the ever-present dangers and went about their business. Scouts kept watch on the Iroquois war trails and Tonti maintained his defenses in good repair, knowing that he could expect little help from the colonists in the St. Lawrence valley.

The Italian kept up a running battle with the authorities in Quebec and Montreal who wanted to close down the fort on the Illinois. Tonti's legal right to maintain a settlement in the interior was questionable, and as far as French officialdom was concerned, the events at Starved Rock were highly irregular and a disgrace. The Montrealers were shocked by the happy-go-lucky attitude of the backwoodsmen who were "all young men without any means of cultivating the soil; every eight days they marry squaws after the Indian fashion of that country, whom they purchase from the parents at the expense of the merchants. These fellows, pretending to be independent and masters of their distant lands, everything is in disorder. This year ten plotted to go off to the English and conduct them to the Mississippi." Complaints like these were posted to France aboard almost every ship that crossed the North Atlantic. Sometimes the criticisms had their effect and orders went out from the Court "officially" relieving Tonti of his command, and "officially" Fort St. Louis was abandoned. But it took more than an order signed thousands of miles away in Versailles to root out a settlement which was so conveniently situated for the fur trade. While the price of peltries remained high, Tonti's home on the Illinois survived; it did not decline until constant hunting, trapping, and trading creamed off the supply of furs which was its life blood. Tonti centered his efforts on the Illinois for almost twenty years, dominating the commerce of the great central valley with his energy, experience, and force of character.

These two decades changed Tonti. The strict young officer who came to Canada with La Salle turned into a grim frontiersman and a hard-working entrepreneur. Tonti was only moderately successful at making money and he failed to amass the fortune he desired. It was as an Indian fighter that he made his mark. The subaltern who trimmed the fragments of his smashed hand at Libisso was not squeamish in his dealings with the Indians. Tonti had seen or heard of too many massacres, tortures, acts of cannibalism, burnings at the stake, and other cruelties to believe in the idea of the "noble savage." Europeans were accustomed in their own continent to public hangings, grisly executions, and bloody tortures; in North America there was no reason for Tonti to treat the Indians gently when they expected to receive the same punishment that they would inflict on anyone else. By modern standards Tonti was excessively harsh and tyrannical in his dealings with the savages, but it would have been surprising if, in twenty-five years of living among the tribes, the Italian were not affected by the everyday bestialities around him. Several times Tonti was captured by the Indians and came close to being burned alive or scalped; once he was almost killed in a poison attempt on his life. After several experiences of this kind, Tonti had no scruples about fighting back under the same dirty rules. He allowed his Illinois allies to torture their captives, burn, and eat them. When two of his men were captured and killed by Indians, Tonti shot down twelve members of the offending tribe in reprisal. On another occasion, when accompanying a French military expedition against the Iroquois, the Italian demanded the execution of an Iroquois slave who was making a nuisance of himself by reviling the French. When his fellow officers refused to have the slave shot out of hand, Tonti was most indignant, and even more enraged when the Indian escaped to warn his tribe of the impending attack.

On the other hand, Tonti could never be accused of underestimating the Indians. He respected their bravery, traditions, and treachery, and he knew a great deal about all three from personal experience. Indeed, as the years went by, Tonti became more Indian and less European. He realized that if he were to deal successfully with the aborigines of the continent, he had to adopt their customs and talk their language. The proof of his success was the awe in which the natives held "Iron Hand"; they believed that he was terrifying as an enemy and honest as an ally. The Iroquois feared and shunned him, while the timid Illinois were prepared to fight under his leadership, sending out war parties at his request. It was indicative of Tonti's knowledge and understanding of the Indians that before he led his savages to battle, he invited them to a "dog feast," which culminated in the warriors' devouring the raw heart of a dog to give them courage for the coming fight. Tonti was brave, loyal, and realistic. Handicapped by the isolation of his post at Starved Rock, he knew that it would be fatal to let the Indians become too familiar with his weakness and he refused to let them take any liberties for fear that they would get the upper hand. His attitude is summed up by a report which he wrote for Governor Frontenac, who wanted to know what steps Tonti had taken to curb the Iroquois menace. In his report Tonti stated in a matter-of-fact tone that during their six years at the fort the Illinois, under his instigation, had sent our numerous raiding forces; these raiders had killed or captured of the Iroquois, 334 men and boys, 111 women and girls. The tally was witnessed by the Jesuit Father Jacques Gravier, dispatched to Frontenac, and forwarded in due course to Paris where it was carefully filed away for the attention of the minister. Tonti was honest about his treatment of the Indians and at a time when the French government was shipping Iroquois prisoners off to Toulon to pull oars in the war galleys, there were few people who thought that the Italian was unduly unjust or brutal toward the natives.

When he was not commanding the fort on the Illinois or campaigning against the Iroquois, Tonti was traveling. By now the canoe trips to Montreal were a routine matter and the Italian was looking south toward the Mississippi delta. He believed in La Salle's idea of a southern exit for the furs and buffalo hides of the Mississippi valley and he felt that he could make the dream come true. Besides, he had promised his captain that he would meet him at the mouth of the river when La Salle's colonizing squadron reached the delta. In the spring of 1686 Tonti took twenty-five Frenchmen, five Illinois, and four Shawnees down the main river to the Gulf. But La Salle was many miles away on the Texas coast and there was no sign of a Louisiana colony. The pillar with the king's arms, which he and La Salle had set up on the beach four years earlier, had been knocked down by the waves; Tonti had it re-erected out of reach of the tide and sent canoes east and west to look for La Salle. But his scouts came back with nothing to report and Tonti reluctantly returned upstream to the Illinois country. He left behind a letter for La Salle saying that he had descended the river to look for his patron and would try to come back as soon as possible. This letter Tonti gave to the Indians of the delta with instructions that they were to deliver it to the white man who came in "the house that walked on water." Fourteen years later when Le Moyne d'Iberville sailed into the mouth of the Mississippi to found a new colony for France, an aged Indian chieftain in a coat of blue French broadcloth carefully handed over the letter to the visitors.

Late in 1689, by which time he had heard of La Salle's death, Tonti again went down the Mississippi at his own expense in an attempt to rescue the survivors at Fort St. Louis of Texas. It was a long difficult journey which took ten months of futile effort. Seven days' march away from the abandoned settlement at Matagorda Bay, Tonti's voyageurs deserted and he was forced to turn back. It was a bitter disappointment; not only was his captain dead and the "Great Plan" crushed beyond hope, but Tonti had sunk his savings in the colonizing venture.

Searching for the vital trade that would sustain his Illinois settlement, Tonti made two more trips down the Mississippi, making contact with friendly tribes and establishing trading posts; once he went upriver to the country of the Sioux Indians. But the tide of colonial progress was turning against his efforts. Count Frontenac, after a brief reappearance as governor of New France, died, and Tonti lost the only ally whose authority and influence could stem the flood of complaints from merchants who were jealous of his fur-trading operations. In Paris Louis XIV's advisers finally made up their minds to consolidate France's possessions in North America by concentrating the colonial population in towns and cities. Tonti's far-flung network of forts and trading stations had no place in their schemes, and the Italian began to feel the full weight of one royal edict after another forbidding settlement in the interior, refusing trade permits, cutting down the number of licensed voyageurs, withdrawing troops, and ordering the wilderness posts to be abandoned. To make matters worse, the quantity and quality of furs being brought into Fort St. Louis and Tonti's other warehouses dropped badly. The Indians had not only killed off the best fur-bearing animals, but as the hunters ranged farther and farther southward, the texture of the furs was inferior to the sleek winter pelts of the north. The Indians had also discovered how to speed up the "greasing" of the fur which made it much more valuable on the European market. In the early days of the trade the Indians had worn the animal skins, fur side against the body, until the guard hair on the pelts picked up a glossy sheen from the oils and grease on the human skin. Now the Indians cunningly counterfeited the greasing process by rubbing in animal fat by hand. While the profits from the fur trade continued to fall, the cost of running his trading posts was rising. Tonti had spent large sums in his search for La Salle and the Crown never repaid him for his expenses in fighting the Iroquois. In a letter to his brother he wrote: "What to do? There is no more trade since it has been forbidden by the Court. . . . All the voyages I have made for the success of the country have ruined me." As a last resort he applied for a royal grant to trade at the junction of the Ohio and the Mississippi, but his request was refused.

Short of money, starved of supplies, and curbed by regulations, Tonti at last recognized the hopelessness of his position and admitted defeat. In 1702 he set off down the Mississippi for the sixth and last time. With a handful of loyal followers he paddled to the delta which he and La Salle had discovered. There, at the new French colony of Louisiana, he offered his services to the commandant, Pierre le Moyne d'Iberville. His offer was accepted, and for the next two years Tonti continued to serve France, advising the settlers and campaigning against the Indians of the lower river. Then, in the summer of 1704, the supply ship *Pelican* arrived with a cargo of marriageable young women for the colonists. The *Pelican* also brought with her the deadly germs of yellow fever. In the epidemic that followed, several settlers contracted the disease and died; among them was Henry de Tonti.

At the time of his death Tonti was sixty-four years old and had spent more than half his active life in the New World. Disappointed and unwanted in Europe, he had chosen to take the chances of a pioneer in the unknown west and in the course of a hard and energetic life he had made his mark on the great central valley of the continent. He did not look back wistfully to France, his adopted fatherland, but by inclination and outlook was the first truly "American" explorer of the Mississippi. Almost 150 years later another Italian came to explore the great river but he never acknowledged his countryman who had preceded him; by then Tonti had sunk into obscurity as "the faithful lieutenant."

8

The Mendacious Friar

DURING THE LAST YEARS OF TONTI'S LIFE THE MIS-
sissippi finally emerged from the shadows of geographical ignorance. Repeated journeys up and down the
river by French voyageurs established its general course
and direction from the mouth of the Wisconsin to the delta.
Their discoveries percolated back to Europe, where the royal
cartographers busily assembled reasonably accurate maps of
the Father of Waters. It was true that many of the large
tributary streams like the Missouri and the Arkansas were
still unexplored, but these would be filled in later; the main
river was known, exploited, and regularly navigated.

Paradoxically, the European politicians failed to use this
new information. Acting privately, a London physician
named Daniel Coxe went so far as to dispatch a ship to seize
the delta, put settlers ashore, and wait for reinforcements.
The English were too late. When the sloop groped her way
up the main distributary, she was met by Sieur de Bienville,
one of Iberville's lieutenants, who persuaded the English captain to turn back at a place still called English Turn. But apart
from warning off interlopers, the French did little to increase

their head start in the Mississippi valley. The policy, initiated
in Paris, of limiting settlement to the St. Lawrence and the
delta was a disaster. The traders, half-breeds, canoemen,
trappers, and adventurers, who maintained the physical presence of French control along the Mississippi, were cut off and
isolated. The great river, La Salle's natural highway linking
Montreal and the Gulf, was neglected; the central valley slid
back into stagnation, known to French statesmen but ignored.
Gradually the idea of "Louisiana" came to include everything
west and south of the Great Lakes—a vast, torpid area which
would one day be useful when France had enough time and
money to colonize it.

But while government enthusiasm for Louisiana waned,
public interest about the exotic Mississippi valley surged to
new heights. People in Europe, and especially in France,
wanted to know a good deal more about this large slice of the
world's surface which had scarcely been scratched by the
wanderings of a handful of literate travelers. Since 1673
when the publication of the annual Jesuit *Relations* was suspended for reasons of state, the public had been deprived of
its main source of information on the climate, terrain, flora,
fauna, and inhabitants of North America which the Jesuit
missionaries had zealously reported as they probed deeper
into the heart of the continent. Armchair travelers in Europe
wanted up-to-date details. They were famished for descriptions of these endless prairies, giant rivers, impenetrable forests, weird animals, and outlandish barbarians. Café gossips
bartered fascinating tidbits culled from official government
publications and these served to whet people's appetites. It
was common knowledge that soldiers, Indian traders, and
priests had been exploring the backlands; now the European
public demanded to hear their wondrous tales of valor and
determination.

The publishers and booksellers of Europe responded
nobly to the demand. By their efforts a whole new race of
travel writers sprang into existence. Some of the authors had
never even crossed the Atlantic or left their firesides; a few

had been to America but never wandered farther than the taverns of Quebec; a mere smattering had seen genuine Indians. It did not matter. Authors and publishers plotted together to decide what the public wanted to buy, and tailored their books accordingly. The new travelogues did not need to be truthful; the chronic reticence of the French government to release official details of their colonies kept the public ignorant and this helped the publishers and writers deceive their audience. Very few people knew what Louisiana was really like and those who did know the facts seldom bothered to speak up for fear of ridicule or government displeasure. The field was left wide open for the profiteers and they made the most of it. Numerous books poured from the presses, claiming to be "Descriptions of Louisiana." Some were written under pseudonyms; a few were anonymous; and others, like an account which was put out under Tonti's name, sailed under false colors, never having been near the pen of the supposed author. The most successful books were those written by real travelers who returned from "Louisiana" and then published a story which was embroidered with exactly those details their readers wanted to hear about. The public had a craving for tales of derring-do, of bizarre tribes, and of the incredible. They snapped up anything that tickled their palate; one author above all others pleased them—Father Hennepin, a Flemish missionary, who produced a series of best sellers that played a key role in molding the popular idea of the conditions and aborigines of "Louisiana."

Between 1683 and 1698 Louis Hennepin published three versions of his American travels, called, respectively, *A Description of Louisiana, newly discovered to the South-West of New France; A New Discovery of a Vast Country in America, extending above four thousand miles between New France and New Mexico;* and *A New Voyage in a Country Larger than Europe.* All three books were colorful concoctions of myth, fact, and imagination; all of them were enormously popular. The *Description,* which first appeared in Paris, ran quickly through three editions and was translated into Dutch, German, and Italian. The *Discovery* was the top seller of the trilogy, appearing in no less than fourteen versions; seven French, four Dutch, a German translation, a Spanish abridgment, and an edition in English. The *New Voyage* also had an international sale with seven editions spread between France, Holland, Germany, and England. As his books rattled off the presses Hennepin's reputation spread throughout Europe. He was acclaimed as the leading authority on the Indians of North America, the navigation of the Mississippi, and the exploration of the continent. He became a man of importance, consulted by the British government on their prospects for colonizing the delta, and held in good repute by his masters in Rome. The worthy friar's books were avidly collected, read, and solemnly discussed. Men of letters, science, and distinction were profuse in their praise for this indomitable and learned missionary. Yet it was all a gigantic hoax. Father Louis Hennepin was a liar with a plainly odious personality whose writings were largely stolen from other authors and who was known throughout Canada as a *grand menteur*. His books were top-heavy with obvious inaccuracies, slanders, flattery, and boasts. To anyone who had the wit to stop and think about his statements, they were a tissue of lies thinly spread over a framework of truth.

The secret of Father Hennepin's success lay in his genius for conjuring up plausible and attractive situations. Like all good liars, he was careful to include a strong element of popular knowledge in what he wrote. As a result his readers recognized those glimpses of reality on which he based his tales; from there Hennepin, who had a lively imagination, led his audience on a wild goose chase of fantasy. An exaggeration here and an embroidery there—these touches sent his rather ordinary narrative soaring into the realms of high adventure. His readers loved it. They liked to learn of bold heroes and strange peoples, so Louis Hennepin obliged them by transmuting his brief Canadian career into a breath-taking account of an intrepid priest facing impossible obstacles, of brave voyageurs battling through incredible difficulties in a land where nature had run riot, and strange savages followed bizarre and barbarous customs. There were clear-cut heroes and villains in Hennepin's Louisiana, neatly arranged in black and white. On the one hand were the forces of evil made up of Jesuits (Hennepin was a Recollet of the Franciscan order), the Iroquois, the English traders, and anyone who had annoyed Hennepin or called him a liar. This group included Henry de Tonti who had snubbed Hennepin during the building of the *Griffin*; the missionary retaliated by accusing Tonti of cowardice and the death of Father Gabriel. Ranged against the wicked stood a courageous band—La Salle, the Recollets or "gray gowns," Governor Frontenac, and, of course, Hennepin himself, the bravest of the brave fearlessly describing the struggle for power in the Canadian backwoods.

It was a shrewd move to line himself up with La Salle, for Hennepin succeeded in attracting the public's sympathy for that unhappy figure, and turned that sympathy to his own uses, basking in the reflected glory. Hennepin had accompanied La Salle on his trip to establish the Illinois post, playing a minor role on that expedition, though in his diary the friar blandly insisted that when decisions had to be made, the initiative came from "Monsieur La Salle and I." Of the thirty or more other members of the team there is seldom any mention. This familiarity with all that La Salle did or thought would have enraged La Salle if he had found out what Hennepin was relating in Europe about their close association, but Hennepin took care to publish his books when La Salle was safely out of range. In reality, La Salle thought Hennepin of no consequence, disliked him, and had few illusions about his character. He warned his colleagues against the priest: "It is necessary to know him somewhat, for he will not fail to exaggerate everything; it is his character . . . and he speaks more in keeping with what he wishes than with what he knows."

Hennepin's version of his relationship with La Salle was only a minor fiction when compared to his treatment of the geography of Louisiana. Here Hennepin was at his best.

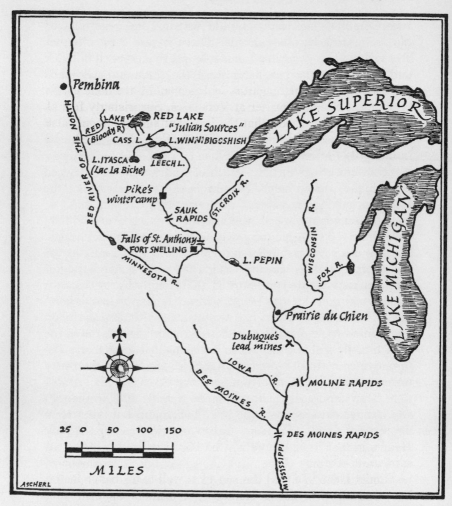

Glibly he filled his stories with one lie after another; he painted glowing pictures of the natural wonders—Niagara Falls, which are now 167 feet tall at their highest point on the United States side, became a "cataract of waterfall beyond belief. The river, here only an eighth of a league wide, is extremely deep in places. So swift is the current above the huge falls that none of the animals which try to cross it there can withstand it. They are all swept away and plunged downward *more than five hundred feet*." His descriptions of the Indians wandered even farther from the truth; he loved to put speeches into their mouths which would have done credit to the most elegant courtier at Versailles. Surprisingly few of his readers found it odd that the ignorant savages should use the same phrases and titles among themselves that were heard in the Hall of Mirrors.

It would be unfair not to allow that Father Hennepin (or his publisher) had an eye for the unusual and coupled it with a flair for putting his observations into attractive words. Here and there are snatches of prose which sparkle; they far out-shine the leaden-footed efforts of some of the more truthful travelogues. For example, when Father Hennepin is describ-ing the Iroquois, he tells his reader that "never did Venetian senators bear themselves more grandly or speak with more pride than the old men of the Iroquois in the assembly." Again, when he mentions the winter life of the Sioux of the upper Mississippi, he says that "the little children are so hard-ened to cold that in mid-winter they run naked through the snow and wallow in it like little pigs." Phrases like these are embedded like nuggets throughout his chapters; his readers were captivated. They knew that these had to be the words of a veteran traveler who in truth had visited Louisiana. At the same time they failed to realize that the qualities which make a man a rolling stone did not necessarily make him an accurate reporter.

Louis Hennepin was the son of a well-to-do baker in the Low Country province of Hainault, then under Spanish rule. When he was about twenty years old Hennepin applied to join the Recollet division of the Order of St. Francis and was sent to study for the priesthood at Bethune. There, by coincidence, his superior was the same Father Gabriel de la Ribourde who was later clubbed to death in the Illinois country. Finishing his studies in 1666, Hennepin was ordained a friar and for the next seven years worked as a missionary priest in the towns along the Channel coast. He proudly told his readers that while at Calais and Dunkirk he preferred to spend his nights hiding behind the doors of seamen's taverns, eavesdropping for tales of distant lands, until the stench and stale tobacco smoke made him retch.

When Louis XIV invaded the Low Countries, Friar Hennepin found himself pressed into service as a chaplain to the troops, burying the dead, taking confessions, and giving the last rites. Finally in 1675, he persuaded his masters to send him overseas to the foreign missions in New France. There he spent three years preaching to the "tame" Indians of the lower St. Lawrence, got to know La Salle, visited Fort Frontenac, and in 1678 wangled the chance to accompany La Salle's western expedition.

Up to that moment in his career, Louis Hennepin had not done anything unusual as a missionary priest working in Canada. It was a short period of six months—from the early spring of 1689 to July of the same year—which gave him his chance to shine as the gallant missionary-explorer who played the leading role in his books. Toward the end of February, La Salle, who was setting up the Illinois post, decided to send a small patrol to scout the upper reaches of the Mississippi. The expedition consisted of three men—two experienced voyageurs, Michel Accau and Picard du Gay, and a priest, Louis Hennepin. Their task was to navigate the upper river by canoe, report on the feasibility of using sailing vessels for trade with the north, and make contact with the Indians. Accau was to command the party, and Hennepin could proselytize among the tribes if there were time, which was unlikely. It was Tonti's opinion that La Salle sent Hennepin off with the expedition in order to get rid of the meddling friar who was making a nuisance of himself on the Illinois.

The three scouts left by canoe on February 29, and paddled down to the junction of the Illinois River with the Mississippi. There they were delayed by drifting ice for a few days before it was safe enough to work their way up against the current on the main river. It was an uneventful trip until, somewhere in the present state of Wisconsin—there is no way of knowing the exact place—they fell in with a large flotilla of river Sioux who were coming downstream to raid the Miami Indians. The Frenchmen were stupid enough to inform the Sioux warriors that they were wasting their time, as the Miami had already taken refuge at the French stronghold on the Illinois. The Sioux were understandably annoyed and the war party decided to seize the French, their canoe, and its contents as a consolation prize. This took place on April 11, and for the next three months Hennepin and the two voyageurs were ignobly shunted up and down the river by their captors, who considered the white men something of a curiosity. Until his capture Hennepin had been boasting of his strength and physical prowess; once he fell into the hands of the Indians he wailed loudly about the agonies he endured while living their way of life. Before long he had so irritated the two voyageurs that they refused to travel in the same canoe with him. Hennepin was relegated to the worst vessel in the fleet under the orders of an aged crone; while the friar glumly bailed the decrepit canoe with a bark dish, he found time to marvel how the old hag managed to discipline the only other passenger, a small child, by thumping it on the head, between strokes, with her paddle.

During the last week of July Tonti's voyageur cousin, the resourceful Sieur Duluth, heard about the prisoners and came down from the north with five soldiers to rescue Hennepin and his companions. Reading between the lines, it seems that the Sioux had already grown tired of the friar whose never-ending complaints and lectures had ceased to be amusing, and they were only too glad to surrender him. Immediately Hennepin's spirits rose; before long he was telling the experienced Duluth how to handle the Indians. Duluth escorted Hennepin to Lake Michigan and sent him on to Michilimackinac. By 1682 the friar was back in France.

Hennepin's real achievements can be numbered on the fingers of one hand: he had explored the Mississippi from the mouth of the Wisconsin to the Falls of St. Anthony near the junction of the Minnesota River; he had named these falls after his patron saint, St. Anthony of Padua; he was then escorted by the Sioux through the previously unknown marshlands around Mille Lacs in the present state of Minnesota; he was one of the first people to live among the Sioux; and he wrote the first popular description of Niagara Falls.

It is a worthy but not spectacular list. However, by the time Hennepin got back to France, he had puffed his achievements into a great froth of importance and heroism. His first report, the *Description* of 1683, did not stray too far from the facts. He restrained himself to writing about La Salle's expedition, described the Canadian countryside, and gave some account of his own captivity with the Sioux. He also grossly overstated his own importance; failed to mention that Michel Accau, not himself, was the leader of the side trip; slandered the Jesuits at every opportunity; and gave out a barrage of incorrect details. But on the whole the *Description* was based on events which actually had taken place and Hennepin's story contained a good deal of fact. And well it should: Hennepin had stolen the bulk of his material from other sources, including La Salle's official account of the Illinois trip.

There is something cloak-and-dagger about the *Description*, which at first glance defies analysis. It is very different from the later books that Hennepin wrote, and there is a hint of mystery in the speed with which it was published. Soon after his return to France, Hennepin dropped out of sight into some secluded retreat where he worked on the draft of his book. One of his superiors must have agreed to this highly irregular course of action for a junior friar, who by rights should have been put straight back in harness. There is also the puzzle of the speed of publication. It is as though the *Description* was rushed to the printers in a frantic hurry in order to meet a deadline. What this deadline was, it is difficult to say; there is a possibility that the *Description* was in fact a piece of propaganda. Hennepin comes out so strongly in favor of La Salle's "Great Plan" and is so overwhelmingly pro-Franciscan at the expense of the Jesuits, that the book smells of a plot to discredit the established religious structures in Canada. Again and again there are paragraphs in which the work of the Recollets is praised; the Indians are made to say how much they prefer the "gray gowns" who do not rob them of their beaver pelts, and no chance is lost to tell the world of the devotion of these selfless Franciscans. One must remember too that La Salle's expedition was on the point of sailing for the delta, apparently with every hope for success. This being the case, there is reason to believe that the *Description* was designed to drum up support for the Recollets as the natural heirs to La Salle's empire, the trusted allies of the visionary who by their earlier faith in him deserved to be allocated the central valley as their exclusive right. If La Salle had succeeded in planting his colony, perhaps the *Description* would have persuaded the Court to send only Franciscans to preach in the new lands. Whatever the outcome, Hennepin could well have received undercover help in preparing his book, and if so, he was probably encouraged to make it as colorful and readable a work of propaganda as possible.

Whether or not the *Description* was propaganda, it sold well. Hennepin was rewarded with positions of responsibility within the Church hierarchy and for a while he thrived. Then his native temperament got the better of him. He made enemies, he quarreled easily, and he became embroiled in theological disputes with the Jansenites. People began to criticize his book and doubt some of his taller stories. Step by step he fell into disfavor until finally he found himself back in the Low Countries. Then from Utrecht he wrote his second book, the *New Discovery*. It was an eye-opener. Fourteen years after publishing the *Description* he had a lot more to say about his experiences in America. He began by refuting all the critics of his earlier book, telling them that they were too provincial if they failed to believe his stories. Next, Hennepin let fly with some startling revelations which he "did not think fit to publish in his *Louisiana*." To begin with, the phenomenal natural wonders were all paraded again, only this time they had all grown like irrigated crops under a desert sun. The height of Niagara jumped from over 500 feet to "more than 600 feet"; the Sioux war fleet, originally thirty-three canoes, now suddenly swelled to fifty canoes; the Falls of St. Anthony put on another ten feet in height; and a six-foot snake which had appeared in the *Description* had profited from the time-lapse to add another couple of feet to its length. Furthermore, Father Hennepin, who had previously appeared as the second most important man in the west after La Salle, now emerged as a combination of Daniel Boone, St. Francis, and Marco Polo. In one of the biggest travel lies ever perpetrated, Hennepin claimed that he and his two faithful voyageurs had not only beaten La Salle to the Gulf, but they had been the first white men to paddle a canoe on the Mississippi. According to Hennepin's new story, Joliet and Marquette had never reached the river.

The magnitude of the lie was impressive; unfortunately Hennepin did not match its sheer size with an equal amount of ingenuity. He opened fire by revealing that one day, while sailing a canoe with Joliet on the St. Lawrence, the famous explorer had confessed that his Mississippi journey was a fraud engineered by the Jesuits and their supporters to gain prestige. From this outrageous beginning Hennepin went on to say that in the time between his departure from the Illinois with the two voyageurs and their capture by the Sioux, the three of them had paddled down to the delta and back, thereby preceding La Salle by two years. To substantiate his story Hennepin produced a point-by-point itinerary of his journey to the sea. The details were extraordinarily accurate. They agreed in every way with La Salle's description of the same trip. The lower river was faithfully portrayed—tribes, tributaries, villages, oxbows, meanders—they were all there just as La Salle had found them two years later as he plodded down in the wake of the intrepid friar. Unfortunately, they were there *exactly* as La Salle found them, right down to the daily campsites and the thudding drums. Even some of the native speeches were much the same; apparently the Indian chiefs had found little new to say to La Salle which they had not already said to Hennepin. The deceit should have been obvious to every reader. Hennepin had brazenly filched the entire story of La Salle's expedition to the delta and had written it up as his own. In all the history of plagiarism there have been few such blatant thefts as Hennepin's tale of his "first," the discovery of the Mississippi and its mouth. Even though La Salle was long dead, the forgery was so crude that it ought to have been spotted by the first well-read critic, yet the *New Discovery* was a runaway best seller. Copy after copy was sold while the presses churned out more editions, and despite the glaring mistakes in his narrative Father Hennepin was acclaimed a great explorer, a man of steadfast courage and sterling worth.

Looking back on the widespread success of this fraud, it is difficult to understand from a twentieth-century viewpoint how Hennepin's readers could have been so gullible. It appears that almost no one stopped to think seriously about his statements. Even the simplest mathematics would have disposed of his claim to have journeyed down to the mouth of the river in the short time available. Allowing for the fact that the European public did not know that the Mississippi ran at least a six-knot current at high-water stages, there was still no possible way in which Hennepin and his two canoemen could have covered the distance he claimed in his book. It amounted to nearly three thousand miles which had to be completed in forty-seven days. To make matters worse, several days were lost, according to the journal, in parleying with the Indians. La Salle and his men had taken several months to travel down to the Gulf and back only as far as the Illinois; Hennepin had much less time to return a great deal farther upstream to the land of the Sioux. In addition, although he did a lot of preaching, Hennepin did very little paddling; such work was best left to his sturdy voyageurs. They must have been a fantastic pair. If one were to believe Hennepin's claims for his paddlers, they performed better than an Olympic rowing eight. Paddling from sunrise to dusk, day after day, with barely a mouthful of food, they fought off Indian attacks, outdistanced runners on the bank, and sped upstream at over twelve knots, a most respectable pace for a modern high-power river cruiser.

Hennepin's mistakes did not end with the superhuman qualities of his voyageurs. He also blundered into a dreadful tangle with dates and distances. For no apparent reason his daily mileage swung wildly between 32 and 140 miles, while the over-all length of the river was subjected to so many alterations and corrections that it stretched and contracted like a huge coiled spring. If this were not enough, Hennepin juggled his dates so preposterously that he finished up with Easter Day one month out of its proper place—hardly the mistake expected from a Recollet friar.

Yet despite all these obvious errors, Father Hennepin got away with it. He successfully hoodwinked most of his audience. To be sure, one or two people saw through the deception, and in Louisiana Tonti dashed off an angry letter from Fort Mississippi, in which he fumed: "I do not know how Father Hennepin had the boldness to lie so impudently in his account. He was insupportable to the late M. de la Salle and all of M. de la Salle's men." But most of those who were in a position to expose Hennepin did nothing, and for fifty years Hennepin's book became a standard text on North America. Such gross lies as the height of Niagara Falls found their way into schoolroom geographies, and learned societies portentously quoted the friar as a sound authority. Encouraged by the success of his second book, Hennepin tried his hand at a third work, *The New Voyage.* This time he merely plundered the available (and true) accounts of La Salle's expedition to Texas, embroidering his own version with such implausible details as the fact that when La Salle fell to the ground with two musket balls in the brain, he had enough life left in him to turn to the accompanying priest and ask for absolution. Nor could Hennepin resist the temptation to underline his role as an "authority" on America by adding a few personal postscripts: he delivered several very trite and in-

coherent homilies on such well-rubbed themes as the benefits
of a Northwest passage (if it were found) and sought to
instruct his peers in their relations with the Indians. This
third monument to the plagiarist's craft completed the trilogy
and followed the previous books as a best seller. One mis-
guided London publisher went so far as to combine the *New
Voyage* with the *New Discovery* in a handsome double edition. It seemed that the public could not have enough of the
lying friar's products.

Even taking into account the ready market for Hennepin's
books, it is clear that something more is needed to turn a
Recollet priest into a plagiarist and a liar. Father Hennepin is
so important in the history of Mississippi exploration that it is
worth pausing to consider the character of this extraordinary
man and the reasons for his extravagant claims. Somewhere in
the combination of personality, circumstances, and opportunity is the formula for his role as a charlatan.

There is no doubt that circumstances played a large part
in determining Louis Hennepin's career. To begin with, he
was living in a world of intrigue. Born in the Low Countries,
he was torn between allegiance to Spain or to France. With
reasonably acute perception for the swing of political fortune,
he aligned himself at an early stage with the French and took
pains to curry favor with Paris. However, this did not end his
dilemma. The French Court seethed with conflicting factions
and pressure groups; it was difficult enough for an experienced courtier to weave his path through the plots and
counter-strategems at Versailles. When Louis Hennepin returned from Canada and chose to dabble in politics, he was
joining a game which he was not equipped, mentally or by
experience, to win. It was all very well for him to publish the
Description in support of the Recollet claim to do missionary
work in the Mississippi valley, but by showing his sympathies
so openly he came under attack from the antireligious groups
at Court as well as the Jesuits who were smarting under the
sting of the friar's gibes. Hennepin aroused too many enemies, and he was neither powerful nor subtle enough to fight

back with any real hope of success. His only weapon was his pen and he used it wildly. He was forced not only to stick by the mistakes he made in the *Description*, which one critic described as "Dom Henpin's wretched book," but to heap on additional claims and exaggerations in his later works in order to promote his political ambitions. When the *New Voyage* and *New Discovery* were written, Hennepin's fortunes were at a very low ebb. His enemies had brought about his disgrace, he was discredited and desperately short of cash. The two new books were intended to restore his status at all costs. It is impossible to say whether the sale of the books brought in much money or whether the publisher took most of the profits; but as far as his political ambitions were concerned, Hennepin failed to improve his fate as a semi-exile. He failed because of a naïve political blunder. At Utrecht he suddenly switched sides. After years of behaving as a loyal French subject, the friar decided to throw his lot in with the English. He publicly dedicated his second and third books to William III, wrote a letter criticizing Louis XIV, who, he felt, had failed to reward him adequately, and volunteered to assist the British in taking over the Mississippi valley. It was a crashing *faux pas*. Hennepin could scarcely have timed his political somersault more clumsily. William III did not feel secure enough to antagonize Louis by harboring a turncoat or by trespassing on France's Mississippi colonies, and the French King was enraged at Hennepin's double-dealing. The English turned a deaf ear to Hennepin's suggestions, and orders went out from the French minister that Hennepin was to be arrested if he ever set foot in Canada again. Despite all his twisting and turning Hennepin found himself worse off than before. Gloomily he made his way to Rome to lay his case before the Pope and was never heard of again.

But Hennepin's literary concoctions cannot be explained solely by his political maneuvers nor by the eagerness of his readers. The real key to the amazing stories in his books is his personality, which was a jumble of conflicting parts. Hennepin was by no means an out-and-out rogue. In his writings he unconsciously reveals himself as a practical and persistent man; someone, indeed, who had several excellent qualifications to be a backwoods missionary. For instance, in one of his more diffident paragraphs he lets slip the fact that when he entered a hostile Indian village to preach to the savages, he usually made a bee-line for the children, knowing that the Indians overindulged the youngsters; once he had got the spoiled brats on his side, he found it easy to pacify their more suspicious parents. It was an effective, simple technique which the friar was sensible enough to employ. Hennepin is also refreshing in that, unlike Marquette who was always inserting long religious supplications in his reports, he seldom allows himself to be diverted from his narrative by spiritual hankerings. There is a great difference between Marquette and Hennepin. The latter was much more a man of the world than his fellow missionaries. The friar fancied himself as a military strategist and a gourmet. When the "Sieur de la Salle" decides to build a fort, Hennepin is there at his elbow, busily jotting down soldierly notes on defensive ravines, scarps, chevaux-de-frises, parapets, and the like. Having served as chaplain to the forces and at the Channel ports, Hennepin loved to flaunt his military and technical knowledge. His readers were served up snippets of information about the rigging of the *Griffin*, the speed of the current in Lake St. Clair which was "as strong as the tide off Rouen," and the battle tactics of the Iroquois. Even his literary images have a martial flavor—the Indian women "sometimes carry 300 lbs. on their backs, throwing their babies on top of their load, which to them does not seem more of a burden than does a sword to a soldier."

Hennepin is at his most endearing when he talks about food. It seems that he regarded his Canadian tour as a heaven-sent opportunity to experiment with new dishes and he did not hesitate to try anything that looked vaguely edible in this strange new continent. He sampled everything: black squirrels; beaver; native varieties of walnut, plum, chestnut, and apple; berries and wild rice; porcupines; sagamité, the Indian corn mush; geese, swans, turtle doves, wild turkeys, and para-keets. Dried blueberries were "as good as currants" and bear's flesh was "succulent." He pronounced the whitefish from Lake Huron "larger than carp and the best-flavored and most wholesome of any fish in the world," and he was overjoyed to discover he could make passable wine from wild grapes, though this meant laboriously chopping down the trees on which the vines climbed. Father Hennepin thought it worth the effort—the grapes were "big as damson plums," and by storing the wine gourds in cool sand he could make his wine cellar last three and a half months without spoiling, definitely a bonus in that uncivilized land. The gourmandizing friar enjoyed himself hugely as he found satisfaction with almost everything he put in his mouth. Indeed, his bitterest complaint about the Sioux was that as their captive he was not given enough to eat, and he hints darkly that the Indians were sneaking off into the bushes without him in order to gorge themselves on midnight feasts.

One cannot help feeling sorry that with these attractive qualities to his credit, Father Hennepin should have spoiled his image with a number of rather repellent character flaws. He was cursed with an overwhelming desire for a glory far exceeding his capabilities. This personal ambition, coupled with a clacking tongue, proved to be his downfall. His boasting is overweening and repetitive. To read the *New Discovery* is to be told that had it not been for Hennepin's help, La Salle would never had got farther west than Fort Frontenac. According to his own version of the trip, Hennepin saves the expedition time and again. Every week he is either pacifying the Indians, soothing mutinous voyageurs, or volunteering for all the unwanted jobs. At one stage he boasts that he saved La Salle's life when their hut, made of reed mats, caught fire. Hennepin found the door first. On another occasion he had the effrontery to claim that if a missionary in Europe suffered the miseries which he had endured among the Sioux, the priest would be a candidate for sainthood. It is no wonder, in Tonti's phrase, that La Salle found Hennepin "insupportable," and that even his fellow priests could not abide him. Dollier de Casson, superior of the Sulpicians and La Salle's old acquaintance, wrote to his opposite number in the Recollets: "For the sake of our union, [send] no Father Louis [Hennepin], I beg of you!"

Unfortunately Hennepin's failings did not end with his boasting and self-pride, which one might almost forgive as they were so blatant and childish. Unhappily he was also a toady. He suffered from the conviction that large dollops of flattery would smooth away all the obstacles to his advancement. The introduction to his *Description* is cloying. He dedicated the book to Louis XIV and groveled before the Sun King.

"It was with this thought [the glory of God and France's monarch] in mind, Sire, that I undertook the long and difficult journey, unafraid of its grave dangers. I even dare to tell Your Majesty that neither the bloody death of one of my companions, massacred by the Indians [Father Gabriel], nor my captivity of eight months [in fact nearer 3½ months], during which I was so cruelly exposed, was effective to overcome my courage, it having been an abiding consolation . . . to serve a King whose glory and virtue are without limit." He then went on to say how he calmed the Indians by telling them "some of the heroic virtues of Your Most Christian Majesty, of your amazing exploits in conquest, of the happiness and devotion of your subjects." Carried away in his adulation, Hennepin goes on to claim that Louis the Magnificent was destined by God to rule the indigenous people of North America. As proof, he states that when the redskins smoke the pipe of peace they first held it up to the sun, which they "respect, adore and worship," saying "Tchendiouba Louis! meaning Smoke, O Sun! . . . Thus the name of Your Majesty is ever on their lips." Despite the widespread sycophancy of his times, Hennepin's efforts at flattery exceeded the limits of decency and did more harm than good. When one of his shrewder opponents heard that the friar was on his way to Rome, he sarcastically remarked that Hennepin's next volume would probably be dedicated to the Pope.

Poor Hennepin was the victim of his vanity. It ruined his relations with La Salle and Tonti, crumpled his political career, and colored his books with extravaganza. Yet it also produced his popular reputation as a courageous missionary-explorer and gave him his share of glory. The sad thing is that if he had been content to rest on his true laurels, he would have achieved the renown which he craved, without adding the stain of a liar. But there was no chance of this. Louis Hennepin was an ambitious and garrulous peacock. He set out to write his name on the pages of history and the results were not quite as he intended. His early fame lost its luster and became tarnished with notoriety, though he would be happy to know that streets, avenues, and buildings in several towns of the upper Mississippi valley still commemorate his name and deeds.

9

Captain from
Connecticut

F**ATHER** L**OUIS** H**ENNEPIN'S STORY CONTRASTS EF-**
fectively with the case of another liar—Captain Jonathan
Carver, a native of New England who followed the menda-
cious friar on the great river nearly a century later. Both men
were explorers, both wrote about their travels, and both were
untruthful about their American experiences. But while Hennepin deliberately planned to dupe his readers, Captain
Carver became a liar more by accident than by design. As
a result, Carver's travelogue withstood the critics far longer
than Hennepin's more slipshod efforts. While Hennepin's
works were popular with the general public, Carver's book
went one better—it influenced the poets Schiller and Byron;
it was read by Coleridge and Chateaubriand; and it may even
have encouraged President Thomas Jefferson to send Lewis
and Clark on the first transcontinental crossing of the United
States. Oddly enough, Jonathan Carver would have been very
upset if he had foreseen the repercussions of his book; he did
not intend it to mislead his readership.

Captain Carver was not the first Mississippi liar to take up
where Father Hennepin left off. He was preceded by the

Baron Louis-Armand Lahontan, a smooth mountebank, who claimed to have ascended the Mississippi in 1701 and discovered a major tributary, the "River Long." This convenient waterway led the roving baron many leagues to lands inhabited by tribes of "civil" Indians who rejoiced in such names as Eokoros, Esanapes, Gnacsitares, and Mozeemleks. According to Lahontan, these distant natives received him courteously, though always warring among themselves, and he was able to observe and record their customs. In many ways his Indian tribes resemble the strange nations in *Gulliver's Travels*, and they were no more real than Jonathan Swift's creations.

Lahontan's tall stories were made a little more credible than they would at first appear because they were published at a time when French voyageurs, having established the north-south direction of the Mississippi and planted a colony at its mouth, were intrigued by the large tributary rivers which flowed in from the west. Once again the French explorers were years ahead of their rivals. While the English thought that it was a great adventure to cross the Appalachians and enter the eastern half of the Mississippi valley, the French were already trying to take their canoes up such rivers as the Arkansas, the Red River, and the Missouri. In 1714 Louis de St. Denis and twelve other Frenchmen set out from the Louisiana colony, paddled their way up the Red River, and then walked across Texas to the Spanish settlements on the Rio Grande. Their journey was the obvious sequel to La Salle's last trip to get help for Fort St. Louis of Texas and it marked the beginning of thirty-five years of intensive French exploration westward from the spinal column of the Mississippi. By 1750 the French had explored the outlines of the huge belt of country which lies between the Rockies and the central river. Their traders paid regular visits to the Spanish mines in New Mexico, sold firearms to the Comanche and the Apache, and had even persuaded the colonial government to build Fort Orleans some three hundred miles up the Missouri. By exploiting the continent's system of waterways the French had pushed the horizon of discovery to its logical conclusion and, superficially at any rate, it appeared that La Salle's "Great Plan" had come true: from the Falls of St. Anthony to New Orleans there stretched a line of ten forts which commanded all navigation along the main river. Control of the Mississippi, as Frontenac and La Salle had pleaded, made France the real power in America's heartland.

In the farthest north, France's authority was challenged only by the semicircle of English fur stations dotted along the shores of Hudson's Bay. Elsewhere the French knew, or guessed, more about the geography of America than the Spanish and English combined. The day when Hennepin could boast of venturing into the "unknown" headwaters region of the Mississippi was gone; explorations by the Sieur Duluth and a horde of trappers had opened up that area as well. Even the enormously complex relationship of the waterways leading west from Lake Superior had been unraveled by the efforts of the Vérendrye family. In 1743 this extraordinary family had crowned their achievements when one of the sons, Louis-Joseph, penetrated overland to the villages of the Mandan Indians living near the middle Missouri. It was a magnificent endeavor, for it meant that French explorers had reached a point that was three years' travel away from their main base on the St. Lawrence. It meant also that the Mississippi, which had so long featured as the limit of their geographical knowledge, was now by-passed. The next generation of Mississippi explorers would not be investigating the course of the river as part of the unknown frontier; in the future the river travelers would be men who regarded the exploration of the river either as an end in itself or as a preliminary step toward a special ambition.

But it was not France that would provide this new generation of explorers, for the French and Indian Wars had exposed the weakness of her American colonies and the initiative passed to the English. England's victories in the northeast made a mockery of France's claim to the continent's central valley, and although French traders and trappers still made up the majority of white men along the river, the British-Americans were the new masters of the Mississippi. Suitably enough, their first representative in the upper valley was an army captain from Connecticut who traveled into strange lands for the love of adventure and from a sense of patriotic duty.

Captain Jonathan Carver had a passion for exploring and thought of himself as a man with a mission. If the French-Canadians had been defeated, then, Carver felt, it was high time for the victors to make an inspection of their spoils of war. But since the English colonial government had little interest in exploration, Captain Carver was obliged to take it upon himself to act as an unofficial government surveyor. His plan was to explore, map, and publicize the West, which he felt sure would eventually become the heart of a great American civilization. He also had the intelligence to prophesy that one day the Mississippi would be the main artery of commerce, and "will enable their inhabitants [of the central lands] to establish an intercourse with foreign climes, equally as well as the Euphrates, the Nile, the Danube, or the Volga do those people who dwell on their banks, and who have no other convenience for exporting the produce of their own country, or for importing those of others, than boats and vessels of light burden: notwithstanding which, they have become powerful and opulent states." In stressing the future importance of the continental river system, Carver was looking much farther ahead than most of his contemporaries in New England. They were content to have crushed the French menace on their northern border, and they were much more concerned about local affairs and paying their taxes to England than the dubious prospects of opening up another troublesome frontier in the West. To the eyes of the coastal settlers, the upper Mississippi, and the whole central valley for that matter, appeared a nasty, inhospitable area, plagued with mosquitoes in summer, bitterly cold in winter, swarming with treacherous Indians, and more suited to French half-breeds than to worthy New Englanders.

This prim attitude did not help Carver, nor did the French colonists offer any encouragement either. They refused to accept defeat, begrudged interlopers, and were surly toward inquisitive strangers. Carver's only support lay in the enthusiasm of a handful of pioneer leaders who held a rough-and-ready authority on the fringe of England's American empire. The most important of these outpost commanders was Major Robert Rogers, the hero of *Northwest Passage* and the founder of the irregular buckskin-clad troops called Rogers' Rangers. Major Rogers had taken command of Michilimackinac when the French garrison was ousted from that hub of the fur trade, and he was keenly interested in opening up the interior at all costs. Luckily Carver managed to meet Rogers when the latter was on a visit to Boston, and offered his services as an explorer and cartographer. Rogers had no authority to hire extra men for the exploration of the West but he gave Carver a vague commission to join him at Michilimackinac. Jubilant over this half promise, Carver packed his bags, said good-bye to his wife and children, and in June 1766 set out from Boston. Traveling by way of Albany and Niagara, he arrived at Michilimackinac in short time and prepared to plunge into the unknown interior.

Carver was not altogether unsuited to be an explorer in Indian country, already having some experience as an Indian fighter. He was born in 1710 at Weymouth, Massachusetts, the son of a prosperous New England gentleman. When he was eight years old, his family moved to Canterbury, Connecticut, and although his father died nine years later, there was enough money to provide young Jonathan with the best education available at that time in the colony. At thirty-six, Carver married Abigail Robbins in his home-town church and devoted his days to the life of a moderately well-to-do colonist; he participated in his civic responsibilities, raised a family, served on the town council, and conducted the humble but respectable trade of shoemaker. The wars between French Canada and British America changed all this. The Canadians were inciting the Indians, arming them, and launching hit-and-run attacks on the outlying New England settlements. The British settlers mobilized and Jonathan Carver patriotically joined the local militia. In 1757 he was a sergeant serving under General Webb in a disastrous campaign which culminated in the capitulation of Fort William Henry. The English garrison, including Carver who had just arrived with reinforcements, surrendered with a guarantee of safe conduct from the French commander. Unfortunately, while the English were evacuating the fort, the French lost control of their redskin allies, who massacred the refugee column. Carver was wounded in the leg by a spear thrust but managed to escape in the confusion while the savages murdered and looted the other prisoners. The following year he re-enlisted, this time in a Massachusetts Bay regiment which was being mustered for an invasion of Canada. From then on his army career was a success. He was rapidly promoted in the ranks of the provincial troops and in February 1761 he was made a captain, holding that appointment for the remainder of the war.

His life as a soldier in the backlands had given Carver a taste for excitement which he found hard to forget. After his discharge from the army he could not settle down to his former civilian life with its placid routine and he hankered for the curiosities and hazards of the frontier. When Major Rogers agreed to give the restless captain a chance to see action once more, Carver accepted the offer unconditionally. Rogers could make no arrangements for putting his recruit on the military payroll, but Carver was so eager to head west that he gladly paid his own expenses, hoping to be reimbursed by the Crown when he returned. It was a mistake which eventually brought him to the verge of ruin and cost him much bitterness and misery.

From Michilimackinac Carver knew precisely what he intended to do. His objective was the unknown source of the Mississippi. But Carver did not pursue the source for the same motives as the explorers who followed him nor in the manner of those Victorians who searched for the headwaters of the Nile. His ambition was to determine the most northerly branches of the river with a view to their usefulness. If the Mississippi was to be the highway of the continent, he realized it was essential to find out just how far into the heart of the country this river was commercially viable. Carver proposed to enter the headwaters region with Indian guides to assist him, criss-cross the area and its approaches, and explore all relevant streams, rivers, and portages with a view to future lines of communication. He also wanted to investigate the tribes of the upper Mississippi. Carver had seen how important the Indians had been for balance of power in the colonial wars between France and England, and he overestimated their future significance in the evolution of the West. He thought in terms of white-redskin alliances, cheap Indian labor coupled with European technology, and a joint development of the land. History was to prove that Carver was very wide of the mark in relying on the continued importance of the native inhabitants, but many a veteran of the French and Indian Wars shared his views, and besides, Carver was curious to meet the various tribes, identify them, and record their customs. Above all, it was his intention to persuade the Indian chiefs of the benefits of allegiance and trade with the British. It was Carver's fear that the Spanish and French agents who still haunted the upper valley might strip England of her gains in the recent wars. The roving captain took it upon himself to forestall the opposition. It was a grandiose scheme for a retired army officer acting on his own initiative, but Carver's optimism reflects the spirit of his times. The expansion of British America was a casual affair. Unlike the French who planned their exploration under geniuses like Frontenac, the English were still content to ramble ahead in a haphazard fashion, relying mainly on the volunteer efforts of men like Carver and Rogers. In no way was Carver a scientific traveler of the type soon to arrive on the scene armed with sextant and barometer; the New England captain was an inquisitive amateur with a lively curiosity and a high spirit of adventure, the sort who was normally dismissed by his acquaintances as a harmless crank.

Captain Carver set out westward from Michilimackinac on September 3, 1766, with a flotilla of French-Canadian traders bound for their customary Indian markets on the Mis-

sissippi. Carver traveled with little equipment to burden him.
He did not have sufficient funds to buy his own supplies, but
relied on Major Rogers who had promised to forward a stock
of trade goods to the Falls of St. Anthony. As soon as these
arrived, Carver intended to visit the local chiefs and win their
friendship with a plentiful distribution of the white man's
gifts.

As he sat back in the canoe and his voyageurs paddled
him across Lake Michigan, Carver was agog at the prospect
of his first meeting with the Indians of the West. Evidently
the New Englander had already made up his mind to give
the natives the benefit of the doubt. Despite his experiences
of the massacre at Fort William Henry, Carver harbored no
resentment toward the Indians. In this respect he was rather
unusual; most of the British settlers were either violently
hostile toward the Indians or veered sharply in the opposite
direction, claiming that the indigenous people of the continent were angels debauched by the newcomers. Carver kept
an open mind. He wanted to be fair and make his own judg-
ments. Therefore, it was all the more startling for him at the
first inhabited island to discover the peculiar and somewhat
dangerous method the Indians used to greet distinguished visitors. He recorded the incident for the benefit of posterity:

> What appeared to be extremely singular to me at the
> time and must do so to every person unacquainted with the
> customs of the Indians, was the reception I met with on land-
> ing. As our canoes approached the shore and had reached with-
> in about threescore rods of it, the Indians began a feu-de-joy;
> in which they fired their pieces loaded with balls; but at the
> same time they took care to discharge them in such a manner,
> as to fly a few yards above our heads; during this they ran
> from one tree stump to another, shouting and behaving as
> though they were in the heat of battle. At first I was greatly
> surprised, and was on the point of ordering my attendants to
> return their fire, concluding that their intentions were hostile;
> but being undeceived by some of the traders, who informed
> me that this was their usual method of receiving the chiefs
> of other nations, I considered it in its true light, and was
> pleased with the respect thus paid me.

Carver's flotilla stayed overnight at the island and then proceeded down the length of Green Bay which, he said, was code-named Stinking Bay by the French in order to mislead foreign spies and exclude the Indians from their conversations. The result, Carver pointed out, was that "the English and French geographers in their plans of the interior parts of America give different names to the same people and therefore perplex those who have occasion to refer to them." It was precisely this sort of confusion in mapping the country which Carver hoped to clear up by his observations during his journey. Making his way up the old Fox River route which Marquette and Joliet had used, Carver reached the "great town of the Winnebagoes," a cluster of about fifty palisaded houses situated on an island in Lake Winnebago. Here he was greeted warmly by the natives and intrigued to discover that the chief sachem of the tribe was a coquettish old woman, at least eighty years old. Casting his New England dignity aside, Carver made a great hit by flirting with the old lady. At every possible occasion he saluted her extravagantly and was amused to see that not only did this delight her courtiers, but the giggling chieftainess assumed "a juvenile gaiety, and by her smile showed that she was equally pleased by the attention I paid her."

Carver was having the time of his life. He scurried about the Indian settlement, sketching their houses, clothing, and utensils. He industriously ran tests to determine the most accurate way of measuring distance when traveling up a winding river by canoe. He began putting together a rudimentary vocabulary of the Indian tongues and he made diligent inquiries about the origin of the tribe. The Winnebagos were enchanted with the attentions of this funny little man—Carver's portrait makes him look like an eager hamster—and to gratify their visitor they fed him full of wild tales about their history and customs. Carver solemnly wrote it all down and stored away the information for use in the book he intended to publish when he got back to Boston.

The only drawback to this assiduous burrowing into Indian life was that it was difficult to draw distinctions between any one tribe and the others. As he accompanied the French traders along their path to the Mississippi, Jonathan Carver found that he was running out of fresh material. The various groups of Indians which they met en route presented the same picture with only minor differences—their lodges, customs, and physical appearance were almost identical. Carver was disappointed to find that their language was uniformly coarse and guttural, an "uncouth jargon," and that the tribes shared many words in common. Only rarely was there an unusual fact for him to jot down: at one village the Indians thought the English were great medicine men who had invented smallpox specifically to wipe out the Indians, and at another settlement there was an Outagamie chief with eleven wives and fifty sons living together in harmony. But on the whole Carver was disappointed. He had hoped to uncover many more exotic facts. Even the countryside was not so weird as he had anticipated. Ruefully he found that nearly everything—vegetation, soil, the size of the settlements—was best described as "indifferent." It was all very dull. Obviously his only hope of finding uncommon information or Indian tribes ripe for treaty-making was to penetrate farther west. Accordingly, when fall came, Carver left his companions at their trading stations on the Mississippi and headed north. He took with him two hired men, a French voyageur and an Iroquois canoeman named Jacko.

Carver's plan was to contact the Sioux. He had read Father Hennepin's account of captivity with this tribe, and he wanted to see them for himself. Paddling upstream, the three travelers made their way to Lake Pepin, the first large body of water which the river crosses after tumbling over the Falls of St. Anthony. Lake Pepin is long and shallow, a treacherous crooked lake caught between bluffs. It interrupts the course of the river abruptly. The Mississippi enters between a necklace of islands at the northern point, slows its pace and dissipates its current, then issues forth with renewed strength twenty-two miles to the south. This interruption was enough to make Carver declare that the lake was "the most proper head of the Mississippi" because the upper stream lost its identity and was the real Father of Waters only after it had left the lake. This was an odd theory, for Carver was certainly not seeking to claim for himself the distinction of discovering the source of the Mississippi. For years there had been a French trading post in the area, and furthermore, Carver named the place "the Lake of Tears," in honor of Hennepin who had described his visit there as a captive of the Sioux, when the Indians had wept and wailed as they were discussing whether or not to kill their white prisoners. Apparently Carver, in his amateur way, was only trying to arrive at the truth about the source of the river, a most unusual example of honesty in view of the claims, counterclaims, and acrimony of the later explorers, each of whom tried to seize the honor of discovery for himself.

Carver's journal of his trip gives the impression that he would have preferred the Indians in his day to be as uncouth as the Sioux who had mishandled Hennepin. But that was not so; by the time Carver visited the region, the Indians of the upper river were well accustomed to contact with the white man, his goods, his liquor, and his demands. It was the usual story—the native culture crumbling before the pressures of the European newcomers. At first the Indians were only too pleased to cooperate with the bearers of metal tools, weapons, cloth, gunpowder, and liquor. While the natives had furs to offer, their lot improved briefly. Then the supply of furs dried up, the traders moved on, and the Indians found themselves with little to offer in exchange for the white man's manufactured articles which by then had become necessities for their new way of life. Carver was witnessing the early stages of this apparently inevitable process. When he visited the nearer nations—Huron, Fox (Outagamie), Winnebago, Menominee, and Chippewa—they were already in decline, weakened by disease and alcohol. He remarked that even "a few trifling presents . . . would tempt parents to give up their daughters to be debauched." Fortunately for the inquisitive New Englander this degeneration had not yet undermined the more westerly tribes who had seen only a few Indian traders. Ironically, Carver proposed to approach these less contaminated natives with the same bribes that had ruined their eastern neighbors. The captain was a dabbler in the study of Indian culture long before the rise of the trained anthropologist with his professional techniques of ingratiation, and he saw nothing wrong in handing out liquor to the Indians in order to make himself popular as quickly as possible. Accordingly on November 10, when he met his first wandering band of Sioux, he presented them with a wampum belt, a "Kegg of Rum and a Prick of Tobacco." These gifts were topped off with a speech on the subject of friendship between the English and the Indians, an exhortation which probably bewildered the Sioux. Carver's words had to be translated first into French, then into Ottawa, then into Winnebago, and finally, much garbled, into Sioux.

The Dakota Sioux, or Naudouwessie, as Carver called them after their name in Chippewa, formed one of the most powerful tribes of the continent. Really a confederation of clans belonging to the same Siouan family which included the Winnebagos and groups of Indians as far east as Carolina, the Dakotas (an Indian word meaning "allies") were a substantial coalition of nomads, living at the extreme limit of the voyageur trade routes. Their territory extended in a great belt from the Mississippi well into the Great Plains. When Carver came into contact with them, the Sioux were already beginning a slow removal westward away from the Chippewa and the white man. The New Englander was lucky to visit them before they had developed in their later hostility toward the white settlers. Tall in stature, striking in their manner, and picturesque in appearance, the Sioux were ideal subjects for Carver's master plan. He was in a unique position to document their behavior and win their allegiance to the British empire. Accordingly he decided to visit their main encampments by turning up the Minnesota River just below the Falls of St. Anthony and following it two hundred miles into the interior. It was a gallant decision which produced his real contribution to the exploration of the country.

The journey to the land of the Sioux proved to be less troublesome than expected. Carver had no difficulty in finding guides, and although his canoe had to be left behind when it became caught in the winter ice, he was able to continue on foot into the heart of Sioux territory. The chiefs of the nearer Dakota tribes greeted their visitor cordially and Carver decided to spend the winter with them. For six months Jonathan Carver lived in the leather tents of the Sioux. It is a feat which has seldom been granted the recognition it deserves. Carver was hundreds of miles from the nearest white man, surrounded by a nation of warlike savages, and exposed to the rigors of a mid-continental winter; all by his own choice. Ill-equipped and with only a handful of presents to distribute, he shared the life of the nomads, and it is to his credit that he never once complained of the discomfort or danger. In fact his journal makes it clear that he enjoyed every minute of his stay. In his opinion the Sioux were "a very merry and sociable people," living together in a "Commonwealth or Republick." Their women were "much handsomer than the Eastern Indians" and their guest found nothing reprehensible in the fact that there was widespread polygamy and wife-swapping. Unlike many of his contemporary travelers, Jonathan Carver respected the Indian customs and sympathized with their behavior; he may even have shared in it. The Sioux reciprocated by allowing him to move about freely so that he could see what he wanted. There was plenty to investigate: buffalo hunts; shamans dancing to the great spirits; bereaved clansmen mourning the death of a relative by lacerating themselves with terrible self-inflicted wounds; tomahawks, tepees, and hieroglyphics. Scarcely a day went by without some new curiosity to report, and Carver steadily added to his notes.

Then on April 26 when traveling became easier, Carver made his farewells to the Sioux chieftains, leaving them with promises of English friendship, and returned along the Minnesota River to pick up the supplies which Major Rogers had promised to send to the Falls of St. Anthony. But Rogers had failed to keep his promise; there were no supplies at the rendezvous. It was the ruin of Carver's hopes for pushing farther west. Without presents he could not return to the Sioux nor penetrate beyond the encampments he had already visited. There was no choice but to abandon his project and return to Michilimackinac to find out what had happened. Traveling back by way of Lake Superior, Carver reached the fort to find that Rogers was not to blame. It was the same story of a breakdown in confidence and communication which had been the bane of La Salle's operations ninety years before. The colonial authorities, especially General Gage, the commander in chief of British armies in North America, had grown suspicious of Rogers' activities. The major had a record of disobeying orders, counterfeiting currency, and misusing his position for his own profit. There was even a rumor that Rogers was plotting to turn over his fort to the Spanish. It was a messy business and Carver was the loser. He could expect no more help from Rogers and there was little chance that he would be paid for services as an explorer and surveyor. Disheartened, Carver wintered at Michilimackinac and returned to Boston the following spring.

By now Carver had been away from home for almost two years and virtually ruined himself in paying for his travels. All he had to show for his efforts was a logbook of his daily mileages, an annotated journal, several sketches, and some rough maps of the country he had visited. In Boston he tried to interest the public in a book describing his adventures. An advertisement appeared in the *Boston Chronicle* for September 12, 1768, asking for subscribers to "an EXACT JOURNAL of his TRAVELS." He promised his backers "Descriptions of the Indian nations—of their manners and customs—Of the soil and produce of the country—Of the great lakes Huron, Michagan [sic], and Superior; &c. &c. &c.—Of the Mississippi and other great rivers that run in that part of the continent; and in particular, a full account of the Naudouwessie Indians, the most numerous nation of Indians in North-America, who live in tents of leather, and can raise 6000 fighting men." The proposed publication would include

"DRAUGHTS and PLANS" together with "curious figures of the Indian tents, arms, and of the Buffaloe Snake which they worship." Each subscriber was asked to put up two Spanish dollars to cover the cost of engraving and printing the work.

To Carver's chagrin the proposal fell flat. The Bostonians saw no good reason to fritter away their money on books about the redskins, and subscriptions were not forthcoming. Carver decided to try his luck in England. Leaving his wife and family behind, he sailed for London on February 22, 1769 aboard the *Paoli*, carrying with him his papers and a batch of good recommendations for his faithful service to the British Crown.

It was in England that Carver's troubles really began. Short of funds, with few friends, and cast up in a strange metropolis, the New Englander was at a loss. The exact story of how this bewildered explorer allowed his genuine and truthful tale to be turned into a highly inaccurate travelogue has never been entirely unraveled. Certain details of his life in London are known and to this day his manuscripts repose in the British Museum. But there is also a great deal that is mystifying about Carver's London days. There are hints that he fell into the hands of loan sharks, gamblers, and unscrupulous booksellers. By piecing together these scraps of evidence it is possible to reconstruct his fate and follow the development of the Carver legend.

When Carver landed in London, his first move was to contact the Lords Commissioners of Trade and Plantations. He offered them all the materials he had put together on his Mississippi explorations with the idea that the geographical evidence they contained would help the British oust their rivals in the central valley. Attached to his petition was a request that the British government defray his expenses on the trip. He asked for £735. 11s. 3d.; the bulk of which had accumulated from an unauthorized warrant signed by Major Rogers allowing his agent eight shillings a day in expenses, provision being "excessive dear." While this petition vanished into the channels of civil service procedure and the Lords Commissioners deliberated on the colonial captain's request, the luckless Carver struggled to pay his way in London. Finally, when it seemed that an answer would never come from the grinding machinery of government, Carver was forced to raise money by making over his original journal to a bookseller. Scarcely had this been done, when the Lords Commissioners informed him that, although they were under no obligation to do so, they were prepared to pay Carver a gratuity for his services. Their terms were generous—something over £1,100—but there was one snag: Carver was obliged to recover his documents from the bookseller, and by the time he had settled this matter, much of his grant had been spent. Still, it was a princely gesture on the part of the Commissioners and £1,100 was a great deal of money. There was no reason why Jonathan Carver should not have shipped back to Boston and gone into comfortable retirement.

However, this was not Carver's style. He was thoroughly smitten with the possibility of developing the region "west of Lake Huron, lying between the Illinois River on the south, and the Hudson Bay Company Terretories [sic] on the North, And as far West as His Majesty's Government may extend." He petitioned to be sent back to this area as Crown agent for Indian affairs, and when this request was denied, he tried to interest Richard Whitworth, Member of Parliament for Stafford, in a scheme for an expedition to the source of the river "Oregan." Carver and Major Rogers were to take part in the venture, but the idea had to be shelved when increasing unrest in the American colonies made it clear that there were more important matters to be considered by the politicians of Westminster. Undaunted, Carver made one more attempt to get back to the wilderness which fascinated him. Taking advantage of the current craze for speculating on the origins of the North American Indians, he volunteered to "a private society of gentlemen" that they send him on a tremendous transcontinental journey across northern Europe and the steppes of Asia and on into North America with the hope that he would thereby trace the ethnic sources of the redskins. It was a monumental plan, which once again came to nothing.

Thwarted at every turn, Carver had been burning through his government money. He was not a frugal man and by 1773 the captain was once again short of cash. In addition, he had acquired another wife by a bigamous marriage (his first wife was still living with her children in New England) and in desperation he returned to his original idea of publishing a book about his American experiences.

How Carver recovered his manuscript from the files of the Commissioners for Trade and Plantations is not known; perhaps they had received fair copies while Carver kept his original notes. At any rate he had enough material to work out a first draft, which was then taken over by an editor, and in 1778 the first edition of his book appeared under the title *Travels through the Interior Parts of North America in the Years 1766, 1767, and 1768. By J. Carver, Esq. Captain of a Company of Provincial Troops during the late War with France*. This book was a mockery of his original script. Somehow a ghost writer had got hold of Carver's journals, embroidered, altered, and enlarged them. The pages of the new book were packed with colorful tales which Carver had never mentioned in his journal. There were long passages copied from other authors, Hennepin and Lahontan included; it was a question of one liar stealing from another. In his *Travels* the details of Carver's original journey had been compressed into the first 167 pages. These were followed by a much more important block of 340 pages bristling with fanciful yarns purporting to describe the life of the savages. Little of this was accurate; most of it was the product of the ghost writer's plagiarism or imagination. For example, Carver's original vocabulary of some 140 words and phrases in the Sioux tongue had been expanded in the book to well over 400 words which claimed to cover both the Chippewa and Sioux languages. Most of the new words were nonsense. Elsewhere the *Travels* recounted such fantasies as snakes with two heads, a viper which shot poisonous darts from its tail, "Tygers," and the dreaded "Carcajou." The latter was a terrible creature that sprang from the trees on its prey and, wrapping its long tail around the victim, sank its teeth into the jugular vein. The only way to shake off this clinging monster was "by flying immediately to the water . . . as the carcajou has a great dislike to that element."

The bulk of the *Travels* was devoted to the Indians. Beginning with various theories on their origins, which included a charming ten-point thesis that the redskins were a lost tribe of Israelites, the book went on to discuss every aspect of Indian life from the "circumspect and stoical Disposition of the Men" to "their manner of dressing and eating their Victuals." Nothing was overlooked: there were descriptions of their utensils, their method of making war, their religions, their dress, their politics, and so forth. Every now and then these comments were interspersed with little anecdotes about this or that "singular occurrence" to illustrate the natural state of these savages. Thus the reader learned that should he fall into the hands of the natives (a not unfortunate fate) he could command their allegiance by demonstrating his compass. On the other hand, he was cautioned not to join their war dances because the frenzied braves "hold their sharp knives in their hands, with which, as they whirl about, they are every moment in danger of cutting each other's throats; and did they not shun the threatened mischief with inconceivable dexterity, it could not be avoided."

Sifting through this deluge of miscellaneous information, it is obvious that just as Hennepin had a propaganda motive when he advocated the Recollet cause and his own fame, so Carver's *Travels* also followed a definite policy. In this case the author, or rather the ghost writer, wanted to portray the "noble Indian" in his happy natural state. Europe was fascinated with the Rousseauesque conceit that the untutored human being was as worthy a creature as his sophisticated fellow man. The "noble savage" was all the fashion. Learned societies discussed his background, beer-mug philosophers extolled his virtues, and poets composed paeans to his glory.

Now, conveniently, from the depths of North America came an informative work to put flesh on the bare bones of the theories. According to the *Travels*, the redskins would be the happiest people on earth if it had not been for the white man and his "noxious juices." Strong drink was their downfall, but until they were offered this devil's brew, the carefree savages lived an idyllic life, untouched by stress and worry. All was shared in their land, all was plentiful, a veritable Garden of Eden before the temptation. From such sentimental descriptions the romantics of Europe found evidence for the eulogies on the condition of the "noble savage." Here Schiller culled the material for his *Indian Death Dirge*, which Goethe claimed was the poet's finest work in that style. Carver's supposed observations on the unalloyed paradise of the American Indian swept Europe off its feet. His *Travels through the Interior Parts of North-America* was a best seller in the entire history of publishing. Edition after edition, more than forty of them, rolled off the printing presses. The book gave the English-speaking peoples the first account in their own language of this newest part of their dominions, and it was translated into Dutch, German, and French. By the end of the century at least half a dozen editions had been printed in the United States (an ironic twist for the Bostonians who had originally rejected Carver's proposed travelogue), and during the next hundred years a new edition appeared on an average of one every thirty-two months. Inaccurate and gaudy, the *Travels* served up precisely what the publisher knew his customers would buy, and he reaped the profits.

But while his book raced through different editions and booksellers fattened on the income, Jonathan Carver was dying in poverty. Before his manuscript had been set into letter press, he had spent every penny he possessed, until he was obliged to beg for help from Sir Joseph Banks, the noted patron of science who at his own expense had accompanied Captain Cook aboard the *Endeavour*. Banks gave money to the derelict, but Carver was still forced to pledge the royalties of his book to moneylenders and take a menial job as a clerk in a lottery office. It was during this time of distress that the captain probably agreed to the idea of trumping up his narrative and doctoring the information it contained. He had no choice. He was literally starving and the least crumb of comfort helped fend off his collapse. The form, contents, and income of his book slipped out of his control and into hands which, as he complained in a letter to Banks, "professed of little Mercy or Justice." Crushed by circumstances, Carver was sucked into the deceit and was no longer responsible for his *Travels*. The book became the raw material for its promoter and his ambitions. The explorer had to stand by helplessly as his work was tailored to public taste.

In this unhappy state, Carver, by now a physical wreck, was found by Dr. Lettsom, a philanthropic Quaker and one of the founders of the Medical Society of London. The doctor took Carver under his care and tried to nurse him back to health. But it was too late. In 1780 Jonathan Carver died, as his physician diagnosed, from malnutrition. It was a strange ending for an explorer who had thrived in the company of the wild Sioux, an honest traveler whose legacy was a work of plagiarism and travel lies, a pauper whose book was already in its sixth edition.

Nor did the contradictions of Carver's life die with him. In the following century critics began to doubt the truth of his writings, and, as a reaction, his opponents declared the entire story a hoax—Carver had never visited the Sioux at all. An academic argument raged for many years, until eventually his manuscripts and personal correspondence came to light, proving that he had in truth reached the land of the Naudouwessie. Even more extraordinary was the legend of the "Carver Grant" which blossomed soon after his death. His descendants came forward with a claim that the Sioux had given the captain a huge grant of land bordering on the Mississippi, and his heirs demanded that the United States recognize the land deed. Three attempts, the last in 1825, were made to persuade Congress that the title was valid, and three times the claim was denied. Captain Carver's name and story found its place in the archives of the American government, and his book was essential reading for every administrator or scholar who followed the frontier as it rolled westward over the lands which Carver was the first British colonial to visit.

10

Enter the Army

ZEBULON MONTGOMERY PIKE, LIEUTENANT OF IN-
fantry in the United States Army, is a misfit in the
ranks of the Mississippi explorers. Marquette, Joliet, La
Salle, Hennepin, Tonti, and Carver—all of them came to
explore the river because it fascinated them and exerted a
powerful pull on their life ambitions. In one way or another,
these earlier explorers all focused their careers on the river
because they wanted to; Lieutenant Zebulon Pike felt quite
the opposite. To him the task of exploring the Mississippi
was a distasteful chore which he would have avoided if it
had been at all possible. As far as the young lieutenant was
concerned, he would have preferred a post on the east coast
where he could surround himself with the luxuries and com-
forts of civilization instead of bucolic boors and frontier log
cabins. Pike's concept of an ideal army career was a life of
cultivated cleverness among his social peers, interspersed with
periods of brilliant campaigning against a civilized foe. It
was only because he was under orders to do so that he found
himself taking a detachment of raw troops to the headwaters
of the Mississippi in a land peopled largely by unwashed

savages. Ironically, he is remembered not so much as an outstanding professional soldier, which he was, but as a brilliant explorer, which he certainly was not.

Pike's reputation as an explorer rather than a soldier was unavoidable in the context of his times. The public of nineteenth-century Europe and America had a predilection for creating hero figures. Usually there was an abundance of military leaders to provide examples of martial virtue, but explorers were at a premium. They were a rare and exotic breed created by mankind's curiosity and not by the fortunes of war. Exploration was held to be the business of dedicated visionaries gallantly piercing the veils of ignorance that hid distant lands. By the very nature of his occupation the lone explorer presented a ready-made idol for all lesser men to see and to praise. It was equally true, in the popular opinion, that there was no such creature as an unpleasant explorer. All pathfinders and pioneers were expected to share certain characteristics, and willy-nilly they were cast in the same mold. Their admirers insisted that each and every explorer worthy of the name be intrepid, self-reliant, and tactful. He had to be good at dealing with the aborigines, brave in the face of hardship, and a superb leader of men. Finally, he was required to get home alive with a well-written and neatly packaged book describing his adventures. Into this praiseworthy category Lieutenant Pike was pulled and prodded without much regard for the reality of his achievements or the truth about his personality.

To be fair, one must admit that the citizens of the fledgling United States had good reason to look for heroes among their pioneers. The country, fresh from the politicians' statutes, needed examples of home-grown virtue, and without a doubt many of the emigrants who were flooding outward across the Appalachians were the stuff from which heroes are made. Time and again there were incidents which involved daring and courage as the Americans pushed their frontier westward into the unknown backlands. Unhappily, these events too often concerned obscure illiterates whose exploits went unsung. By contrast, Lieutenant Pike was a well-publicized figure: he traveled as an official representative of the governor of upper Louisiana; his progress received full coverage; the President of the United States supported his activities; he kept a logbook of every incident on his journey; and, when he returned, the Department of the Army sponsored the printing and publication of his travelogue. As a consequence, Pike could scarcely have failed to emerge as one of America's foremost explorers.

If the American public was eager to create its explorer-heroes, the North American land mass was equally ripe for journeys of discovery. Half a continent lay exposed to the energies of a young and vigorous republic whose activities were soon to change the entire character of western exploration. In previous years the soldiers, priests, and traders of France, Spain, and England had laid the groundwork of the new era by outlining the structure of the central valley. Now it was time to push out beyond the hundredth meridian, north into the Canadian borderlands, southwest to the frontiers of New Mexico, and perhaps most important of all to fill in the gaps which the earlier explorers had left behind them. So, like a signal gun, the Declaration of Independence heralded the two most important innovations of this new style of exploration: it forewarned the permanent settlement of the interior and it coincided with the beginnings of "saturation exploration." Both innovations depended on the same phenomenon—the extraordinary migration of people across the mountain barrier which had separated them from the Mississippi valley for more than six generations. It was as though some rising tide of eastern settlement had been lapping against the mountain crest and sending the occasional trickle over the rim, until suddenly the upper half of the dam collapsed and a flood of immigrants poured through the wreckage. Although this movement was a general one and took place over several decades along the length of the Appalachians, the main migration followed the line of the Ohio. There an increasing number of broadhorns, flatboats, keelboats, and assorted weird home-made vessels drifted down on a current which had formerly known only the canoes of Indian traders traveling on their transcontinental journeys. The voyageurs, "long hunters," and *boschlopers* had explored a delicate network of routes which criss-crossed in narrow threads from one end of the Mississippi valley to the other; now the migrating Americans filtered along these same trails and spread outward between them, sprinkling the gaps with tiny villages, cabins, and cleared fields.

Farther west, beyond the line of the Mississippi itself and to the north of its junction with the Ohio, the expansion of settlement across the Appalachians also had an effect, though it was more of a political one. Seeing the successful occupation of the eastern part of the central valley, the politicians of the United States began to be interested in a similar exploitation of the poorly known western and northern sectors of the valley which now belonged to the republic by reason of the Louisiana Purchase. Their hopes bore some resemblance to La Salle's dreams for an empire of the West and to Carver's plans for an Indian–white man alliance, but there was one great difference—the settlement and development of the outback was within the capacity of the American nation whereas previously it had been beyond the power of the colonial governments. By the time of Pike's expedition along the Mississippi, the interior was no longer the plaything of ministers in faraway London or Paris, but the immediate concern of the federal authorities in Washington, who by the Louisiana Purchase had recently paid a great deal of money for the Mississippi valley and now wanted to find our precisely what they had bought. Of course, there were those politicians of the coastal states who believed that their new nation should restrict its efforts to developing the seaboard and not dissipate its resources with blind adventurism inland. But opposing this caution were men of importance in federal affairs, in particular President Thomas Jefferson, who were prepared to launch forth with daring and to send scouting parties westward.

For this task of reconnaissance there was one obvious

federal agent—the army of the United States. For years the military had been active on the frontier, garrisoning the outer fringes, pacifying the Indians, and protecting the settlers. They had the time and experience necessary for exploration and they were relatively free from local favoritism and niggling political interference. The shrewdest argument of all— one that silenced even the most critical opponents of expansion—was that if the country was to afford the luxury of a peacetime army, it might as well be employed profitably rather than being left to kick its heels in barracks. It is no surprise, therefore, that the opening years of the nineteenth century saw the impact of American soldiers on the progress of American exploration. In the van came the most famous of the uniformed pathfinders, Captains Meriwether Lewis and William Clark, sent by President Jefferson to cross the breadth of the continent until they reached the Pacific. Close behind was Lieutenant Zebulon Pike, probing the international frontiers to the north and southwest of the United States.

Pike made two exploring trips: the first up the Mississippi from St. Louis to seek the river's source in present day Minnesota; the second to the headwaters of the Arkansas River and down as far as the Mexican border. The Mississippi journey was without doubt the easier venture as it covered an area which was already sparsely settled by fur trappers and Indian traders, American as well as Canadian, so that during his trek the young officer was never more than a day's journey from the nearest white man. The Arkansas expedition, on which he saw (but failed to climb) the mountain now named after him, was much more difficult. It took a random route across dry barrens known only to wandering Indians and the occasional Spanish cavalry patrol. On this second trip Pike's party suffered considerable discomfort, most of which could have been avoided with a little more foresight. Today Pike's reputation as an explorer is very sensibly based on this second expedition. However, to his contemporaries Pike was at least as well known as the man who visited the source of the Mississippi, and it was the apparent success of his river trip which brought about his selection as commander of the Arkansas journey. His fame began with his expedition to the "Headwaters of the Mississippi River, Through Louisiana Territory" during the years 1805 and 1806, and his story illustrates the creation of an artificial hero out of poor material. It also heralds the arrival on the great river of the U.S. Army acting as agent for a new nation which had come to claim its own.

Physically Zebulon Pike was not cut out to be an explorer. He was the second child of Isabella Pike whose first baby survived only nine days. Zebulon was not a strong child and his family seems to have suffered from chronic tuberculosis, a common enough malady for the time, usually diagnosed as "consumption." Only four of the Pike children reached maturity and even then the youngest boy, George Washington Pike, died at the age of nineteen from the family illness. This left Zebulon's brother James, who was never able to support himself or his brood of eight children, and the only surviving daughter Maria, who also seems to have been afflicted with poor health. In later life Zebulon was described as having a ruddy complexion, blue eyes, light-colored hair, and good features. Somehow he must have avoided or overcome the family weakness because the same description mentions that "his stature was about five foot eight inches, tolerably square and robust for his age," an unusual physique if he had been consumptive. He also had the odd habit of holding his head tilted to one side so that his hat brim touched his right shoulder. Apparently this particular observer was beating the drum for Pike, because the lieutenant's own journals repeatedly show that he experienced the utmost difficulty in standing the physical strain of his journeys, and his portrait, an unhappy likeness, shows a shifty-looking character with a pointed nose and a wide mouth set in a faint sneer.

But what Pike really looked like is of little consequence. His personality is much more interesting and can be deduced from contemporary reports, his letters, and his travelogues. Contemporary reports are the least trustworthy, as the authors, writing after Pike's rise to fame, were obviously bent on displaying their hero in the best possible light. The sum of their opinions is that Zebulon Pike had a strong will, a retiring disposition, and a high sense of duty starched with decorum. This opinion, from a more cynical point of view, could equally well describe a prig, and this suspicion is unexpectedly strengthened by the evidence of Pike's private correspondence. His letters are full of blue-nosed morality. In a note to sister Maria, then only thirteen, he discusses her loneliness in the following vein: "I console you on the solitary situation in which you are placed, but hope that it may be the source of improvement of your mind, the grace of which shines in the countenance and beautifies the body. You should employ what leisure time you can command in reading and writing. Your words are generally well spelt, but the writing is bad. Practice more and learn to write without so much flourish." In another letter, he informs Maria: "Your letter is wrote [sic] well with respect to language, but it is too much crowded and wants a little more attention in the stops. . . . Again let me entreat your attention Maria to the cultivation of your mind—not for youth alone, but a long life, is all too little to acquire the art of learning." Here and later, it is evident that Zebulon was insensitive to the feelings of others. Even consumptive brother George received his share of sermons and was exhorted to "make rapid advances in learning for the time you are [sic] lost." Disregarding the self-righteousness of these letters, it is evident that elder brother Zebulon was not practicing what he preached; his letters and logbooks were consistently misspelt, ungrammatical, and turgid. When the time came for his book to go to press, the printers threw up their hands in despair and a London editor was called in to disentangle the rambling chaos which Pike called his manuscript.

Of course, Pike was not without his virtues. He was utterly loyal, giving complete obedience to his military superiors and expecting the same from his men. He must have also had great stamina in pushing himself as far as he did, both on his expeditions and in his army career. As a regular officer he reached the rank of brigadier-general at the dazzingly early age of thirty-four, before losing his life gallantly leading his men in the storming of York (Toronto), during the War of 1812. Throughout his life Pike was driven by an insatiable desire to succeed in all that he did. With ambition he overcame his early handicaps and survived the rigors of his exploring trips. Sadly, in striving for the pinnacle of success he became an introvert and an isolate from his colleagues. He was blind to the weakness and warmth of human beings, whether in the army or at home. He spied on his troops, hoping to catch them breaking regulations, and he relegated his wife to second place in the interests of furthering his own career. In the final analysis there is something coldly inhuman about Lieutenant Zebulon M. Pike. He is too machinelike, too prone to chide others for their shortcomings, and too quick to promote his own aims regardless of the effects on his fellows. This unlucky combination of traits contradicts the ideal picture of the dashing, generous explorer which his public was determined to see in him.

Pike began his military career at the earliest possible age. When he was still fifteen he enrolled in his father's company of infantry. The elder Pike, also confusingly named Zebulon, was a professional soldier who had fought in the Revolutionary War and was at that time commanding a small army post in the frontier village of Cincinnati. For the next five years, as cadet, ensign, and lieutenant, young Zebulon was employed in running the humdrum business of army supply lines. Sometimes attached to his father's command and sometimes operating independently, he spent his days purchasing supplies from private contractors and shipping the matériel by barge and flatboat to the "chain of forts" which the American government, unconsciously mimicking La Salle's original scheme, had erected along the Ohio and the Mississippi as far as the delta. In 1799 he was made second lieutenant and in November of the same year received his commission as first lieutenant. Two years later he married Clarissa Brown, the daughter of a rich Kentucky planter. Captain Brown, the girl's father, disapproved of the match, so the young couple were forced to elope. It was the beginning of a long and vindictive correspondence between the Browns and the Pikes, as the planter had little use for his son-in-law.

For five more years Lieutenant Pike followed the routine postings of a young infantry officer. The army was thinly spread in tiny forts across the country. Officers were regularly switched from one outpost to the next and Pike found himself at Fort Wilkinsonville on the Ohio (where he probably met Meriwether Lewis), Fort Knox in Indiana, and finally in 1805 at Kaskaskia, an old French missionary settlement only six miles from the Mississippi. During these years Pike was unhappy. He had a high opinion of his own capabilities, which he felt were being wasted. He detested commonplace drills and the paperwork of an adjutant's job. For a while he even thought of leaving the service and working as a private supply contractor, but later discarded the idea. Army life was indeed grim. Pay was bad, the conditions poor, equipment indifferent. The forts were filled with riffraff who drank, gambled, and cohabited with camp followers, squaws, or the local women. The ordinary soldier frequently absented himself from duty without permission, and the officers quarreled among themselves or cursed their decision to take up military careers. Awash in all this discontent, Pike, a stickler for military deportment, a nonsmoker, and a very temperate drinker, felt lonely and misused. Typically, he fended off depression during those gloomy years by studying French, Spanish, and mathematics, for he was gifted with a certain academic intelligence and believed unquestionably in the benefits of education.

From this soul-destroying position Pike was rescued by a dispatch sent by General James Wilkinson, C-in-C of the western army and governor of Louisiana Territory. The letter was written on June 24, 1805, and contained orders for Lieutenant Pike to relinquish his duties at Kaskaskia and to report to St. Louis immediately. There he was to assemble a river expedition and embark, as soon as convenient, to explore the Mississippi River to its northernmost source. Pike knew that this was the opportunity he had been waiting for. His mission was a heaven-sent chance for an obscure officer to make a name for himself and display his talents in full view of his commanding officer. There is no way of knowing why General Wilkinson selected Pike, rather than any other sub-altern, to lead the Mississippi trip; he was probably influenced by Pike's experience as a barge commander during his term as a supply officer. But whatever the reason for his being chosen, Pike lost no time in following up the general's letter. He wound up his affairs at Kaskaskia, picked a squad of men to accompany him, and by the end of July arrived in St. Louis eager to carry out his instructions.

The diplomatic and political background of Wilkinson's decision to send an army patrol to the source of the Mississippi is tainted with intrigue and treachery. On April 30, 1803, American delegates in Paris, led by James Monroe, had purchased the Louisiana Territory for $15 million. It was President Jefferson's master stroke and France's final renunciation of all that Frontenac, La Salle, and Tonti had worked for. But Napoleon Bonaparte needed the money and preferred to see the United States, rather than his archrival England, control the Mississippi valley. The size of the acquisition startled even the most sanguine expansionists in the United States, who were presented overnight with more than 828,000 square miles of new territory. Jefferson decided not to delay but to forge ahead briskly with its exploration. He had long dreamed of opening up the interior, and as early as 1783 had been in touch with an old friend, George Rogers Clark, suggesting an overland journey from the Mississippi to the Pacific in order to discover the extent of the American landmass. The Louisiana Purchase accelerated Jefferson's plans. Using his authority as President, he promptly dispatched Lewis and Clark to cross the continent by following the line of the Missouri River, and appointed two governors to rule the new province: W. C. C. Claiborne and General James Wilkinson.

Within a year of buying Louisiana, Congress split the region into two portions—the Territory of Orleans which included the area south of the thirty-third parallel, and upper Louisiana, which extended northward to a vague border with British Canada and was governed by General Wilkinson at St. Louis. Due to the hurried manner in which the purchase had been drawn up, the northern boundary was not accurately specified. Too little was known about the geography of the interior, and Napoleon may have hoped that a disputed border would be a bone of contention between the British and the Americans.

Whatever its legal boundaries, upper Louisiana was thinly populated and scarcely mapped. Furthermore, it was a long way from Washington and General Wilkinson was left to his own devices for governing the territory. How he used or abused his responsibilities as governor has been hotly disputed by historians. It is known for certain that Wilkinson kept in constant touch with the Spanish and played a sly double role, on the one hand officially representing the government of the United States, and on the other hand plotting to benefit himself. He blandly spied on the strength of the Spanish forces and at the same time furnished them, for a price, with military intelligence concerning the movements of American troops. He also became entangled in a plot with Aaron Burr, a former Vice-President of the United States and now a thwarted and discredited politician. The details of this plot are not at all clear, but it seems that Burr, with Wilkinson's help, planned to seize New Orleans and declare independence from the United States.

Pike's role in this treachery is puzzling. He was ordered to explore the headwaters of the Mississippi just when Wilkinson's machinations for secession from the Union were at their height. The general may have been scheming to seize the upper river as well as the delta. But Pike knew nothing of his commander's plans, if such plans existed. Lieutenant Pike was no Machiavelli. He executed his orders to the best of his ability and did not question Wilkinson's motives. In so doing,

Pike may have been the general's dupe, but he had every excuse for believing that he was acting in the best interests of the United States. Only a year earlier the President himself had ordered Lewis and Clark to explore westward, so there was no reason why General Wilkinson should not send a similar expedition to scout the northern parts of his province.

Fitting out a river-borne expedition to the source of the Mississippi should have been a straightforward task for a man accustomed to organizing barge traffic. But Pike had one great handicap to face—he wanted to leave St. Louis in time to reach the source of the river before winter cut off his retreat. In consequence, the lieutenant's preparations were rushed. Brusquely he deposited his wife, who by then had a baby daughter to look after, at Fort Bellefontaine near St. Louis. Then he turned to the task of putting together his exploring team. His twelve men from Kaskaskia formed the nucleus, to which he added soldiers from Bellefontaine, bringing the strength of his command to twenty regulars—seventeen privates, two corporals, and a sergeant. For supplies, Pike drew on the assistant military agent at St. Louis who furnished him with standard equipment from the quartermaster's stores. The most important item, which had to be specifically prepared, was his vessel—a 70-foot keelboat. Long and slim, the keelboats were considered to be the most sophisticated of river craft until the advent of the paddle steamer. Most of the boats which plied the Ohio and Mississippi were designed for one-way trips, squat, ugly vessels like the Kentucky broadhorn or "ark" which were nailed together on the upper reaches of the rivers and floated down the current to their destinations. There these makeshift tubs were unloaded and knocked apart to sell as raw lumber or to make a homestead for its emigrant owner. By contrast, the graceful keelboat was designed to make several round trips. The "keels" were carefully designed for they needed to be stout enough to withstand frequent groundings on shoals and beaches as well as a constant battering from logs and other snags that littered the river. The keelboat's slender length made her easier to push up against the current on return trips and was an asset when it came to picking a channel through rapids. Pike's own craft carried a sail for use with a following wind, but frequently the keelboats had to be rowed or poled against the force of the current. When progress became really difficult it was customary to "cordel" the vessel, a back-breaking procedure in which the crew was put ashore at the end of a long bow hawser and dragged the boat by brute force against the rush of water.

Equipment and food for the projected four month journey presented little difficulty. The keelboat could carry several tons of cargo and Pike's only problem was to avoid lading her so deeply that she could not be worked over the river shallows. Pike had enough experience in organizing barge traffic to know the optimum load and there were plenty of traders from upriver posts who could advise him on the conditions he would encounter. Most of the supplies—flour, pork, gunpowder, corn meal, salt, and tobacco—were packed in barrels, which were cumbersome and heavy but had the great advantage of keeping the stores dry when handled carefully. For the most part these supplies were standard army issue, but Pike was also provided with several kegs of rum for his troops as well as the Indians, and a quantity of calico, knives, powdered paint, and colored bunting, to be distributed as presents. In addition, there were tents, spare clothing, blankets, lead shot, carpenter's tools, extra weapons, and the thousand and one items necessary to make his command self-sustaining during their voyage. For his private use, Pike took along his personal rifle and pistols, some special double-battle Sussex powder, and a copious supply of pens, ink, and paper. By contrast, his scientific apparatus was primitive, for the lieutenant was neither a trained surveyor nor an accomplished draughtsman. He had only a watch, a thermometer, and a crude instrument for determining latitude. All three items later proved to be unreliable and inaccurate. Finally, there were a number of American flags to be handed out to the chiefs of friendly tribes as their tokens of allegiance to the United States.

There were several significant omissions to Pike's preparations, none of them really his fault but rather the result of the army's niggardly cheese-paring. For a start, there was no interpreter. As Pike was to deal with Indians who seldom spoke any language except their native dialect, it is hard to understand how he was expected to negotiate with the tribes. Perhaps it was understood that he would acquire an interpreter en route, though a reliable man selected from the Indian traders of St. Louis would have been a more intelligent choice. Also his party did not include a surgeon or another officer. It is true that doctors were hard to come by and expensive to employ, but it would not have been difficult to provide Pike with a subaltern to share the burden of command and to help with the multitude of tasks which the expedition was supposed to undertake. It is possible that Pike was confident that he could handle the entire command on his own, and it would be in keeping with his character that he preferred not to share the glory of the exploration with anyone else. At any event, by the second week in August after less than three weeks' preparation Pike felt that his patrol was equipped and ready to go. On August 9, 1805, the expedition pushed off from Fort Bellefontaine and headed up the Mississippi.

Pike's instructions from General Wilkinson were clearcut. He was ordered to travel upstream to the source of the main branch of the Mississippi, unless the winter ice forced him to turn back. On the way he was to proceed with maximum diligence, map the course of the river, calculate his daily mileages by time, and note "rivers, creeks, highlands, prairies, islands, rapids, shoals, mines, quarries, timber, water, soil, Indian villages and settlements in a diary to comprehend reflections of the winds and weathers." He was asked "to procure specimens of whatever you may find curious, in the mineral, vegetables, or animal kingdoms," and it was General Wilkinson's wish, perhaps with a view to making some profit for himself, that Pike gather data on the "population of the several Indian nations, of the quantity and species of skins and furs they barter per annum, and their relative price of goods, of the tracts of country on which they generally make their haunts, and the people with whom they trade." In fact, the Indian question was uppermost in the general's mind. He wanted to make sure that the savages were curbed by a line of strategic army forts along the river. Therefore he ordered Pike to select the sites of two forts; one between St. Louis and the mouth of the Wisconsin River, the other on the Wisconsin itself, which would also serve to block the path of Canadian fur traders who still used this traditional short cut from the Great Lakes. Having selected these two sites, Pike was to obtain the consent of the Indians to the construction of forts on the land. Furthermore, he was empowered to purchase any other strategic locations for military strongpoints or trading posts which "may fall under your observations; these permissions to be granted in formal conferences [with the Indians], regularly recorded, and the ground marked off." On the whole the subaltern was to have a relatively free hand in directing the enterprise for "your own good sense will regulate the consumption of your provisions, and direct the distribution of the trifling presents which you may carry with you, particularly your flags."

With these broad terms of reference in his pocket, Pike lost no time in traveling up the great river to seek his fame. The keelboat behaved well and there were few complications to slow down his patrol. A daily routine was established. The party would rise early and make several miles before stopping on a convenient sand bar for breakfast. Then, alternately rowing or using their large square sail, the expedition traveled as much as forty miles in a day despite halts for meals and the occasional excursion on the bank. At dusk Pike ordered his men to beach the boat and the soldiers would go ashore to cook their evening meal, set up their tents, and play cards or saw away on their violins until it was time to sleep. For food they depended on the rations which had been taken on board at St. Louis, improved with fresh fish from the river. Now and again they were held back by headwinds and when the boat ran onto shoals or "sawyers," water-logged trees lurking just below the surface of the water. Once it was necessary to send men over the side to hack away a large tangle of dead wood that became jammed under the bow, and another time a log punctured a hole in the hull so that Pike had to call a halt while the damaged plank was replaced and the seams recalked with oakum. Sudden rainstorms were more troublesome. They caught the men unawares in their open boat, soaking crew and cargo so that the expedition was forced to stop and dry out. Despite this precaution some of the men began to complain of galls brought on by damp clothing, and several barrels of biscuits were found to be faulty and therefore ruined by the rain.

Pike's first real obstacle was the Des Moines Rapids, a succession of ridges, shoals, and broken water which extended from shore to shore for eleven miles. It would have been sensible to have found an experienced pilot to guide the keelboat through the rapids, but Pike did not hesitate to press forward without assistance. The first shoal was crossed only after great difficulty, and as the channel zigzagged from one bank to the other, it looked as if the young lieutenant had rushed into more trouble than he knew how to handle. Just at that moment, to Pike's relief, he saw several canoes, one flying the American flag, running downstream to help. His rescuer proved to be William Ewing, the local Indian agent, who brought with him an interpreter and twenty Sac Indians. With their help fourteen of the heaviest supply barrels were transferred to the native canoes, and the keelboat, considerably lightened, was worked through the rapids under the guidance of two experienced canoemen.

Not the least chastened by this escape, Pike decided to stay with Ewing and take advantage of the interpreter's presence to explain the purpose of his mission to the Sacs. "I spoke to them of the following purpose," he recorded in his diary, "That their Great Father, the President of the United States, wishing to be more intimately acquainted with the situation of the different nations of the red people in our newly acquired Territory of Louisiana, had ordered the General [Wilkinson] to send a number of his young warriors in different directions, to take them by the hand." To underline this brand of paternalism, Pike distributed tobacco, knives, and whisky to the Indians, who probably had not the least idea what he had been lecturing them about but were happy to accept the bounty of this rhetorical young white man in his strange uniform with the shiny buttons. Pike, however, was exhilarated. At last, he felt, he was getting to grips with the aborigines. Before re-embarking he took pains to set down in his journal the precise text of his first attempt at Indian diplomacy and then wrote a full account of his voyage so far to be sent by canoe to General Wilkinson.

There followed several days of smooth sailing, marred only by the disturbing realization that the trip would take much longer than had been anticipated. Already there was a cold snap in the night air, and although the summer days allowed plenty of daylight for navigation, the expedition had fallen way behind schedule. Also, to Pike's annoyance, the local Indians were shy of the white men in their big boat. Nearly every day the party saw canoes loaded with natives approaching downriver, but seldom came face to face with them for the Indians either paddled off behind an island or ran their canoes ashore and disappeared into the forests.

On August 28 the Americans arrived at the camp of James Aird, a Scots trader who had recently come down from Michilimackinac with his flotilla of trade canoes. Throughout his trip Pike held a very unfavorable opinion of these Canadian traders on the Mississippi. He regarded them with almost neurotic suspicion as sinister agents of a foreign power and seldom passed up an opportunity to defame them. Aird proved to be a sociable fellow who invited the lieutenant to breakfast with him on shore, gladly supplying all the information which Pike demanded. The Scot was encamped at the foot of Moline Rapids, which had damaged or delayed several of his canoes, but Pike did not hesitate to run the rapids without help. Once again his luck held; the rudder of the keelboat was carried away on the first reef but at the critical moment a strong wind sprang up from the south and the expedition scraped through safely. Pike smugly noted in his diary: "Met Mr. Aird's boats, *which had pilots*, fast on the rocks." There was a good reason for Pike to be grateful to Aird. Two of the lieutenant's soldiers had become separated from the main party on the twenty-fourth. They had volunteered to look for Pike's two favorite hunting dogs that had wandered off into the prairie. Pike refused to wait for the men, hoping that they would catch up with the boat by nightfall. Now, five days later, the lieutenant was worried; his two soldiers had failed to appear, and he feared that the Indians had caught and killed them. In fact, the missing pair were having a miserable time. For six days they scrambled along the bank, living off raw river mussels and hoping to catch up with their commander. Aird found them half-starved and exhausted. The trader very kindly attended to their needs and then arranged for them to be taken by canoe to their commander, who had reached the famous Dubuque lead mines about seventy miles farther upstream.

Julien Dubuque was a legendary figure. A canny French trader, he had learned of the lead veins which the Indians mined to provide shot for their muskets. The savages had only the crudest notion of smelting the ore. They were content to hack at the surface deposits with digging sticks, throw the broken rock into campfires, and gather up the molten residue. Dubuque saw his chance to make a fat profit in the lead trade and introduced efficient mining methods so that very soon he was not only supplying all the lead the Indians could use but also sending rafts loaded with the metal down to St. Louis. Pike's arrival must have alarmed the Frenchman, because, strictly speaking, his mining operations were illicit as they were being conducted on Indian territory. In the past the Spanish authorities had turned a blind eye to the illegalities of Dubuque's position and had recognized his claim to the lead-bearing region. Now, after the Louisiana Purchase, he was under the jurisdiction of the Americans and he had no idea whether they would allow him to continue his business. Fortunately for Dubuque, General Wilkinson was more interested in the commercial possibilities of the lead trade than in the legal technicalities; Pike had only been instructed to note down the amount of lead mined annually. Furthermore, when he called to see Dubuque, the lieutenant was suffering from dysentery and this stopped him from inspecting the mines in person. Evidently relieved, Dubuque entertained the young officer lavishly and sent him on his way with the idea that the mines produced a bare twenty to thirty thousand pounds of lead per annum—a gross underestimate, as Dubuque was probably shipping twice that amount. The Frenchman was shrewd enough to realize that his best policy was to divert the cupidity of his new masters with a smokescreen of inaccurate information.

From Dubuque's mines to the mouth of the Wisconsin River was a three-day journey which the expedition accomplished without incident. At the confluence of the Wisconsin and the Mississippi stood the frontier village of Prairie du Chien, formerly a French trade rendezvous and still the most important settlement upstream from St. Louis. Here Pike stopped to rest his men and meet the local United States representatives. Prairie du Chien was a raw place, a straggle of houses and shanties populated by five or six hundred whites, mostly of French-Canadian extraction heavily diluted with Indian blood. The fur traders used the village as their supply base and a convenient spot for meeting one another, exchanging information, or carousing. Semicivilized Indians drifted in and out with the seasons or set up their lodges on the outskirts of the settlement to beg and barter the white man's goods. Liquor was in great abundance and there were no restrictions on its sale, so that drunken brawls were common and the village had a well-earned reputation for violence and murder. Despite these drawbacks Prairie du Chien was so obviously the key to control of the Wisconsin portage route that here, in accordance with his instructions, Pike selected the sites of two forts, one on the west bank of the Mississippi opposite Prairie du Chien and the other three miles up the Wisconsin.

The inhabitants of Prairie du Chien received the Americans hospitably. They supplied all Pike's requirements with good grace even though an official U.S. scouting party boded ill for their continued prosperity which flourished on a laissez-faire attitude. Already there was a power struggle between the French and American settlers for control of the river trade and this rivalry extended into private feuds. Pike could not help noticing that after a sports meeting between his soldiers and the locals, the American population was openly jubilant when the soldiers "beat all the villagers at hopping and jumping."

By now it had become clear that the keelboat would have to be abandoned. She was too unwieldy to take much farther up the river, and although there was plenty of water to float her, it was out of the question to manhandle the seventy-foot vessel around the Falls of St. Anthony. If the expedition was to travel by boat to the source of the Mississippi, smaller and lighter craft would have to be used. Accordingly Pike obtained two handier bateaux which he described as "Schenectady barges." These were serviceable craft but so small that it was only with much repacking that the keelboat's cargo could be transferred into them; even so there was precious little room to move about on the new boats. At Prairie du Chien Pike also decided to hire an interpreter, a man by the name of Rousseau, who was probably an out-of-work French voyageur. For the rest of the journey Rousseau was to prove invaluable as a guide and translator. Up to now Pike had either been hopelessly cut off from the natives by the language barrier or had fumbled along with makeshift interpreters using mutilated English, French, Sioux, and Sac. Rousseau filled the gap. He scouted, hunted, guided, and negotiated for the inexperienced Americans, though Pike seldom acknowledged his help.

On September 8 the expedition set out once more. Their barges were escorted by several light craft under the orders of Mr. Frazer, a fur trader of some note who, although American by birth, had learned his trade in Canada. With Frazer's help the soldiers made good time and three days later reached their first large Sioux encampment near the mouth of the Iowa River. Here Pike and his men were startled by the same sort of *feu de joie* which had once greeted Carver; on this occasion the welcome was all the more hair-raising because the Sioux marksmen were gloriously drunk and took pride in seeing how close to the visitor's boats they could fire. Their musket balls spattered the water around the slow-moving barges. Pike was not impressed; he took the precaution of going ashore with sword in hand and a brace of pistols in his belt, while his men nervously fingered their blunderbusses. Fortunately the savages sobered down enough to talk sense with the lieutenant, who asked the Sioux to end their feud with the Chippewa. After the usual peroration Pike persuaded the chief to restrain his young men from the warpath, shook hands on the deal, and presented two carrots of tobacco, four knives, a quart of rum, and a half pound of vermilion paint. Frazer, who knew the Indians better, added eight gallons of "made" whisky in the usual proportions of three parts water to each part spirits. To top off the general bonhomie, Pike unbent so far as to allow his gawking soldiers to shake hands all around with the uncouth savages so that his homespun conscripts would have a tale to tell when they got back home.

Lake Pepin was the next landmark on the journey. Rousseau, who had been there before, was worried about the passage of lake, which was notoriously dangerous. He recommended crossing at night when the waters were usually calmer than by day, a phenomenon which all later pilots confirm. Pike, however, pooh-poohed the idea and accused his guide of wanting to avoid the fierce lake tribes under cover of darkness. Subsequent events more than proved Rousseau correct. Pike ordered the flotilla to sail by daylight with pennons flying and fiddles playing. Scarcely had the boats reached open water than the wind freshened, a swell sprang up, and the barges were wallowing with their bows almost under water. Pike's own vessel became almost unmanageable. He had rigged up the keelboat's large sail on a twenty-two-foot mast so that the little bateau was grossly overburdened. She pitched and swooped atrociously. Pike had no choice but to turn aside and run for shelter before his command was swamped out of existence. The expedition reached the east shore of the lake in disarray; the boats ran aground and had to be dragged by brute force into a safe anchorage; the men were soaked to the skin and exhausted. All thought of crossing the lake that night, according to Rousseau's original suggestion, had to be put aside.

Next morning Pike still had not learned his lesson. The sky was overcast with lowering storm clouds and there was every indication of an imminent gale, but Pike stubbornly insisted on trying again. He roused his men and ordered them to sail. Before the leading boats were clear of the land a squall hit from dead ahead, sails were hastily struck, and with thunder and lightning rolling through the surrounding hills the barges were hard-pressed to scud for shelter behind a convenient headland, a mere three miles along their route. Here Pike found a more sensible traveler, Murdoch Cameron, another of that clan of wandering Scots traders. Cameron was comfortably ensconced on the beach, waiting for the weather to improve before tackling the lake. He had his tent in position, his canoes upturned on the shore to protect their cargo, and was living, to use Pike's phrase, "in all the ease of an Indian trader." Cameron helped the Americans sort themselves out. For the second consecutive day they had suffered a drenching and their commander was in an evil humor. Pike was not to be soothed by the Scotsman's hospitality. In his diary the American ungratefully noted that his host was a "man of tolerable information, but rather indolent in his habits; a Scotchman by birth, but an Englishman by prejudice." Even when Cameron piloted his expedition across the lake next day and lent Pike a canoe to poke around the smaller tributaries, the lieutenant saw no reason to amend his harsh report which remained in the official log.

Nothing of interest occurred for the next three days. Then the expedition reached the mouth of the Minnesota river. This was a strategic point, so Pike stopped to investigate. At the first Sioux village all but one of the menfolk were absent, and their squaws flocked around the visitors, chattering excitedly. Pike was taken aback by their jabber; at other camps he had observed that the Indian women kept silent and very much in the background. He ascribed their sudden curiosity and babble to "the absence of their lords and masters." Landing again a few miles farther on, he settled down to await the return of the chiefs. The Sioux warriors arrived at six o'clock the next evening and were invited to attend a grand council at Pike's camp on the beach. Here, twenty-four hours later, in the shelter of a sail spread across spars, Pike persuaded the Sioux sachems to part with 100,000 acres of tribal land, including the commanding bluffs that overlooked the junction of the Minnesota and the Mississippi. This grant included the present site of Minneapolis and was valued in Pike's private estimate at $200,000. He purchased it by making a private deal with the chiefs and giving them $200 worth of paltry presents.

From start to finish there is something uncomfortably suspicious about Pike's dealings with the Indians. To begin with, the Sioux were notorious procrastinators. Any experienced Indian agent knew to his cost that the Indians loathed to rush tribal business. Under normal conditions the Sioux would refuse to make agreements of any kind without long consultations beforehand. These deliberations took a highly formal pattern, set out by tribal custom. There should have been arguments, counterarguments, pleas, circulocution, grandiose oratory, and vacillation, all lasting several weeks. Yet, in Pike's case, a young army lieutenant managed to force through in the space of a single day a treaty which gave the white man effective control of the upper Mississippi. Pike

achieved this by negotiating directly with the chiefs and brib-
ing them with presents and liquor. The most charitable conclusion, if Pike is not to be branded a cheat, is that neither he
nor the Sioux sachems had any understanding of each other's
motives. Pike was thinking in white man's terms: he was content to buy the largest area of land at the cheapest possible
price. The chiefs were happy to receive his $200 worth of
baubles without the least idea of what they were giving in
exchange. As it happened, the Sioux leaders were in no position to barter away their lands. By tribal custom, the rivers,
prairies, forests, and all they contained, were public domain,
free for everyone's use. The chiefs probably had no inkling
that as a result of accepting Pike's glittering presents the U.S.
Army would soon arrive to claim sovereignty and build a fort
on their territory. They were equally puzzled by Pike's in-
sistence that they put their mark on his treaty paper. As far as
the chiefs were concerned, their spoken word was a binding
contract, and the two leading sachems "touched the quill"
only after Pike had stressed that signatures were in their best
interests.

Naturally Pike was elated by the success of his negotiations. He dashed off a letter to Wilkinson, exulting that he
had bought the vital 100,000 acres "for a song." He also
pointed out with much self-congratulation that he had drawn
up the treaty document with the price of the land left blank.
Now that the chiefs had signed, Congress could fill in any
price they wanted over the Indian pictographs. The ambitious
subaltern was jubilant. As a bonus he allowed sixty gallons of
liquor to be made up and distributed to the chiefs, who happily returned to their separate villages rejoicing in the white
man's bounty which they felt had been so lightly given.

At the mouth of the Minnesota there occurred an odd
little drama that illustrates the fanatical chauvinism that was
to dominate the remainder of Pike's trip. On the morning
after the council, he discovered that the large American flag,
which normally flew from the jackstaff of his barge, was
missing. Not knowing whether the flag had fallen overboard

or had been stolen by the Indians, Pike lost his temper. Summoning the local Sioux chieftain to the beach, Pike harangued the discomfited Indian on the importance of the loss. Then, before the eyes of the savage, the American guard was produced and flogged for dereliction of duty. Next morning Pike was awakened in his tent by a timid chieftain who came to report that the flag had just been found floating in the water some way downstream, still attached to its broken staff.

By now Pike had been more than six weeks on the river. In this time he had ascended a well-traveled section of the Mississippi from St. Louis to the Falls of St. Anthony. Now he was faced with finding his way around the Falls and taking his command along the relatively unknown upper reaches of the river. Though his route would now be more difficult and it was already late September, Pike was still confident that he could reach the source of the Mississippi and return to St. Louis before the ice closed in. Accordingly he pushed ahead as fast as possible with his arrangements for the portage. Sleds were made to haul the barges around the cataract; the stores were unloaded and carried to a convenient beach upstream; and the bateaux were pulled up onto the bank. The first barge was transported without a hitch, but when the second boat was halfway over the portage, the supporting props collapsed and she slid all the way back down to the bottom of the slope. As it was raining hard and only fifteen of his men were fit for duty, Pike left the barge where she lay until the next morning, when she, too, was pulled over to the upper river.

From now on it was a race against the onset of winter. Pike drove his men hard. While the soldiers pushed, poled, or paddled their craft against the strengthening current, Pike would take the best marksman in the party and go off into the prairie to hunt game. The lieutenant was a good shot, and using his special rifle seldom came back without a brace or two of geese and swans. On good days he might even bag a wolf or deer. Fresh meat of any kind was badly needed. The men were beginning to feel the strain of their efforts and they were losing heart in the fight against innumerable shoals and rapids which punctuated the course of the river. By October 16, two weeks after portaging the Falls of St. Anthony, the boats had been knocked about so badly that it was essential to call a halt for repairs. To make matters worse, the sergeant, a man called Kennerman, who was later to accompany Pike on his Arkansas trip, broke a blood vessel and vomited nearly two quarts of blood. About the same time one of the corporals suffered a rupture so that he was passing blood with his urine. Pike realized belatedly that he was demanding too much of his men; they could never manhandle the clumsy barges to the source. There was no choice but to build a stockade, garrison it with the invalids, and press on by foot and canoe.

For fifty-five precious days the expedition was bogged down by a combination of bad luck and poor management. At the outset it was discovered that there were only two felling axes and three hatchets in the baggage and this made the construction of the stockade a slow operation. Then the party set about building canoes for the dash to the source, only to make such a botched job of one canoe that it sank like a stone an hour after launching, taking down Pike's personal gear and ammunition. This cargo was retrieved from the water, but while he was trying to dry his special powder in a makeshift rig suspended over the campfire, Pike succeeded in blowing up the whole contraption and the explosion nearly took a tent and three men with it. After that the snows came down and game became so scarce that the lieutenant had to scatter his command over a wide area in order to survive. Hunters got lost; the soldiers caught frost-bite; and Pike himself began to suffer fits of black depression. In his diary he recorded that he was "powerfully attacked with the fantastics of the brain called ennui." The same comment could have been made many years earlier by La Salle or De Soto when they too found themselves hemmed about by obstacles which slowed their feverish energy. For Zebulon Pike in these straits there was a special burden, as it had now become obvious to everyone in his party that the canoes, so laboriously built on the lieutenant's instructions, had been left until too late; jagged ice floes were already beginning to block the river and the canoes would be torn to shreds if they were launched. Pike decided to make the best of a bad job and to haul the useless canoes overland. Grimly he set all hands to making sleds.

On December 10 a slight thaw set in and the snow around the stockade began to melt. Pike, who had been poised for just such an opportunity, decided to make his lightening trip to the source. Sergeant Kennerman and ten men were detailed to hold the stockade with strict instructions to hunt food rather than eat the last of the packed supplies. Then Pike, eleven men, and Rousseau set out.

This final leg of the journey is reminiscent of Scott's epic dash to the Pole. Pike himself led the way, scouting and hunting. Behind him came the main party with two sledges, each loaded with supply barrels and drawn by a pair of soldiers harnessed abreast, and the two canoes which a team of six men dragged over the frozen ground. Rousseau and the best hunter covered the flanks of the march. It was a grueling ordeal for everyone as the expedition stumbled forward, often no more than five miles a day. All the elements of intrepid exploration were present: the piercing cold, frequent falls into ice holes, short rations, and the numbed men collapsing into their tents at nightfall. Christmas Day was celebrated in a dreary landscape of rocks and snow, dead timber, and ice hummocks. Each man was given two extra pounds of meat and flour, a gill of whiskey, and some tobacco. Pike wrote: "Never did I undergo more fatigue performing the duties of hunter, spy, guide, commanding officer . . . sometimes in front, sometimes in the rear and frequently in advance of my party 10 or 15 miles. At night I was scarcely able to make my notes intelligibly." Day after day he records the gallant progress of his command and the obstacles that were overcome. His journal makes stirring reading but cannot camouflage the basic fact that all this suffering was unnecessary. The end of their labors was not the source of the fabled Father of Waters, hidden away in some unknown corner of the continent, but the warm fireside of a fur trader's home and an invitation to breakfast.

Pike's course along the line of the river led him through upper Minnesota in an arc which curved from northeast, through north, to south and southwest. Dotted along the circumference of this arc were trading posts, most of them owned by partners in the North-West Company, the largest of the Canadian fur-trading concerns. Thus as Pike and his men trudged along through the snow, they found themselves being intercepted by white men or half-breed messengers who invited the Americans to drop in at the trading posts for hot meals and coffee. To make the trek even more ridiculous, one of the traders, yet another Scot, named Grant, arranged to make the expedition welcome along his chain of trading houses by greeting them in person at each place. This meant that he would see Pike and his expedition safely on their way from his first home, send them a keg of spirits en route to cheer them up, and be at hand to greet them when they struggled in to his next post. Pike was mortified, and decided that Grant was a dangerous spy who needed to be watched.

By rights Pike should have been extremely grateful to the Canadian furmen. It was only with their assistance that he finally learned the elementary aids to winter travel through the snowbound land. They showed him how to make decent sledges instead of his own amateur efforts, taught him how to use snowshoes, and even lent him valuable teams of sled dogs. More important, they at last persuaded Pike to see that his dozen inexperienced soldiers formed a miserable exploring team. He was far better off with a good guide, a pack of supplies, and his rifle. His soldiers could follow later.

The much abused Grant took Pike under his wing. The weary lieutenant was fed roast beaver and boiled head of moose. His men were given comfortable billets—even though this meant that Grant had to give up his own quarters—and their every need was attended to without hint of repayment.

The Canadian then volunteered to guide Pike to the source, a
tedious process for Grant since the American officer could
only cover one-third of the trader's daily mileage. The Scot
made the best of it by dashing off on side errands while Pike
plodded forward along the designated path. In this fashion
the lieutenant at last reached Leech Lake on Saturday,
February 1.

To the confusion of geographers and explorers, the Mississippi rises in an area where the drainage pattern is a maze of
ponds, lakes, marshes, and streams, spread over several hundred square miles. The run-off of surface water is so complicated that the most painstaking observations of slope and
channel are needed before one can determine which lake or
spring is the true source of the great river. Further, when
Pike visited the region in the depths of winter, the drainage
network was hidden under the ice and snow. Therefore it
would be churlish to blame Pike for his decision that Leech
Lake was the ultimate source of the Father of Waters. In fact,
the Mississippi rises in Lake Itasca, eighty miles and five more
lakes to the west. Pike, however, was not to know this as he
stood on the ice of Leech Lake at half-past two that Saturday
afternoon in 1806. With unaccustomed restraint he entered
into his logbook: "I will not attempt to describe my feelings
on the accomplishment of my voyage, for this is the main
source of the Mississippi."

Even if Leech Lake had been the true source, Pike would
have been hard put to claim the honor of discovery; scarcely
twelve miles from where he stood, on the opposite shore of
the lake, was another comfortable trading station owned by
the North-West Company. Here Pike went to meet the proprietor, Hugh M'Gillis, who lived in considerable comfort,
surrounded by a small but choice library and supplied, even at
that time of year, with such delicacies as butter and cheese.
As usual, the trader welcomed Pike and did everything in his
power to succor the American, whose soldiers trickled in six
days later. Pike was in need of help. His health had given out
and his legs were so badly swollen that he could not wear his

own clothes but had to borrow larger garments from his host. M'Gillis, seeing that Pike had to rest, send runners to summon the local chiefs to hear what Pike had to say, in the meantime providing his uninvited guest with books on philosophy, geography, and travel. By all the tenets of frontier hospitality, M'Gillis was uncommonly polite. He even asked the prickly lieutenant if he had any objections to the Union Jack being flown over the company's post. Pike gave his tacit approval but promptly ordered his soldiers to raise the American flag alongside.

A man less self-confident than Pike would have found himself in an awkward position. The American had penetrated into territory that was technically under dispute between the United States and England. Both countries claimed the land, but in point of fact it was firmly in the hands of the English through the presence of the Canadian fur companies. To drive home this reality, Pike must have known that he was at the mercy of the British traders, and only their unstinted help had brought him to Leech Lake. Without their cooperation he could neither meet the Indians nor survive the snows. Surprisingly, Pike chose this moment to overstep his authority, assert United States sovereignty, and snub his host. On February 10, four days after giving permission for the flying of the Union Jack, Pike assembled a firing squad in the trading-post square. Then, in the presence of visiting Indians, he ordered his men to shoot down the offensive British flag. The musket balls broke the iron pin that fastened the standard to the masthead, and the gaudy square of bunting came fluttering to the ground. With that gesture, Pike went indoors to continue reading a book from his host's library. One wonders that M'Gillis did not send the obstreperous lieutenant packing out into the snow.

It is difficult to explain Pike's behavior in the flag incident. He had no instructions from General Wilkinson to force the British out of upper Minnesota. His mission was merely to reconnoiter the headwaters of the Mississippi as an official representative of the governor of upper Louisiana, and to gather information on the Indian trade. In written orders Wilkinson had stressed the distribution of American flags with the "trifling presents" but had not suggested removing the flags of other nations. It was on his own authority and by his own judgment that Pike set about destroying the symbols of English presence in the north country. He did so in a singularly loutish manner, which can only be ascribed to his youth —he was only twenty-seven years old—and to his rabid distaste for the easygoing traders. In his opinion they were a queer, lonely group who survived, in Pike's words, "by contenting themselves in this wilderness for 10, 15 and some of them for 20 years, by the attachment they contract for the Indian women. It appears to me that the wealth of nations would not induce me to remain secluded from the society of civilized mankind, surrounded by a savage and unproductive wilderness, without books or other sources of intellectual company, or being blessed with the cultivated and feeling mind of a fair [one]." Unfortunately, his self-righteousness fails to excuse the shabby way he treated the traders who helped him.

The return trip to St. Louis began on February 18. Naturally it was a much quicker journey than the northward march. With the help of guides and snowshoes (provided once again by the Canadian fur traders) the expedition made good time. Pike himself rode in a dog sled while his men marched through the snow ahead of him. A direct route across the loop of the upper river brought them to Sergeant Kennerman's stockade on March 5. There, to Pike's chagrin, he discovered that Kennerman had disobeyed his orders, broken open the store barrels, sold whisky to the Indians, rifled the contents of Pike's personal trunk, and "used all the elegant hams and saddles of venison which I had preserved to present to the commander-in-chief and other friends." To punish the sergeant, Pike, who seems to have had a soft spot for the rogue, merely reduced Kennerman to the ranks. Then for more than a month the expedition came to a standstill, waiting for the ice to clear from the river. On April 7, they set out from the stockade after a farewell party when "the men cleared out their room, danced to the violin, and sang songs until eleven o'clock, so rejoiced was every heart at leaving this savage wilderness." Precisely three weeks later, after a journey of more than five thousand miles and about nine months, the Mississippi expedition returned to its starting point, St. Louis.

Although he would have been the last to admit it, Pike's journey to the headwaters of the Mississippi was a signal failure. He had neither found the source of the river nor gathered any scientific or geographic information of value. His maps of the country were inaccurate and poorly drawn, his journal a jumble of contradictions and gaps. The Canadian fur traders ignored his admonitions and continued to trade with the Indians. The tribes who had accepted Pike's presents or listened to his long-winded speeches nearly all fought for the English in the War of 1812. Pike himself was glad to get out of the north country and the frontiersmen were equally willing to see him go. His influence on the river was fleeting. Behind him came the scores of little men, the faceless surveyors, cartographers, and draughtsmen who would reduce the river's course to an orderly explanation neatly executed with plane table and inclinometer. Their work was more durable than any result of the lieutenant's visit. Not that Pike cared; his Mississippi venture had given his career that vital push which brought him into the limelight. From then on he never faltered—the Arkansas trip and his meteoric rise through the ranks followed in rapid succession. Like Meriwether Lewis and William Clark, who both received high office after their journey, Zebulon Pike, the third army explorer, benefited from his reputation as a pioneer to achieve national prominence in his chosen profession.

11

The Red Silk Umbrella

AFTER PIKE'S TEDIOUS SELF-SATISFACTION, THE AR-
rival of the next Mississippi explorer is a breath of
fresh air. He is Giacomo Costantino Beltrami, an Italian
of comic-opera proportions. Following closely on Pike's heels,
Beltrami with his antics underscores the American solem-
nity. Both men praised their own achievements; both took
themselves seriously; and both wrote books to publicize
their own importance. But while Pike is the natural heir to
American ambitions for the interior and conforms to the
pattern of Mississippi exploration, Beltrami is a glorious
misfit. He is wayward, unpredictable, and humorous. It is
impossible for the Italian to be anything but a charming
maverick, the lone dilettante setting forth to discover the true
source of the Mississippi in a gush of hyperbole. His narrative
is so bombastic and so extravagant that a thread of absurdity
carries Beltrami gaily into the depths of Minnesota and
enlivens every page of his adventures.

Beltrami was forty-two years old when he began what he
described as his "Pilgrimage." A citizen of the Venetian republic, he had been a vice-inspector of the army, a judge in

the civil and criminal courts, and an unsuccessful political conspirator. As a well-known supporter of the French puppet regime, the Italian saw his career crash when the Austrians marched back into northern Italy after the Battle of Leipsig in 1813. Beltrami retired to his estates at Filotrano, not far from Macerato in the Marches. There he fell under suspicion as a conspirator in the "carbonari" plots for a separate Italian kingdom, and in 1821 he was exiled from his homeland. Deeply hurt, Beltrami packed his bags on one mule, and, like Don Quixote, set out to seek adventure as a "promeneur, solitary, unprotected, struggling by his own unaided efforts with every sort of difficulty, privation and danger." Before he left, he promised to send back full reports to his old friend, the Countess Guilia Medici-Spada. His book finally appeared as a collection of these letters, suitably arranged and embellished.

Determined in his exile to see and do everything expected of a gentleman traveler, Beltrami began his "Pilgrimage" with a grand tour of Europe. He poked and pried everywhere, delighting to show off his erudition with Latin tags and technical phrases. In Languedoc he rode an ass along the shore and collected sea shells. In Provence he gaped at Roman aqueducts and quoted the classics. In Aquitaine he took a steamer trip up the Gironde with several Gascons, a German who spoke French, a Frenchman who spoke German, and a group of Englishmen who apparently spoke only English but were dutifully observing the moon in bright sunshine in order to make an almanac. From Leghorn to Brussels, Beltrami sauntered and mused. Nothing escaped his notice, and every subject, from Napoleon's battle tactics to the German national character, was treated to his opinions. Paris was declared to be the "metropolis of the world" and Baden "the temple of the mystival Esculapius." At Karlsruhe he drew a sketch of the Grand Duke's palace and at Bonn he peered at the "curious circumstance" of a woman with an artificial nose. Finally, via Ghent and Ostend, he found himself in London during the summer of 1822.

London, Beltrami decided, was a very confusing city. Large palaces belong to public institutions; obscure-looking houses were royal residences. Dukes dressed like servants; footmen like lords. In the streets the common people rubbed shoulders with the greatest in the land; the city exuded democracy; and in the public taverns there were "men sitting in the midst of women, and women surrounded by men, all completely absorbed in their glass of beer or cup of tea." Such overfamiliarity disturbed Beltrami, who took refuge in the solid elegance of the men's clubs, particularly the Traveller's Club. From there he sallied out to see the sights: St. Paul's ("too long for its width, or, if you will, extremely narrow for its length"); the Bank of England ("a prison"); the Mint ("simple and majestic"); the Customs House ("already decrepid, though it is not six years old"); and the Guildhall ("an architectural miscellania"). He also found time to discuss a variety of topics ranging from the system of government and the aristocracy, through the quality of the newspapers, to a boxing match. Some of his comments were shrewd ("the individual Englishman does not, in all cases, recommend his country"), but for much of his time in London Beltrami was handicapped by his poor knowledge of English. Although he had studied the language in school, he found it almost impossible to use in real life: "If you speak it as you read it," he wrote to the countess, "it is a charming jargon; your mouth and eyes are thrown into the most beautiful grimaces; every limb of your body is convulsed in the struggle to pronounce all these consonants, these strings of monosyllables. You give utterance to sounds which come from your stomach like volcanic eructations, shaking your whole frame like an electric shock, and, by sympathy, those of all who have the patience to listen to you. I forgive the English from the bottom of my heart, if sometimes they cannot refrain from laughing at the novelty of the exhibition. Often indeed I anticipate them, and laugh myself, to encourage them to give vent to a convulsion which, if repressed, might do them harm."

The Red Silk Umbrella

From London Beltrami proceeded to Windsor and then on to Oxford—"the sanctuary of learning." The university was almost as confusing as London. No one seemed to know or care about the inner workings of the academic system, and the best that his guide could offer was "what I least cared for, a good dinner." However, the colleges were there for inspection in "their Gothic character—severe, gloomy, majestic— the fit abodes of meditation, learning and wisdom." Beltrami confessed that his soul thrilled "with a holy veneration," and, lamenting that he was unable to visit Cambridge, he continued on his way to Liverpool, there to take ship for America.

Beltrami had a miserable passage across the Atlantic. He loathed sea voyages and was violently seasick. Furthermore, because the regular packet service sailed to New York where a yellow-fever epidemic was raging, he decided to travel directly to Philadelphia aboard a small American merchant vessel. The change of route was a disaster. The ship's cook had deserted and the regular cabin steward was removed from his duties in order to do the cooking. To replace the steward, an ordinary deckhand was detailed to look after the passengers. As a result, Beltrami noted that "the hour of dinner discovered . . . that we had neither steward nor cook." Later, conditions went from bad to worse. The cabin was filthy, the meat putrid, and the captain a drunken rogue. The newly appointed steward turned out to be a thief, and the food ran out. For weeks they were delayed by storms off the Irish coast. While the ship tossed and heaved, Beltrami clung to his bunk, refusing to eat the rotten fare and imploring the captain to put in to the nearest port. His fellow passengers, two Spanish-Americans who Beltrami firmly believed to be off-duty pirates, alternately prayed for salvation from Our Lady of Cuba or raided the Italian's private stock of wines until it was all gone. Finally, after fights among the crew, gales, and near shipwreck, they reached Philadelphia where Beltrami thankfully scrambled ashore, convinced that he had narrowly escaped the most terrible death by drowning and seasickness.

Once he was safely on dry land, his high spirits bubbled back. He "promenaded" briskly around Philadelphia and Baltimore, then moved on to Washington. There he inspected the Capitol and other public buildings, made his customary comparisons to the senate of early Rome, and was immensely pleased to meet President Monroe in person. Traveling westward by stagecoach and hired wagon, Beltrami continued his "Pilgrimage," carefully jotting down his impressions of the country: Kentuckians were "brave, industrious and active" but also "coarse and insolent"; the roads "detestable"; and Pittsburgh a "little Birmingham of the United States." Few details escaped his eye and he did not hesitate to give personal opinions. He found that American women were superior to their menfolk, being "agreeable without forwardness, modest without affectation, well-informed without pedantry, and are excellent housewives," but he was not so enthusiastic about coeducational schools, where, he feared, "opportunity will prevail over the most austere principles."

By April 20, 1823, Beltrami had reached the confluence of the Ohio and Mississippi, intending to take a steamboat down to New Orleans and then continue to Mexico. Quite by chance, the first boat to call was the *Calhoun* bound for St. Louis in the opposite direction. On board was Major Taliaferro, Indian agent at Fort St. Anthony,[1] the army post which had been built on Pike's purchase site at the mouth of the Minnesota River. Beltrami seized on Taliaferro and bombarded him with questions about the north country. The Major's descriptions of the up-river Indians captivated the romantic Italian. Impulsively he threw over his plans for visiting New Orleans and took passage on the *Calhoun*, determined to visit those tribes whose "extraordinary character had, from infancy, excited my astonishment and my incredulity." Thus, in a fit of whimsy, Beltrami joined the ranks of Mississippi explorers.

Beltrami made a good river commentator. From the start

[1] Beltrami called it Fort St. Peter. In 1825 the name was changed to Fort Snelling.

he resolved to ignore "hydraulics, hydrometrics, hydrostatics, hydrodynamics, and a whole dictionary of such hard words . . . for all this is Greek to me." Instead, he was interested in Indians, pioneer figures, the scenery, and of course "antiquities." It was difficult to apply classical quotations to frontier America, but Beltrami tried hard. At St. Louis he put the Indian burial mounds in the same class as the Parthenon, Mithraic temples, and the Pyramids of Giza. He also never lost a chance to mention the Italian contribution to American history, invoking Columbus, Verrazano and "Cabot or Gaboto," and the small river town of Herculaneum naturally called forth a fulsome comparison to its Italian counterpart. Nothing could deflect Beltrami from his chosen role as a gentleman traveler of grace and education. When he was not sauntering round the deck of the *Calhoun*, he was sweeping dandified bows to astonished frontier farmers' wives in their log cabins, and in St. Louis he minced happily through "a very brilliant ball, where the ladies were so pretty and so well dressed, that they made me forget I was on the threshold of savage life."

At St. Louis Beltrami and Major Taliaferro transferred to the *Virginia*. It was to be a momentous trip. The *Virginia* was the first steamboat to attempt the upstream journey to Fort St. Anthony and no one knew whether she would manage to battle through the rapids. Beltrami loved the drama of the venture. In great excitement he hung over the rail to watch the paddle wheel push the stubby vessel against the rushing water, and day by day he pestered the crew for details of the boat's progress. The *Virginia's* captain was taking no chances and proceeded cautiously, so Beltrami had plenty of time to go ashore en route. Each sortie into the forest was an adventure. The Italian, draped with rifle, pistols, and sword, trod gingerly through the undergrowth, looking for a lurking savage behind every tree. He blazed away at wild turkeys, pondered on the beauty of nature, and managed to bag a rattlesnake which "at first fled from me; it then stopped, and was in the act of looking at me, when I shot it through the head." Of course Beltrami preserved the reptile's skin, for he was an inveterate souvenir hunter and was busily putting together a magpie collection of Americana, ranging from tomahawks to dried Indian scalps.

The *Virginia* was having a rough trip, even without Beltrami's pen to exaggerate the dangers. She hit a rock in the Des Moines Rapids, fortunately without puncturing her hull, and narrowly escaped a forest fire which threatened to destroy her. There were repeated delays while the crew cut firewood for the boilers or pulled their vessel off sand bars. Beltrami did not complain; each halt was another opportunity for more "exploring." On one excursion he lost his bearings and used his compass to return to the landing place, only to find the boat gone. Imagining himself abandoned forever in the "wilderness," he rushed frantically along the bank, firing his gun to attract attention. To his immense relief, the *Virginia* was just around the next bend, firmly aground on yet another sand bar.

To supplement his excursions on shore, he compiled notes on his fellow passengers. The prize exhibit was a Sac chief named Great Eagle. The Indian was returning from his first visit to St. Louis and had been presented with a military uniform to wear on the way home. To Beltrami's delight, the chief's first act on coming aboard the *Virginia* was to remove his uniform and strut around "in statu quo of our first parents." Great Eagle did not stay long. Exasperated by the steamer's slow progress, he dived into the river and swam to the bank. Next day he was waiting to greet the boat when she reached his encampment and he came aboard to collect his belongings. Beltrami, still playing the tourist, shook him by the hand and persuaded him to sell a scalp lock that dangled from the handle of his war club. Great Eagle's departure was a sad loss to Beltrami's "Pilgrimage," but the Italian had other passengers to entertain his curiosity, including a female missionary on her way to convert the savages. Evidently she was practicing on the ship's crew with total lack of success. She was, Beltrami concluded, "one of those women who devote themselves to God when they have lost all hope of pleasing men." Passing his time with such gentle prattle in his reports to the countess, Beltrami rode the steamer northward until the *Virginia* at last reached her destination, Fort St. Anthony, and the garrison unloaded her cargo of military supplies.

When Beltrami visited the upper river, the semi-savage conditions which Pike had encountered were much diluted. The army had moved into the area, a smattering of settlers had arrived and set up homesteads, and the Indian threat was more imaginary than real. Fort St. Anthony, 180 miles up-river from Prairie du Chien, was now the northern outpost of the white man's civilization. Beyond the fort the wilderness was still dominant. Poor soil, bad drainage, and an inhospitable climate discouraged immigrants, so the land was left to isolated bands of Sioux and Chippewa, who eked out a meager livelihood, fishing, hunting, and trapping. Since Pike's visit the power and prestige of the fur companies had greatly declined as their supply of pelts dwindled, and many of the Scots-Canadian traders had moved elsewhere. The only real significance of the headwaters region was its position as the frontier zone between the United States and Canada; this was enough to interest the American government in sponsoring further exploration of upper Minnesota.

Beltrami's visit to Fort St. Anthony coincided with the arrival of an official American expedition under Major Long to define and map the line of the U.S.-Canadian border. This was a great stroke of luck for the wandering Italian. Normally he would have been turned back at the fort by its commandant, Colonel Snelling, who could not allow casual "tourists" to venture unescorted into tribal lands. As it was, Beltrami made friends with the colonel and through Taliaferro's help managed to get himself attached unofficially to Long's expedition. Beltrami was elated. He sent an exuberant letter to the countess, sold his fine repeater watch to raise money to buy a horse and provisions, distributed presents to the colonel and his family, and informed Long that he was ready to go. The major was not pleased. He was running a military expedition under the auspices of the War Department and he did not relish the prospect of a civilian hanger-on. Major Long made his feelings brutally clear. He tried to dissuade Beltrami with descriptions of the dangers the expedition would encounter, the privations they would endure, and the expense of the trip for a private individual. Beltrami refused to be put off by Long's rudeness. His intention, he wrote, of "going in search of the real sources of the Mississippi, was always before my eyes. I was therefore obliged to sacrifice my pride . . . to the desire of seeing places which one can hardly expect to visit twice in one's life."

On the seventh of July the expedition, Beltrami included, left the fort and started up the Minnesota River. The party consisted of Major Long, a lieutenant, twenty-eight soldiers, an astronomer to determine their route, a zoologist, a professor of mineralogy and chemistry to take rock samples, and a landscape painter to help with the mapping and draw pictures of Indian life. For guides they had Joseph Snelling, the colonel's son, and Joseph Renville, one of the most famour frontiersmen in the northwest. Renville's mother was a full-blooded Sioux of good family and the scout himself was highly respected by the Indians for his courage and tact. In the War of 1812 Renville had fought for the British and had risen to the rank of captain in the irregulars. Now he was working as an independent fur trader and guide. Naturally Beltrami was fascinated by the swashbuckling half-breed, who seemed to epitomize the courage and dash of the fearless Indian scout. Throughout the trip Beltrami took care to cultivate Renville's friendship and he basked in the slightest word of praise from the guide, carefully noting down every utterance from his hero's lips.

Unfortunately, although the trip went smoothly apart from one or two upsets in the Minnesota rapids, Beltrami was unhappy. The source of his troubles was his relationship with Major Long. The two men, the verbose Italian and the crisp West Point officer, took an instant dislike to one another. Beltrami thought the soldier stupid and over-

bearing, and Long considered his supernumerary a trifler.
There was constant bickering between them. Beltrami could
not refrain from criticizing the management of the expedition, and Long naturally resented the Italian's interference.
By the end of the first week even the pettiest frictions became
insupportable. Beltrami complained that he was not being
given his fair share of food from the common stock even
though he had contributed generously at Fort St. Anthony,
and he privately suspected that Long assigned him the wettest
sleeping place in the tent whenever a thunderstorm was brewing over the camp. Matters finally came to a head when Beltrami and another man returned to camp after a hunting trip
to learn that Long had failed to warn them of a threatened
Indian attack. Beltrami was incensed and decided that he
could no longer tolerate the major. He resolved to leave the
expedition as soon as possible.

His chance to strike out on his own came when the expedition reached Lord Selkirk's settlement on the Red River.
This was a pioneer attempt at planned colonization in which
Selkirk, operating through agents, had induced European
immigrants to start a new life on his lands near Pembina. One
of Long's tasks was to determine whether the Red River settlement lay within the United States or Canada. From there
he was under orders to proceed eastward to Lake Superior,
moving well to the north of the Mississippi headwaters. Up to
this point Long had refused to tell Beltrami the exact path
that the expedition had been following, but at Pembina Beltrami knew that he was north and west of the Mississippi's
source. He reasoned that if he went southeast up the course
of the Bloody River, as he called the Red Lake River, he
would reach the swampy region in which the Mississippi was
known to rise. Accordingly, he sold his horse, hired an interpreter and two Chippewa Indians, and separated himself from
Long's command despite "the dangers which I was going to
brave among the Indians, who are generally described as
being very ferocious."

Although he was undoubtedly exaggerating the Indian

menace, Beltrami had made a bold decision. The journey up the Bloody River was not an easy task. The stream ran strongly and there were numerous rapids, all of which had to be portaged knee-deep on the slippery rocks as the little group dragged its canoe forward. The interpreter turned back almost immediately and Beltrami was left to communicate with the Chippewa by his own gesticulations. At first the two Indians behaved well and Beltrami's little party made good progress. Then on August 14 they ran into trouble. The Chippewa were ambushed by a marauding band of Sioux, and although Beltrami escaped injury (the Sioux fled as soon as they saw his white skin), one of his guides was shot through the arm. The ambush gave the Chippewa a bad fright and they refused to go any farther by water, insisting that the Sioux were likely to attack again. Beltrami tried to be firm. He insisted that the only way to reach the source of the Mississippi was by canoe and assured his guides that he would protect them. It was useless. After a brief argument in sign language, the two Indians gathered up their belongings and decamped into the woods, leaving Beltrami sitting disconsolately on the bank with his baggage and a canoe he did not know how to paddle. "I imagine, my dear countess," he wrote, "that you will feel the frightfulness of my situation at this crucial moment more strongly than I can express it. I really can scarcely help shuddering, as well as yourself, whenever I think of it."

According to his own version of that momentous day, Beltrami rose magnificently to the occasion. First he mused on the fate of Robinson Crusoe and next he loaded his musket in case he had to defend himself against the white bears "which abound near the Red River" (and which, he stated, sustained themselves during their winter hibernation by sucking the fat from their paws). Then he resolved that at all costs he would continue his journey in search of the mysterious source. From that moment forward, his adventures took a comic turn, which he had the grace to describe:

"I jumped into my canoe and began rowing. But I was

totally unacquainted with the almost magical art by which a single person guides a canoe, and particularly a canoe formed of bark, the lightness of which is overpowered by the current, and the conduct of which requires extreme dexterity. Frequently, instead of proceeding up the river, I descended; a circumstance which by no means shortened my voyage. Renewed efforts made me lose my equilibrium, the canoe upset, and admitted a considerable quantity of water. My whole cargo was wetted. I leaped into the water, drew the canoe on land, and laid it to drain with the keel upwards. I then loaded it again, taking care to place the wetted part of my effects uppermost, to be dried by the sun. I then resumed my route."

For some hours this erratic progress continued, and, if we are to believe the incurably optimistic Italian, he was thoroughly amused by his efforts at paddling. Indeed, he told the countess that he could "scarcely help incessantly smiling," even though it was obvious that he was making little or no headway. Unabashed, he decided to try another means of locomotion:

"I threw myself into the water up to my waist, and commenced a promenade of a rather unusual kind, drawing the canoe after me with a thong from a buffaloe's hide, which I had fastened to the prow. The first day of my expedition, the 15th of the month, was employed in this manner, and I did not stop till the evening. It was natural to expect that I should be fatigued; but I was not in the least so. While thus dragging after me my canoe, with a cord over my shoulder, an oar [sic] in my hand for my support, my back stooping, my head looking down, holding conversation with the fishes beneath, and making incessant windings in the river, in order to sound its depths, that I might most safely pass; I must leave to your imagination to conceive the variety and interest of the ideas which rapidly passed in review before my mind!"

Despite the discomforts of his situation, Beltrami was having the time of his life. He saw himself as an heir to the intrepid heroes of Roman legend, sternly pushing forward to his goal against all obstacles. From time to time he was forced to resume his feeble attempts at paddling, but always found that he could not master the art and made more headway by wading upstream. Everything was soaking wet—his baggage, provisions, weapons, bedding, and himself. At night it was impossible to light a fire to dry out his belongings, because the renegade Chippewa had stolen his flint, so he slept in his sodden clothing and relied on the morning sunshine to warm his chilled body. To add to his discomfort, the weather was sultry and there were many thunder showers. Beltrami himself did not care; wading in the river, he could hardly have been wetter, but his baggage was drenched and began to grow moldly. Therefore on the third day of his extraordinary trek he unpacked the ultimate item in his gentleman traveler kit—a large umbrella, covered with red silk. This he unfolded and stuck upright in the canoe so that his luggage was sheltered from the rain. Then he plunged back into the water, took up the tow rope, and proceeded on his "promenade."

The progress of Beltrami and his red silk umbrella is the last flamboyant episode in the story of Mississippi exploration. There is something captivating about the idea of this lighthearted Italian coxscomb trudging purposefully up the river bed, waist-deep in water, towing his canoe behind him because he did not know how to paddle. The exact location of the Mississippi's source was no longer important to anyone except a cartographer or the most romantic dreamer. Yet Beltrami was utterly absorbed in his mission to find the source. To him, the remotest feeder stream of the Father of Waters was a glittering prize, an exercise in adventure for a "cultivated man." Typically, he expressed his feelings in terms of classical scholarship; wading against the current, he noted that his baggage was "conveyed thus in the stately style and manner of China, while I myself was condemned to travel in that of a galley slave."

But Beltrami's labors were almost over. After one more lonely night on the bank, tormented by mosquitos, he encountered at noon the following day two canoes of Indians paddling downstream. The natives were thrown into confusion by the sight of the half-submerged explorer. Beltrami, shouting and hallooing with relief, persuaded them to approach the extraordinary spectacle of the "great red skin" and the crazy white man walking in the water. The Indians, Chippewa from Red Lake, came forward nervously, and the Italian had to distribute odds and ends of cloth and food to all of them before they would take him seriously. After much haggling Beltrami succeeded in enticing one of the Indians, an old man, to paddle him up to Red Lake. It was a pleasant relief from wading, but the philosophical Italian still had some conclusions to draw from his adventures. "You have experienced," he told himself, "complete solitude, you have tasted genuine independence, you will from this time never enjoy them more. The independence and solitude represented in books, or to be found among civilized nations are vain and chimerical. . . . I, at that moment fully comprehended why the Indians consider themselves happier than cultivated nations, and far superior to them."

On the journey to Red Lake, Beltrami was nearly abandoned a second time. His "patriarchal companion" was an accomplished canoeman and paddled the explorer upstream at a fast pace. Beltrami shot a brace of wild duck for dinner, and after the meal settled down to sleep on the bank, taking the precaution of tying the bowline of the canoe to his ankle in case the Indian stole his boat during the night. He was awakened by something tugging at the rope, so raising his musket he let fly into the darkness. With a loud yelp his elderly guide, who had been sleeping peacefully, leapt to his feet and scampered off into the forest. Realizing his mistake, Beltrami blundered about in the dark shouting at the man to come back, and firing his gun. This encouraged the Indian to believe that they had been attacked by Sioux and it was not until next morning that he timidly emerged from cover. In daylight they found the cause of the commotion—a scavenging wolf whose carcass lay a few yards away from where Beltrami had shot him.

This incident served to confirm the old Chippewa's impression that he was dealing with a lunatic, and all next day he tried to exchange places with any Indians they met on the river. But Beltrami did not relish another bout of haggling and urged his "Charon" to continue. Dusk saw them almost at the entrance to Red Lake, and, as the guide wanted to paddle all night, Beltrami curled up in the bottom of the canoe to get some badly needed sleep. He awakened to find himself alone in the canoe, which had been concealed in the rushes. The guide had very sensibly returned downstream to rejoin his friends, leaving Beltrami to the care of the nearest family of Chippewa. These arrived and led him to their hut, where he was immediately set upon by the household pet, a tame wolf who tore the visitor's last serviceable pair of pantaloons. Beltrami's stay with the Chippewa was not a success. He was eager to travel on toward the source of the Mississippi but had to wait while a half-breed guide was fetched from the other side of the lake. In the interval his hosts stole anything they could carry off from his belongings and held a funeral party for a relative who had been killed by the Sioux. The funeral consisted of the family yelling, eating, drinking, and dancing without intermission until Beltrami, heartily sick of the din, wished that he could leave before the Indians consumed all the provisions he had brought with him. The "*bois-brûlé*," as Beltrami called anyone of mixed blood, put in his appearance on the twentieth and immediately the Italian realized that he was going to have trouble with his new guide. The half-breed was intelligent and could read and write, but he was a shifty character and it took all Beltrami's bluster and wheedling to induce the guide to lead him to his destination.

On the morning of the twenty-sixth Beltrami, the *bois-brûlé*, and an Indian porter set out. The Italian was highly excited; at last, he felt, he was approaching the goal of his wanderings—"the sources of a river which are most in a right line with its mouth." His little band crossed Red Lake and headed up a small tributary river which flowed in from the south. On the other side of the gently rising ground which faced them, Beltrami was told he would be entering the Mis-

sissippi drainage basin. There he was confident he would discover the most northerly source of the Mississippi. It was a
moment of personal triumph for the traveler and he made the
most of it. He savored the scenery, enthusing wildly about
the marshy countryside covered with low brush and clumps
of "cypress-trees." He compared himself with Aeneas wandering into the unknown. A small, isolated lake reminded him
of the Sibyl's grotto at Cumae, so he dubbed it "Lake Aver-
nus of the new world"; a scattering of other ponds was
promptly given a string of names in honor of a family he
knew back in Italy. At last, after a final portage, he came to
the crest of the divide. There, cradled in the top of the low
hill, lay a small heart-shaped lake. It had no streams flowing in
or out of it, but a few paces to the north a small spring issued
from the boggy ground and flowed north to the Red River;
on the south slope there was a second rivulet draining in the
opposite direction to join the Mississippi. After dangling
sounding lines in the lake, Beltrami came to the conclusion
that the lake and the two streams were interconnected
"through long subterranean sinuosities." Thus at one stroke
he had discovered the sources of the Bloody River and the
Mississippi!

Sitting down on the shores of the lake, already named
Lake Julia after another of his heroines, Beltrami pulled out
his pen and began: *These are the actual sources of the Mississippi!* This lake therefore supplies the southern sources of
the Red, or, as I shall in the future call it (by its truer name)
Bloody River; and the most northern sources of the Mississippi—sources till now unknown of both. . . .

"Oh! What were the thoughts which passed through my
mind at this most happy and brilliant moment of my life! The
shades of Marco Polo, of Columbus, of Americus Vespucius,
of the Cabots, of Verazini, of the Zenos, and various others,
appeared present, and joyfully assisting at this high and solemn ceremony, and congratulating themselves on one of their
countrymen having, by new and successful researches,
brought back to the recollection of the world the inestimable

services which they had themselves conferred on it by their own peculiar discoveries, by their talents, achievements, and virtues."

Beltrami was in ecstasies. He had found the source and before him the Mississippi was "but a timid Naiad, stealing cautiously through the rushes and briars which obstruct its progress. The famous Mississippi, whose course is said to be twelve hundred leagues, and which bears navies on it bosom, and steam-boats superior in size to frigates, is at its source merely a petty stream of crystalline water, concealing itself among the reeds and wild rice, which seem to insult ever its humble birth." Carried away with his success, the excited Italian hurried along the course of the infant stream, scattering new names like confetti on every pond the Mississippi crossed; the countess was given her own lake, and such names as Monteleone, Torrigiana, and Antonelli were firmly inked in on his sketch map.

The downstream journey became a march of triumph. Beltrami now regarded himself as the intrepid explorer who was returning to civilization to announce the success of his mission. True to his role as a gentleman traveler, he was magnanimous in victory, making a detour to view Leech Lake as the farthest point Pike—"a bold and enterprising man"—had reached, but he would brook no rival for glory. He carefully examined the efforts of previous explorers and rejected their claims to discovery; denounced government expeditions, after the manner of Major Long's group, as top-heavy; and of course advocated the ideal explorer as a "single individual, possessed of practical philosophy and genuine philanthropy, with a moderate knowledge of geography and astronomy." He could hardly wait to get back to Fort St. Anthony to advertise his accomplishment. He chafed at every delay and urged his half-breed guide to go faster. But the *bois-brûlé* refused to be rushed and led Beltrami southward via a succession of Chippewa encampments.

The Chippewa of the upper river were embroiled in one of their periodic squabbles. Weakened by disease and liquor, the tribe depended on government handouts and had lost its former power. The war leaders, nearly all of them inveterate alcoholics, were quarreling over who should be chief. The reigning warrior, a lazy drunkard named Wide Mouth, was being challenged by an equally indolent usurper, Cloudy Weather. By the time Beltrami stumbled in on the dispute, Wide Mouth had craftily suggested that if Cloudy Weather wished to prove his prowess, he should lead a war party against the Sioux. Cloudy Weather was eager to be chief but he did not want to risk his neck in order to oust his rival. As a result, the two factions welcomed the Italian as an impartial arbitrator. Beltrami was thrilled; to his reputation as an explorer he now proposed to add the role of peacemaker. His first efforts were extremely sensible—he advised the quarreling chiefs to take their problems to Major Taliaferro, the Indian agent, who would decide between them. This suited Cloudy Weather, who saw a convenient excuse to avoid leading the proposed war party, but Wide Mouth was disappointed. Summoning Beltrami to his hut, he tried to persuade the Italian to send Cloudy Weather off against the Sioux. Beltrami replied with a solemn lecture of the responsibilities of leadership and the public benefits of peace. It was no use— the "noble savage" was stone drunk.

On the night of the twelfth, Beltrami's negotiations collapsed when the tribe managed to get hold of several barrels of whisky. A terrific orgy ensued. The men and their squaws, all of them roaring drunk, rushed about the encampment brandishing knives, clubs, and muskets. The baying of their half-savage dogs added to the general din and Beltrami's *bois-brûlé* prudently hid himself. Poor Beltrami was terrified. He found a safe spot just outside the camp and stayed there "standing on a mound of earth with my cutlass in my girdle, my gun in my hand, and my sword half-unsheathed at my side, I remained a spectator of this awful scene, watchful and motionless. I was often menaced, but never answered except by an expressive silence, which most unequivocally declared that I was ready to rush on the first who should dare to

become my assailant." Once he had to venture into camp to
rescue Wide Mouth who was drunkenly defending himself
with a piece of wood against two opponents. With the help
of the *bois-brûlé*, who conveniently reappeared for a brief
moment, Beltrami pushed the raving chief into his hut and
sent in one of his own faction to protect him. Wide Mouth
promptly went berserk, seized a knife, and repeatedly stabbed
his guard, until he was pulled away. Next morning Beltrami
counted the casualties of the previous evening's excitement:
twenty-four wounded and two dead. Understandably, his
bois-brûlé had decided to withdraw, and no amount of pleading could persuade him to continue the trip. Beltrami was
forced to employ Wide Mouth as his guide to Fort St. Anthony, and left the rest of the tribe to sort out their own
problems.

The explorer's homecoming was not as glamorous as Beltrami had hoped. Wide Mouth, suffering from a monumental
hangover, proceeded slowly. He also stole Beltrami's cooking
pot so the Italian was reduced to eating from a tin cup. But
the returning "promeneur" refused to be daunted. He set up
his red umbrella as a flag of peace; shot a skunk and cut up its
corpse to see what made the animal smell so strongly, getting
himself soaked with the animal's fluid in the process; and
clutched the sides of the canoe as Wide Mouth shot the rapids
"with an intrepidity and dexterity truly surprising." Eventually, they reached the fort, where Beltrami scrambled jauntily
ashore, dressed for maximum effect in moccasins, clothes made
from skins, and a home-made hat of bark. Colonel Snelling
and his family greeted this bizarre figure kindly and listened
patiently to the flowery account of his adventures. Then, on
October 3, Beltrami, complete with his jumble of Indian
souvenirs, took passage by keelboat down to St. Louis and
from there traveled to New Orleans determined to write a
book about his heroic Mississippi "Pilgrimage."

Beltrami's book did not receive the acclaim he had anticipated. Two editions were printed, one in New Orleans and
the other in London, and neither sold well. Despite his de-

scriptions of the "Julian sources" of the Mississippi, few people took his discovery seriously. It was obvious that the Italian had approached the source from the wrong side of the watershed. He had merely ascended the Bloody River, crossed the divide, and claimed the first southward flowing stream as the head of the Mississippi. To make his disappointment more acute, Beltrami found that the public was no longer interested in the whereabouts of the source of the Mississippi. The topic was stale, and after a few invitations to high society parties in New Orleans and a handful of favorable notices in the popular newspapers, the luckless Italian was ignored. Only the professional academics and the serious mapmakers read his book carefully, and of course they demolished his claims with biting sarcasm. He was ridiculed in their journals, and his applications to join their learned societies were snubbed. Crestfallen, Beltrami made one more attempt at fame. He went to Mexico, traveled widely in that country, and wrote a book about his journey. This publication was also a failure. In 1826 he returned to Europe and, because he was still exiled from Italy, wandered between London, Heidelberg and Paris, pathetically attending geographers' conferences, writing letters to the leading philosophers, and working to restore a republican system in his beloved Italy. Finally, when he was seventy years old, he was allowed to return to his estates at Filotrano, where he died in February 1855. Eleven years later, the legislature of the State of Minnesota, at the suggestion of the State Historical Society, established a county of about 4,000 square miles which included the "Julian sources of the Bloody River and the Mississippi" and named it Beltrami County. Of his red silk umbrella there was no mention.

12

The Silly Season

BELTRAMI'S JAUNTY "PILGRIMAGE" USHERED IN THE final phase of Mississippi exploration, a time best described as the "silly season" of discovery. It lasted seventy years and embroiled a random assortment of "explorers" in a hunt for the ultimate pond, spring, or freshet which they could stretch their imaginations to call the extreme head of the Mississippi. These eager protagonists included a Protestant missionary, an agent for Indian Affairs, a French surveyor, and a professional adventurer whose fraudulent claims rivaled Father Hennepin's swindle for sheer audacity.

This silly season began three years before Beltrami appeared in upper Minnesota. In 1820 Governor Lewis Cass of Michigan obtained permission from the Secretary of War to investigate the sources of the Mississippi, and with the United States government paying the bill, Cass took a large expedition up the river to within three days' journey of the source. At that point he abandoned the project, though he had learned from the local Indians that the Mississippi rose in a certain Lac la Biche which lay farther upstream. It was left to the mineralogist of this expedition to return to the area and discover that the Indians were correct and that their Father of Waters really did rise in this mysterious lake.

Henry Rowe Schoolcraft, mineralogist, Indian agent, author, politician, and anthropologist, first received public attention when he wrote a travelogue describing a trip he made to the lead mines of Missouri. On the strength of this book he was invited to accompany the Cass expedition as its geologist, and upon his return published a semi-official account of the governor's venture entitled *Narrative Journal of Travels*. This work revealed that Schoolcraft had developed a fascination for the Indians of the Northwest and with the help of Lewis Cass he was soon afterward appointed Indian agent at Sault Ste. Marie in charge of the tribes living near Lake Superior. This position was the springboard which he used to become a leading authority on the geography, wild life, and aborigines of the upper Mississippi.

By all accounts Henry Schoolcraft was a formidable character. Within a year of taking the job as Indian agent, he married Jane Johnston, the half-breed granddaughter of a powerful Indian war chief, and through his wife he acquired an intimate knowledge of Indian customs and legends. At the same time he became markedly difficult to deal with. As his expertise increased he grew more and more scornful of the efforts of his colleagues in the Indian service, quarreled easily, and leaned more and more toward religious bigotry. During his administration he dealt harshly with traders who sold liquor to the Indians, ranted against the evils of strong drink, and, like Zebulon Pike, nurtured a rabid distaste for the Canadian fur traders who were still crossing the border to visit the headwater tribes. Prickly and authoritarian, he resented interference in his territory by any outsiders and relished displaying his power and lore.

After his return from the Cass expedition, Henry Schoolcraft resolved that he would be the successful explorer who finally discovered the source of the Mississippi. It appears that in coming to this conclusion, the Indian agent was motivated by the fact that the headwaters of the river lay within his domain and therefore he felt that it befitted his reputation as an "authority" to discover the actual source. This arrogant approach to the undertaking was part and parcel of Schoolcraft's self-appointed role, and he was prepared to launch any scheme in order to further his ambition. Accordingly, in 1832, he wrote to his superiors in the Office of Indian Affairs, suggesting a government-sponsored expedition to the Chippewa for the declared purpose of settling intertribal disputes. In reality Schoolcraft wanted the opportunity and financial backing for a journey of exploration, and he had already made private arrangements for military assistance from Lewis Cass, who was by then the U.S. Secretary of War. In May, Schoolcraft received a grant of $3,200 for his trip and immediately started his preparations.

Schoolcraft's determination to have the honor of finding the source is shown by the size of his expedition. It was a sledgehammer to crack a rather insignificant nut. The party comprised Schoolcraft as leader; a surgeon-cum-naturalist, Dr. Douglass Houghton, who was to vaccinate any Indians they met; Lieutenant James Allen of the Fifth U.S. Infantry to command the escort and draw maps; the Reverend William Thurston Boutwell of the American Board of Foreign Missions; a half-breed interpreter who also happened to be Schoolcraft's brother-in-law (though the agent took care not to mention this relationship in public); and no less than twenty boatsmen who had been specially hired for the trip. Supplies were purchased on the same lavish scale: a small fleet of canoes; forty kegs of pork and beef; firkins of sugar, butter, dry bread, coffee, rice, and green China hyson tea; 350 pounds of sweet-scented Virginia tobacco for the Indians, and an ample collection of fishhooks, axes, mirrors, blankets, and sewing materials. Together with muskets, fowling pieces, tents, cooking gear, oilcloth, baggage yokes for the portages, paddles, gum and red lead for mending the canoes, mess baskets, and other paraphernalia this added up to a huge accumulation of matériel which had to be dragged laboriously upstream. But Schoolcraft had no intention of failing; as he wrote in a letter to Cass, "If I do not see the 'veritable course' of the Mississippi, this time, it will not be from want of attention."

As expected, the journey itself presented no difficulty except for the soldiers who repeated Pike's mistake of using Schenectady barges and wasted a lot of time manhandling their boats over the shallows. Otherwise the expedition plowed stolidly against the current until upper Red Cedar Lake (by now called Cass Lake) was reached. Here Schoolcraft called upon the local Indians to guide his party to the Lac la Biche, which they had described to Cass. The Chippewa were glad to oblige the Indian agent but pointed out that his ponderous expedition would make heavy work of the swampy region they were proposing to enter. Yellow Head, the chief guide, suggested that a smaller group of men using lightweight canoes would travel without hindrance and promised not only to supply canoes, but also, in his words, "My own canoe shall be one of the number."

On July 10 Schoolcraft, Allen, Boutwell, Houghton, Yellow Head, and the interpreter set out for the lake. Each white man ensconced himself in the center of a hunting canoe and was paddled forward by two Chippewa braves. For their comfort the "gentlemen" took along provisions for ten days, tent, groundsheet, mess basket, medicine chest, and their "travelling beds." The final assault group had more of the appearance of an African safari than an exploring team, and apart from the annoyance of the mosquitoes, they suffered little inconvenience. Schoolcraft's only complaints concerned the weather, which was showery, and the difficulty of finding a suitable spot for their picnic meals. On July 13 the travelers came to the head of the small stream they had been ascending, and, in Schoolcraft's words, Yellow Head "pushed his canoe into the weeds and exclaimed, *Oma mikunna* (here is the portage). A man who is called on for the first time to debark, in such a place, will look about him to discover some dry spot to put his feet upon. No such spot however existed here. We stepped into rather warm pond water, with a miry bottom."

After squelching through this morass the expedition climbed a portage trail and "followed our guide down the sides of the last elevation, with the expectation of momentarily reaching the goal of our journey. What had been long sought, at last appeared suddenly. On turning out of a thicket, into a small weedy opening, the cheering sight of a transparent body of water burst upon our view. It was Itasca Lake[1]— the source of the Mississippi." The Chippewa guides carried their canoes down to the water's edge, the white men stepped aboard, and the entire party coasted round the small Y-shaped lake. In a brief ceremony the American flag was raised, the Indians fired a volley from their guns, and the expedition hurried back downstream. The ultimate source of the Mississippi had been discovered, marked, and proclaimed with the minimum of fuss; there the matter should have rested.

But it did not. Four years later, in 1836, a French surveyor, Joseph Nicollet, visited the source streams of the Mississippi armed with sextant, barometer, portfolio, thermometer, chronometer, pocket compass, tape line, spy glass, and artificial horizon. He was making a hydrographic chart of the upper river and stayed three days at the lake, taking observations and drawing a map of the surrounding ponds and swamps. Nicollet was a remarkably accurate and modest surveyor, working under extremely trying conditions. He scarcely complained when the mosquitoes swarmed so thickly about his lantern that they extinguished the flame, and he took scrupulous care to mention that "the honor of having first explored the sources of the Mississippi . . . belongs to Mr. Schoolcraft and Lieutenant Allen. . . . I come only after these gentlemen; but I may be permitted to claim some merit for having completed what was wanting for a full geographical account of these sources. Moreover, I am, I believe, the first traveler who has carried with him astronomical instruments and put them to profitable account." But although Nicollet conducted his survey with admirable detachment and a lack

[1] Schoolcraft concocted this name from the Latin *Veritas Caput*, meaning Truth Head.

of self-interest, his map did show that there were several small feeder streams flowing into Lake Itasca, which Schoolcraft had failed to mention. One of these rivulets was to cause some trouble.

For another forty-five years little happened. In 1846 a friend of Schoolcraft's canoed up to look at Lake Itasca; in 1872 a New York journalist named Julius Chambers visited the source on a trip which he was taking for reasons of health; and three years later a surveyor under government contract "platted" the area, hacking crude roads through the forest so that his ox team could haul in supplies. By 1881 the source had been visited by a representative of the U.S. Forestry Service, a university professor, a Louisville journalist, and an Episcopalian missionary who took the chance to deliver a sermon on the text, "Then had Thy peace been as a river," Isaiah 48:18. All these casual visitors examined the headwaters out of curiosity, noted the profusion of ponds and streams, and went home with pleasant memories of their excursion mingled with a vague sense of adventure. At this juncture, just when it seemed that the source of the Mississippi was quietly evolving into a commonplace tourist attraction, the calm was shattered by a well-publicized figure who claimed to have discovered the "true source" of the Mississippi. He insisted that Schoolcraft had mistakenly identified Lake Itasca as the head of the river, whereas he, the newcomer, had found an entirely different lake, which now bore his own name.

This bombastic pronouncement would have passed unnoticed if the claimant had not been such a flamboyant personality. He was Captain Willard Glazier, who had spent the greater part of his life keeping his name in the public eye. As the gallant author of such works as "*Soldiers of the Saddle*"; "*Capture, Prison Pen and Escape*"; and "*Ocean to Ocean on Horseback*," the captain made a business of plunging into various farfetched escapades and regaling his audience with the resultant tales of daredevil excitement. He now came forward with a book describing a canoe trip down the length of the Mississippi; its subtitle was *An Account of the discovery of the True Source of the Mississippi*, and it announced to his readers that the writer had located another, hitherto unknown, lake upstream from Lake Itasca.

Glazier's account of his expedition made stirring reading. His venture began, he wrote, when he learned "that many Indians denied that their ideal river had its origins in Lake Itasca, but that there were other lakes and streams above and beyond that lake. These reflections led me to conclude that there was yet another rich field for exploration in the wilds of Minnesota." On this optimistic note the worthy captain assembled a small expedition (his brother and a journalist) and made haste for the mysterious source, sweeping his reader along with him in a surge of bold, military prose, neatly enhanced with elegant illustrations. His book had pictures of a forest portage, a meal with the Chippewa, a night encampment deep in the lonely forests, and a splendid vista entitled, "Embarking for the Source of the Great River." It showed Glazier standing in a canoe paddled by two feathered warriors. In one hand he held his trusty musket and with the other he waved his chapeau to acknowledge the huzzas of a multitude of painted savages assembled on the bank.

Naturally the pioneering soldier did not lose his opportunity to stamp new names upon the land he was exploring. Thus, "learning from my guides that these beautiful lakes had never before, to their knowledge, been seen by white men, I named them successively Bayard, Stoneman, Pleasanton, Custer and Kilpatrick, as a tribute to the favorite Union cavalry leaders of the war—patriot soldiers who deserve well of their country, and to whose calls I had often responded in the campaigns of the Army of the Potomac." When his repertory of martial reminiscences was exhausted, Glazier turned to his own family; his brother, sister, and daughter were all commemorated with similar panache, as the expedition pushed ahead to Lake Itasca, "erroneously located as the source of the Mississippi."

The following morning their guide, Chenowagesic, led them to a patch of reeds on the far shore. There he thrashed about in great perplexity with his paddle until at length he "gave a characteristic 'Chippewa yell,' thereby signifying that he had found the object of his search. Returning, he seized the bow of my canoe and pulled if after him through the rushes out into the clear, glistening waters of the infant Mississippi, which, at the point of entering Itasca, is seven feet wide and from twelve to fifteen inches deep."

This conveniently hidden stream carried Glazier and his accomplices to a small lake, concealed several miles away. This, of course, was the *true head* of the Mississippi, and there the captain delivered with deep emotion a lecture on the importance of having successfully completed the task which De Soto had begun. A fusillade rang out to celebrate the occasion; the Indian guide folded his arms, struck an oratorical pose facing Glazier, and delivered a speech which ended: "When I again roam through these forests, and look on this lake, source of the Great River, I will look on you." To conclude this touching ceremony the journalist, Paine, proposed that the source be named Lake Glazier after the man "whose energy, perserverance, and pluck carried us through many dangers." This proposition, which Glazier said "gave me a surprise," was "carried by acclamation." With that, the explorers turned about and commenced their journey to the Gulf.

The downstream trip was a triumphal junket, artfully stage-managed by Glazier. The newspapers (who had been forewarned) hailed his achievement, armadas of skiffs and other pleasure craft put out to welcome his canoe, and he was greeted with massed bands playing "See the Conquering Hero Comes." At New Orleans the guns boomed and flags waved, the mayor offered Glazier the freedom of the city, and a public reception was held in his honor. The highlight of this function was a speech by the president of the New Orleans Academy of Sciences eulogizing the explorer's shining example to the youth of America. Then Captain Glazier proceeded to St. Louis where he gave a lecture to a distinguished gathering of savants meeting under the auspices of the Missouri Historical Society. The vice-president of the Society introduced the guest speaker with a little poem he had written for the occasion. It ran:

To Captain Willard Glazier—*Greeting*
With triple wreaths doth fame thine head now crown,
The patriot soldier's, in fierce battle won;
The "Pen's" than the "Sword's" mankind's greater boon;
The bold Explorer's finding where was born
The River's King, till now, like Nile's unknown.
May years of high emprise increase thy fame,
And with thy death arise a deathless name.

This verse was greeted with applause, and after his lecture Glazier made the Historical Society a present of the canoe which he had used to discover "Lake Glazier." The only discordant note came from one of the newspapermen covering the meeting who churlishly noted in his column next day that the canoe appeared to be in remarkably good condition for a vessel that had undergone the hardships Captain Glazier described.

While all this had been going on, Glazier's pen had not been idle. He wrote about his trip, published articles in learned journals, and even produced a map of Lake Glazier which was approved by the president of the American Geographical Society and duly published in the New York *Herald*. As late as 1885 the *Monthly Journal* of the Royal Geographical Society in London printed a letter from the captain explaining the success of his trip into Minnesota. Furthermore, friends of Glazier had been making the rounds of the publishing houses, pressing his claim to a new source. Several of the more reliable publishers, including Rand McNally and the Macmillan Company were convinced and prepared to restyle their atlases and schoolbooks to include the newly discovered lake. At this stage, when Glazier appeared to be riding high on the crest of academic and literary success, he was unmasked as a fake by a firm of publishers who produced geography textbooks for children.

In October 1886, Ivison, Blakeman, Taylor and Company put on public sale a special extra edition of the *Educational*

Reporter. It contained a deadly attack on Captain Glazier's honesty written by a geographer named Henry D. Harrower. In his introduction Harrower stated that his intention was to arrive at the true story of Mississippi exploration rather than pillory the captain, but the pages which followed amounted to a damning accusation of fraud. Point by point Harrower proved quite conclusively that "Lake Glazier" was nothing but a large pond which Nicollet had mapped forty-five years earlier for all to see on the regulation government maps of the Itasca area. Not only had Glazier inflated this pond into a "lake," but he had also shifted its position and failed to mention that several of the earlier "tourists" had visited it. One of them, Chambers, the New York journalist, had gone so far as to dub it "Dolly Varden," a joking reference to the name of the canoe he was using on his health trip. Further, Glazier's tale of his journey to the source was largely stolen from Schoolcraft's reports. By arranging extracts from Glazier's and Schoolcraft's books side by side, Harrower had great fun pointing out the more obvious thefts. He demonstrated how Glazier's Indian guide had offered the use of a canoe with the phrase, "My canoe shall be one of them," a ridiculous parallel to Yellow Head's speech under similar conditions half a century earlier. So it went on; Glazier's narrative was riddled with plagiarisms, ranging from the *"Oma mikunna"* of his guide leading the captain into "rather warm pond water with a miry bottom," to the very words Glazier used to describe his "lake"—they were essentially the same as those Schoolcraft had used when he first saw Itasca. As a final indictment, Harrower revealed that Glazier had filched his table of meteorological statistics from Schoolcraft's observations on the Cass expedition. Both sets of readings were identical in every respect, including the coincidence that Glazier's ended on August 2, 1881—the anniversary of the day Schoolcraft had broken his thermometer in 1820!

The publication of Harrower's article caused widespread consternation. Glazier's friends and those whom he had duped tried hard to defend their position, and Glazier, piqued by the criticism, led a small army of witnesses to his supposed "source." There five newspapermen, a librarian, a botanist, a photographer, and a senator vouched for the captain. But by now other magazines had joined in the hunt and the game was up. A surveyor was hired to remap the Itasca area and failed to find "Lake Glazier"; the captain's Chippewa guide was tracked down, shown Glazier's account of his trip, and he denied the story of his supposed oration; even Paine, the accompanying journalist, confessed that Glazier had invited him along to provide publicity, and that far from naming the pond "by acclamation," the party had only responded to the captain's earnest and repeated entreaties that they call the "lake" after him. Other investigators now spoke up, including several from the Minnesota Historical Society which had always been suspicious of Glazier, and they revealed that the explorer's intrepid journey had been spent comfortably traveling by train to within eighty miles of the source and that to approach the lake he had used one of the roadways opened in 1875 by the government surveyors. In short, Glazier's "discovery" was nothing more than the fraudulent embellishment of a straightforward canoe trip into an area which already had been visited many times.

With this exposé the silly season came to an end. Glazier dropped from public view and the story of the Mississippi exploration finally petered out. It had lasted more than three centuries, which was far longer than it should have survived. Even by the time Nicollet was industriously making his notes on the hydrography of the headwaters, the Mississippi was much better known for its paddle-wheelers and river gamblers than for Itasca and the Chippewa. The work of the explorers no longer mattered, and the little Y-shaped lake seemed a long way from the place where, according to Charles Latrobe sailing out of the Mississippi on his way back to Europe in 1843: "Long after we had lost sight of the land, the turbid waters heaving around us told us that we were still within the domain and influence of the Mississippi. At length we shot over a line clearly defined and distinct—passed from a yellow wave into one of sea-green hue—and bade adieu to the mighty Father of Waters."

Selected Bibliography

GENERAL

Adney, Edwin Tappan, and Chapelle, Howard I: *The Bark Canoes and Skin Boats of North America.* Washington, D.C.: Smithsonian Institution; 1964.

Beers, Henry Putney: *The Western Military Frontier, 1815–1846* (dissertation). University of Pennsylvania; 1935.

Brebner, John Bartlet: *The Explorers of North America, 1492–1806.* New York: Meridian; 1964.

Carter, Hodding: *Lower Mississippi.* New York: Farrar & Rinehart; 1942

Clemens, Samuel Langhorne (Mark Twain): *Life on the Mississippi.* New York: Harper; 1917.

Freeman, Lewis R.: *Waterways of Westward Wandering.* New York: Dodd, Mead; 1927.

Hartsough, Mildred Lucille: *From Canoe to Steel Barge on the Upper Mississippi.* Minneapolis: University of Minnesota Press; 1934.

Havighurst, Walter: *Voices on the River.* New York: Macmillan; 1964.

Hosmer, James K.: *A Short History of the Mississippi Valley.* Boston: Houghton, Mifflin; 1901.

Hyde, George E.: *Indians of the Woodlands.* Norman: Oklahoma University Press; 1962.

Long, Major Stephen H.: *Voyage in a Six-Oared Skiff to the Falls of St. Anthony in 1817.* Philadelphia: H. B. Ashmead; 1860.

Margry, Pierre: *Découvertes et Établissements des Français.* Paris: D. Jouaust; 1876–1886.

Ogg, Frederic Austin: *The Opening of the Mississippi, a*

Struggle for Supremacy in the American Interior. New York: Macmillan; 1904.

Parkman, Francis: *A Half Century of Conflict.* New York: Collier Books; 1962.

Shea, John Gilmary: *Early Voyages Up and Down the Mississippi.* Albany: J. Munsell; 1861.

———: *Discovery and Exploration of the Mississippi Valley.* New York: E. Maynard; 1890.

Tousley, Albert S.: *Where Goes the River.* Iowa City: Tepee Press; 1928.

Winsor, Justin: *Cartier to Frontenac, Geographical Discovery in the Interior of North America.* Boston: Houghton, Mifflin; 1894.

Publications of the Missouri, Minnesota, Wisconsin, and Louisiana Historical Societies.

DE SOTO

Bourne, Edward Gaylord (ed.): *Narratives of the Career of Hernando de Soto by . . . A Knight of Elvas, . . . Luis Hernadez de Biedma, . . . Rodrigo Ranjel, his private secretary.* New York: A. S. Barnes; 1904.

Dunbar, Rowland (ed.): *A Symposium on the Place of the Discovery of the Mississippi River by Hernando de Soto.* Publications of the Mississippi Historical Society, Special Bulletin No. 1; 1927.

Graham, Robert B. Cunninghame: *Hernando de Soto.* London: Heinemann; 1903.

Maynard, Theodore: *De Soto and the Conquistadores.* London: Longmans, Green; 1930.

JOLIET & MARQUETTE

Delanglez, Jean: *Life and Voyages of Louis Jolliet.* Chicago: Institute of Jesuit History; 1948.

Eifert, Virginia Louise: *Louis Jolliet, Explorer of Rivers.* New York: Dodd, Mead; 1961.

Gagnon, Ernest: *Louis Jolliet, découvreur du Mississippi.* Montreal: Beauchemin; 1946.

Hamy, Alfred: *Au Mississippi.* Paris: H. Champion; 1903.

Michallet, E.: *Voyage et découverte de quelques pays et nations de l'Amérique Septentrionale par le pere Marquette et Sr. Joliet.* Paris: 1681.

Steck, Francis Borgia: *The Jolliet-Marquette Expedition, 1673* (dissertation). Washington: Catholic University of America; 1927.

————:*Essays relating to the Jolliet-Marquette Expedition, 1673.* Quincy, Ill.: August Reyling (ed.); 1953.

————: *Marquette Legends.* New York: Pageant; 1960.

Thwaites, Reuben Gold: *Father Marquette.* New York: D. Appleton; 1902.

LA SALLE

Anderson, Melville B. (trans.): *Relation of the Discoveries and Voyages of Cavelier de la Salle from 1679 to 1681.* Chicago: Caxton Club; 1901.

Cox, Issac Joslin (ed.): *The Journeys of René Robert Cavelier etc.* New York: A. S. Barnes; 1905.

Gaither, Mrs. Frances: *The Fatal River, the Life and Death of La Salle.* New York: Holt; 1931.

Jacks, Leo Vincent: *La Salle.* New York: Scribner; 1931.

Joutel: *Journal of La Salle's last voyage* (reprint of the first English translation), London, 1714. Chicago: Caxton Club; 1896.

Parkman, Francis: *La Salle and the Discovery of the Great West.* Boston: Little, Brown; 1879.

Roncière, Charles de la: *Cavelier de la Salle, explorateur de la Nouvelle-France.* Tours: Mame; 1943.

Viau, Roger: *Cavelier de la Salle.* Tours: Mame; 1960.

TONTI

Anderson, Melville B. (trans.): *Relation of Henri de Tonty Concerning the Explorations of La Salle from 1678 to 1683*. Chicago: Caxton Club; 1898.
Legler, Henry E.: *Chevalier Henry de Tonty; His Exploits in the Valley of the Mississippi*. Milwaukee: Parkman Club; 1896.
Murphy, Edmund Robert: *Henry de Tonty, Fur Trader of the Mississippi*. Baltimore: Johns Hopkins; 1941.

HENNEPIN

Delanglez, Jean: *Hennepin's Description of Louisiana, a critical essay*. Chicago: Institute of Jesuit History; 1941.
Dumont, Georges H.: *Louis Hennepin, explorateur du Mississippi*. Brussels: C. Dessart; 1942.
Hennepin, Louis: *Description de la Louisiane, etc.* Paris: Chez la Veuve Sebastion Húre; 1683.
————: *A New Discovery of a Vast Country in America, etc.* London: for M. Bentley, J. Tonson, H. Bonwick, T. Goodwin, and S. Manship; 1698.
————: *A New Voyage, etc.* London, 1698.

CARVER

Carver, Jonathan: *Travels Through the Interior Parts of North America, in the Years 1766, 1767, and 1768*. London: C. Dilly; 1781.
Lee, John Thomas: *Captain Jonathan Carver, Additional Data*. Madison, Wisc.: State Historical Society of Wisconsin; 1912.
Parker, John: *The Great Lakes and the Great Rivers: Jonathan Carver's Dream of Empire*. Lansing, Mich.: Historical Society of Michigan; 1965.

Also American Historical Review, January 1906, v. II, pp. 287–302, and manuscript copy of *Carver's Travels*, British Museum (microfilm copy courtesy of John Parker, Bell Collection, Minneapolis, Minn.).

PIKE

Hollon, W. Eugene: *The Lost Pathfinder*. Norman: University of Oklahoma Press; 1949.

Jackson, Donald: *The Journals of Zebulon Montgomery Pike*. 2 vols. Norman: University of Oklahoma Press; 1966.

Pike, Zebulon Montgomery: *The Expeditions of Zebulon Montgomery Pike, to Headwaters of the Mississippi River, Through Louisiana Territory, and in New Spain, During the Years 1805–6–7*. Commentary and edition by Elliott Coues. New York: Harper; 1895.

BELTRAMI

Beltrami, Giacomo Costantino: *A Pilgrimage in Europe and America, Leading to the Discovery of the Sources of the Mississippi and the Bloody River, with a Description of the Whole Course of the Former, and of the Ohio*. London: Hunt and Clarke; 1828.

Iacomini, Wally Braghieri: *Giacomo Costantino Beltrami, pelegrino alle sorgenti del Mississippi*. Bergamo: Edizioni Orobiche; 1955.

Keating, William Hypolitus: *Narrative of an Expedition to the Source of the St. Peter's River, Lake Winnepeak, etc. ect.* Philadelphia: H. C. Carey & I. Lea; 1824.

Masi, Eugenia: *Giacomo Costantino Beltrami e le sue esplorazioni in America*. Florence: Tip. de G. Barbèra; 1902.

Selected Bibliography

THE SILLY SEASON

Baker, James H.: *The Sources of the Mississippi. Their Discoverers, Real and Pretended.* Minneapolis: Minnesota Historical Collection, vol. VI part 1; 1894.

Brower, J. V.: *The Mississippi River and Its Source.* Minneapolis: Minnesoto Historical Collection, vol. VII, 1893.

Dobie, John: *The Itasca Story.* Minneapolis: Ross & Haines, Inc.; 1959.

Glazier, Capt. Willard: *Down the Great River.* Philadelphia: Hubbard Brothers; 1889.

Latrobe, Charles Joseph: *The Rambler in North America.* New York: Harper; 1935.

Mason, Philip T. (ed.): *Schoolcraft's Expedition to Lake Itasca.* Michigan State University Press; 1958.

Also "Captain Glazier and His Lake: An Inquiry," in *Educational Reporter, Extra.* New York and Chicago: Ivison, Blakeman, Taylor & Co.; October, 1886. "The Source of the Mississippi," in *Science*, December 24, 1886; and a paper on Joseph Nicollet read to the Society for the History of Discoveries in 1965 by Martha Bray, St. Paul, Minnesota.

INDEX

[i]

INDEX

TIMOTHY SEVERIN, explorer, traveler, author, filmmaker, and lecturer, made his first expedition while he was still a student at Oxford: following the route of Marco Polo on a motorcycle. He has also re-created the journeys of Ulysses, Jason and the Argonauts, Sinbad, and Hsu Fu (which required sailing across the Pacific on a bamboo raft). He now lives in Ireland.

In 1965, as he was conducting research and writing this book, he traveled the length of the Mississippi to better appreciate the difficulties faced by the explorers. He began at the source of the river, Lake Itasca, but was obliged to change vessels when the Sauk Rapids obliterated his canoe. He doggedly continued on to New Orleans by "decrepit launch."